Robert Dwyer Joyce

Irish Fireside Tales

Robert Dwyer Joyce

Irish Fireside Tales

ISBN/EAN: 9783741133800

Manufactured in Europe, USA, Canada, Australia, Japa

Cover: Foto ©Andreas Hilbeck / pixelio.de

Manufactured and distributed by brebook publishing software (www.brebook.com)

Robert Dwyer Joyce

Irish Fireside Tales

IRISH FIRESIDE TALES.

BY

ROBERT D. JOYCE, M.D.

BOSTON:
PATRICK DONAHOE.
1871.

CONTENTS.

	PAGE
THE GERALDINE AND HIS BRIDE, FAIR EILEEN.	5
THE PEARL NECKLACE; OR, THE BEAUTY OF THE BLOSSOM-GATE.	28
CREEVAN, THE BROWN-HAIRED; OR, THE SEVENTH SON.	52
THE FISHERMAN'S DAUGHTER. A TALE OF RINDOWN CASTLE.	68
THE BUILDING OF MOURNE.	83
MADELINE'S VOW.	113
A LITTLE BIT OF SPORT.	
No. 1. DUCKS AND DIVERS.	140
No. 2. HUNTING DOWN THE WALRUS.	159
No. 3. OTTER-HUNTING ON THE BLACKWATER.	177
No. 4. THE ENCHANTED FOX OF DARRA.	193
THE BUCCANEERS' CASTLE.	207
MUN CARBERRY AND THE PHOOKA; OR, THE RETURN ON NEW YEAR'S EVE.	231
THE OLD BACHELOR.	250

CONTENTS.

The Golden Butterfly.	263
The Adventures of Hugh and Brian.	277
Winifred's Fortune. A Story of Dublin Life in the Days of Queen Anne.	302
Legend of Tiernan; or, The Blue Knight.	331
The Rescued Bride. A Legend of the Cummeraghs.	342
The Bible Oath.	352

IRISH FIRESIDE TALES.

THE GERALDINE AND HIS BRIDE, FAIR EILEEN.

A sudden blinding brightness shone —
    O! the purple mountains!
As sudden it was past and gone;
But hearts were throbbing, and cheeks were wan,
For the bonnie bride stood in the dance alone,
    'Mid the purple, heathery mountains!

ONE calm autumnal evening, long, long ago, Cnoc Feirinna, with its bright mantle of purple heath, looked down smiling upon the brown forests and romantic plains that lay extended like a many-tinted panorama around its feet. The peasant, as he plied the sickle amid the yellow corn, the creachadore, as he drove the lowing herds across the valley, and the swarthy hobeler, or horseman, with his glittering arms and accoutrements, as he rode slowly through the rocky pass, looked up occasionally, with reverential awe, to the ancient hill; for they thought — they knew, good, simple hearts as they were in these old times, that Donn the Fairy King sat on his golden throne on its summit, and that his Queen, with all her fair ladies, was perchance at that hour looking down with her piercing eyes from her happy dwelling upon the poor mortals toiling beneath. Ah, these good old days! when the poor peasant and the mail-clad knight, the lowly maid and high-bred damsel, alike believed in the existence of the merry people of fairy-land; when the green haunted mound and picturesque rath were passed by one and all with becoming reverence; when faith and patriotism were strong, and the simple heart and brave arm did their devoir on many a red plain and smoking rampart, amid the "fair fields of Holy Ireland," better than the crafty brains, the faint bosoms, and the flattering tongues that plot and hold forth so loudly on the day of security, and leave their native land to her fate in the night of misery or of danger.

Beneath that mellow autumnal sky, Gerald, the young Earl of Desmond, sat with his betrothed bride, the fair Eileen, beside a little rill that danced down with its numerous and merry songs through a shady dell on the southern side of Cnoc Feirinna. Both were very young. Twenty summers had scarcely rolled over the noble brow of the earl, but the wisdom of many years seemed to lie in his large, calm eyes, and the strength of mature manhood appeared in his finely-moulded limbs and stalwart frame, as he sat on a mossy fragment of rock near the edge of the little rill. His helmet, all chased with gold, with its long plume, was thrown carelessly at the foot of a mountain ash beside him, and he wore the light armor used, almost continually, by young nobles at the time, namely, a gorget and corselet, all ribbed with silver and gold, and flowered and ornamented with strange devices at the joints; tassets, or hip armor, of ribbed steel, also inlaid with gold; while from a large and gorgeous belt around his slender waist hung his sword and dagger, with their rich chasings; and that good sword and that keen dagger, young as their owner was, had seen hard service in many a stubbornly contested field.

His betrothed, the fair Eileen, sat at his feet upon the flowery sward, her large, dark, and lustrous eyes gazing upward occasionally upon his face, and sparkling with the love and joy that reigned in her innocent and devoted heart. The dark and glorious eyes, the queen-like brow, and the small but beautifully moulded face, were rendered still more beautiful by the glossy masses of raven hair that descended upon her lovely shoulders; and, as she sat with her gorgeously colored riding-dress flowing around her in light folds, and with a small white wand in her snowy hand, she looked, indeed, like a young queen — perchance the fair queen of Fairyland, that all believed in in those romantic days, and that the poet now dreams of in the golden hour of his sweetest inspiration. Three richly caparisoned steeds stood near, browsing carelessly by the rill, or anon arching their noble necks, and amusing themselves with various gambols and curvettings, as they listed, for the page to whose care they were consigned had played the truant, and climbed upwards to have a view from the summit of the hill.

"Dost see yon glorious cloud, Gerald?" said Eileen, as she looked southward across the Limerick plain. "See, it rests upon the far-off hill-top, and assumes the form of a castle with its many battlements — a golden palace. Ah! could we live together in some heavenly palace like that, floating away forever and forever over the silver seas, through the bright paths of the sky, eternal happiness would be ours for love —"

"Stay, lady mine," said the earl, gayly interrupting her — "doth not love live here, as well as in yon bright regions? As for me, my heaven, my happiness, I can find not so far away. And," he continued, playfully tapping her on the cheek, "I would be well content to live on and on forever on this earth, — dull as some call it, — and, God wot, could find amusement and employment enough in fighting betimes, and happiness the sweetest in loving thee amid the glades of my own good green woods, and in the gay halls of mine own castles."

"But the wars — the wars, Gerald. Ah, me! when we are married, what between this great war thou art going to engage in against the English king, and thy many raids beside, I shall oft be left alone in some one of thy great castles, and thou knowest that out of thy presence I cannot be happy; and perchance," she continued, looking on her lover with a smile, "I may pine, and fret, and long to be back again to my father's gay halls of Kilmoodan; and that, my heart tells me, would be unjust to thee, though I could not avoid the sorrow."

"But canst thou not, thou little faint heart," answered the earl, laughing, "canst thou not follow thy wedded lord to those wars? Have we not gay tents roofed with the saffron cloth for thee and thy train, wherein we can hold revel before battle, and laugh in triumph and in joy when the day is done? Ah, love, should the war time come, thou shalt follow thy young soldier, and share his dangers. But hark! the wild spirits of the air are awaking!" he exclaimed, as a rushing, stormy sound rolled downward from the crest of the hill. They looked upward, but no cloud, no darkness appeared; and yet the wild rush and roar of many whirlwinds grew louder and louder, till the green earth beneath them seemed to tremble, and the merry voice of the little rill to grow faint and indistinct in the wild murmur and tumult. Yet the leaves of the forest trees around seemed still and quiescent, save of one, the rowan tree, or mountain ash, whose trunk rocked and groaned, and whose branches whizzed to and fro in weird-like undulations, as if all the whirlwinds of heaven were blowing around and tearing it from its roots. The face of Eileen became wan with fear, but the young earl laid his hand upon his sword, and looked calmly on.

"Hush, love!" he said; "though the fairy people be above, they cannot hurt one so good and pure as thou. And the storm-blast is hushed up. See, the rowan tree is still, and silence has settled on the forest once more. But, by our Lady! what's this?" he exclaimed again,-as a snow-white fawn emerged from a green copse hard by, and trotted down the little dell towards where they sat. As it drew nigh the lovers, without any indications of fear or shyness, it gave a few lithe and playful bounds, laid itself down gently at the earl's feet, and looked up with a strangely intelligent look to his face.

"Ah, pretty thing!" said Eileen, attempting to pat the fawn upon the head, and smooth its glossy back. "Art thou not fitter companion for a gentle lady than for this rough, bold warrior? Come to me, darling one, and thou shalt have a little palace in my bower, and follow me betimes through the gay green forest." But the fawn bounded up, shy and angry, and laid itself down again at the other side of the earl. At this the earl laughed heartily.

"Ha! ha! little wood-sprite, and so thou preferrest this rough hand of mine to the lily fingers of my lady love. Here — so, my dainty little rambler," and he patted the fawn upon the head, at which it started up with a wild aerial bound, commenced gambolling up and down in the most extravagant delight, and again laid itself at the feet of the earl. "By the gray towers of Crom!" he exclaimed, "but it seemeth to have more than the intelligence of a mortal in its eyes. It is passing strange. And see, Eileen, more marvels still!" and he pointed up the mountain to the page, who now came running down towards them with frantic haste, and with fear and wonder in his look.

"Speak, Thomas," continued the Desmond; "out with it, man, and stand not gaping thus, as if thou wert going to swallow us and this rock beneath us!"

"My lord and lady," said the page, recovering himself, "I can scarcely tell what hath happened. When I gained the top of the hill I seemed to be in an enchanted land. Towers and domes of palaces appeared before mine eyes, and anon a great hall, where I beheld gay lords and ladies fine, and a great king upon his throne amongst them. A glimpse only. Anon a castle hall grew bright and plain before me, — a hall I know well, — and there suddenly thronged it a bridal train with plumes and gay dresses, all dancing merrily to the sounds of the gay harp, the pipe, and the merry gittern. Alas! in the midst of that festive hall I saw a dead bridegroom and a weeping bride, and then all faded from before my bewildered eyes. Then arose a loud, roaring wind, and whirled and swept around me, and tossed me hither and thither, like the light down of the moorland thistle, till I turned and ran — and ran, indeed, with fear, for I knew the fairy people were around me, and I am here!"

"Gerald," exclaimed Eileen, arising, her cheeks at the same time becoming pale with fear, "let us be gone. I shall swoon — I shall die, should we remain here, and see those wondrous and fearful sights that Thomas the Rider speaketh of."

"Fear not, fair lady," answered the Desmond. "The fairies seemed not in an angry mood, and yet it is best that we should speed away. Besides, the sunset will be faded ere we reach thy father's castle of Kilmoodan, and the dark forest paths are not meet for the journeying of a gay lady. Thomas — Dost hear me, Ride-the-wind? Bring up the steeds, and we will speed away, and I promise thee the sight, at the end of our journey, of a hall with pleasanter and more substantial merry-making than thou sawest to-day upon Cnoc Feirinna."

The steeds were brought up by the page, and the little cavalcade started away through the forest towards the castle of Kilmoodan. Still, as they went at brisk trot or gallop through the paths and glades, the white fawn followed close behind the earl's horse, till the gray towers of Kilmoodan appeared looming above the forest. In a little dell near the castle they halted, and the earl proceeded to fasten a clasp on the trappings of Eileen's horse.

"Kiss me, darling one," he said, looking into her eyes with a loving gaze when the clasp was arranged — "kiss thy poor knight as a guerdon for saving thee from fairy thrall; for the Fairy King must have fallen in love with thy glorious face, and those red lips of thine, and would have taken thee away, and made thee queen of his bright regions, were not my good sword beside thee to keep thee for mine own;" and he bent forward, and kissed his betrothed upon the cheeks and lips. At this moment the fawn gave a wild and angry scream, and, bounding away, disappeared amid the thickets of the forest.

"It is gone," said the earl, as they rode along once more; "and I am glad on't, for its presence seemed to discompose thee, Fair Eileen, and, by our Lady, its keen, strange eyes disturbed mine own breast too But here is thy father's house," he continued, after riding on farther, "and, by my good sword, a pretty large house it is too, somewhat like mine own old tower of Kilmallock even, so full of towers, and bastions, and gables. Here, Skim-the-forest," he said to the page, as they passed through the barbican, and entered the court-yard of the castle, "hold the reins of thy lady's palfrey till I assist her down. And now for a revel with thy father, my Eileen, and a dance with thee and the young gallants and fair maids in the hall;" and with that the two lovers entered the castle, and sat down side by side to a good Irish feast of the olden day, and told their adventures of the evening, and danced afterwards, and talked and laughed, with merry hearts of love, till the black rafters of the old castle rang with the revel and merriment of them and their gay companions.

When the brown woods of September spread before the forester's eye, when the pheasant crowed in

the tangled copse, and the wild grouse clapped his
wings, and called merrily to his companions on the
heathery moorlands, the marriage day of the Geraldine and his fair Eileen came on. The castle of
Kilmoodan, hall, court-yard, barbican and all, was
decked out with the garlands of merry autumn, as
the bridal train rode over the drawbridge, and took
its way to the ancient abbey in the woods hard by.
The gray-haired abbot raised his withered hands
above the heads of the two young lovers, and blessed
them, and made them one; and the long train, with
their caparisoned steeds and ambling palfreys, with
glittering dresses and waving plumes, and with glad
hearts and blithesome laughter, returned to the hall
of the old lord of Kilmoodan. And O, that festive
hall and gay bridal evening! The ancient armor
around the walls, the sheaves of spears, and the
gilded banners, flashed and glittered in the broad
glare of the burning lamps; while, on the floor,
belted knights and high-born dames moved to and
fro in merry converse, or, with gladsome laugh, preparing for the dance.

"Come, sweet one," said the Desmond to his bride,
as he took her by the hand and led her to the end of
the great hall; "we will dance a merry measure, and
begin the revel. See yonder. There is Brian the
Harper sweeping the bright strings with his enchanted
fingers, and my heart is dancing to the tune; and, by
our Lady, my feet are tingling to keep it company;"
and he led his beautiful bride to the tune down the

hall, followed by many gay and brave gallants, with their laughing partners.

Now, this old hall was very bright with the light of the burning lamps, the glitter of the gilded armor, and the steely spears, the sheen of dancing plumes and gorgeous dresses, and the sparkling of many love-lit eyes; but suddenly a brightness that seemed to extinguish all blazed in through loophole and windows, and filled the hall with its excessive splendor, dazzling the eyes of the revellers, and striking their hearts with sudden and portentous fear. In a moment it was gone, and the lamps seemed to start into life again, and the revellers raised their eyes with throbbing hearts, and looked upon their lord and lady — the brave Geraldine and his bride. There stood the bride, looking down with a fixed and stony gaze upon her Gerald, who lay prostrate and lifeless at her feet upon the floor. All gathered round and tried to awake him from his swoon, but it was of no avail. The lord of Kilmoodan took his daughter by the hand, and led her to her bower, and there her maids wept around her, and besought her to speak; but no word repaid their endearments, for the poor bride only looked upon them with her large and fixed eyes, and raised her lily hands to heaven, and wept and wept while the white stars of that woful night glittered in the sky, and the great autumnal moon looked down with its everlasting smile upon the silent woods. And the Geraldine was borne to his couch, and his followers gathered round, and loud rose the wail of the wild pipe, and the lament of the melancholy harp; but louder still swelled up into the windless sky, and out over the mournful woods, the wild Irish *caoine* from the followers of the Desmond. And the hardy kerne, and the giant gallowglass, bent above his couch; but all in the midst of their sorrow and desolation, the same overpowering brightness flashed again upon them for a moment, and when they raised their dazzled eyes once more, the body of their beloved lord was gone!

"By the ancient Crom, the God of thunder and battle!" exclaimed Diarmid of the Rock, the favorite gallowglass of the earl, "but the fairy King Donn, and he only, could have ta'en him thus. Follow me," he continued, rearing up its gigantic form, and drawing his ponderous sword from its scabbard, "and we will up to the crest of Cnoc Feirinna, and storm the enchanted palace, and bring back our young prince!" and he rushed from the hall, followed by his comrades. On they went upon their rushing steeds in frantic and furious haste through the moonlit forest, and to the crest of the enchanted hill, and looked around, with vengeance blazing in their fierce eyes, for the fairy palace; but nothing met their gaze save the gray cairn, and the purple expanse of heath lying still, and lonesome, and melancholy, beneath the ghostly moonlight.

When the morning sun arose over the flat Limerick plain, Fair Eileen of Kilmoodan awoke to the full consciousness of her sorrow and bereavement.

"Bring me back my gallant lord!" she cried — "bring him back to my broken and desolate heart, or I shall die!" But her maidens only looked upon her and wept, till she knew there was no hope, and she laid herself down, and wept again, and spoke no word till the golden sun had sunk to rest beyond the western billows, and the mournful moon looked down from the blue and silent heaven upon the woody plains and solitary hills.

And the good lord, her father, brought the wise men from town, and village, and castle. The white-bearded gatherer of the painted herbs; the fairy woman, with her withered face and red mantle; the doctor, with his looks of melancholy wisdom, from the great town, were brought to the couch of the weeping bride; but none could cure the sad sickness of her heart, or ease her sorrow.

A great war arose in Desmond. Earl Gerald's cousin usurped the princedom, saying that the Desmond had died, perchance by the steel of some vengeful rival, or by the plotting of the English king, — he cared not which, — but that he himself was next in succession. But the followers of the young earl knew better, and believed that he was in Fairyland, and would return to his blithe castle once more, and so they would not submit. Then battles were fought, plains were ravaged, and towns sacked; and thus they continued till another moon shone out with its silver crescent upon the scenes of their contention.

The loyal army of the young prince passed one day

through the hoary town of Kilmallock, with their shrill war-pipes playing before them, and their brave banners waving, and encamped upon the height of Cnoc Sonna, or the Hill of the Moon, from the summit of which, centuries before, ere Patrick lighted the lamp of the gospel in the land, the ancient inhabitants paid their adoration to the mild queen of the night. And the sun had set, and all had composed themselves to sleep, save the sentinels around the foot of the romantic hill. Many a reckless laugh arose from the watchers, as they sat around their camp fires in merry converse.

"We will keep our own," said Brown Redmond, a wiry-looking kerne, to a tall gallowglass who sat near — "we will hold our own for our rightful lord, for the fairy woman of Lough Gur told me yesterday that he would come back."

"Yes," answered the gallowglass; "and in battle we will henceforth lead before us into the onset the gallant steed of the young prince, caparisoned in his war trappings, and perchance the Desmond may suddenly appear among us, and then he would soon retake his own. And royally would he reign over the fair lands of Munster with his young bride; but they say the wise man and the leech cannot cure her, and she will be dead ere her lord comes back."

"I have found a wise man that can cure her, and tell where the Desmond remains in thrall, too," said Diarmid of the Rock, from the other side of the fire; "and that man is Ronan of the White Beard — the

prophet of Kilmore. They say he has power over
the fairy people, and over death, too, and when our
watch is over this night I will ride to his home amid
the forest, and take him to the castle of Kilmoodan
to cure our young lady."

"If he knows the right leaf upon the herb," said
another, "he may well have power over the good
people; but how is he a prophet? and how hath he
got power over death, Diarmid?"

"O," said Diarmid, with an ironical grin, "Theigeen
Ruadh believes in nothing but the good people, whom
I cannot relish since they took away our prince; and
by the bright cross of my sword, if King Donn himself came within reach of me since they did that bad
deed, I would lop off his head as I did to Saxon Will
in yesterday's battle. But I will tell you, Theigeen,
who Ronan of the White Beard is. No one knows
his parentage, for he was found by a young girl, just
after he was born, beside the hill of Corrin Beg,
wrapped up in a red mantle, with no one nigh to
claim him. The girl found a raven's skull beside a
spring, and, filling it with water, gave the child a
drink, and so he became, after the lapse of years,
a prophet; for thou knowest that he who drinks his
first draught from the skull of a raven can pierce the
future with keen eyes, and foretell. And now, comrades, here comes Garrett of the Tower, with his men,
to hold the next watch, and I will away to Ronan of
the White Beard, and take him to Kilmoodan, to cure
my lady."

And so Ronan of the White Beard was brought next day into the presence of the fair Eileen. The roses had faded from her cheeks, and the lustre of her eyes had been quenched in many tears, when the prophet entered her bower. Her maids surrounded her couch, with tears sparkling in their sorrowful eyes, and she looked, as she lay, like a white rose in the midst of its dewy companions.

"Hast thou come to bring back my true love?" said the fair Eileen, as the wise doctor entered.

"No, lady," answered Ronan of the White Beard; "but I have come to cure thee of sorrow, and tell where thy noble Geraldine lies in thrall."

"And O, he is not dead!" exclaimed Eileen, joyfully. "I knew it could not be. Death himself would not deprive me of my love, for he would have pitied my everlasting sorrow."

"Death had pity on thee, great lady," answered Ronan; "and thy husband dwells not in his mansion, but lies in thrall in the great palace of Cleena, the Fairy Queen of Desmond. She marked thy noble lord for her own — she loved him, and took him on the night of his bridal away into her palace of Carrig Cleena, by the haunted shore of the Blackwater. None can bring him back but thee. Go thou to the Fairy Rock of Cleena, and ask the great queen for thy husband, and perchance she may take pity on thy sorrows, and give him back. She may refuse thee first, but persist in thy demand, and thy brave prince will return to thee and his broad domains; for love and sorrow such as thine, bright lady, will conquer all."

And Ronan of the White Beard departed, with a great guerdon for his trouble, and Fair Eileen lay back upon her couch, and bethought how she might touch Queen Cleena's heart with pity, and regain her lost love.

"We cannot go to the Fairy Palace with sword and spear, and the waving of warriors' plumes and banners, and force the queen to give back my love," she said to her favorite maiden, when the others had left her bower; "but thou and I will go to Carrig Cleena, my good Oona, and I will bathe its foot in tears, till the heart of the Fairy Queen will grow soft with pity, and she'll give me back my brave Geraldine."

But the lord of Kilmoodan would not let his daughter go thus out into the wild forest of Moyallo, far away, where the merciless Englishman had power; and so he shut her up in her chamber, and set a guard upon her, as one demented. Yet—for love is a crafty lord and a strong—Fair Eileen blinded the watchfulness of her guards, and, one golden sunset, stole out with her maid Oona into the wild forest. On they went, through lonely pathway, green glade, and flowery dell; but the loveliness of the forest scenery was lost upon Eileen and her maid, for their way was growing weary, and they had yet far to travel. At length, when the yellow moon had ascended high over the peaks of the tall Galtees, they beheld a forester's little hut at the bottom of a solitary hollow.

"We will abide here for the night, Oona," said Eileen, "and the good forester will direct us on our way on the morrow."

But the poor forester had also been an outlaw, and the ruthless Englishman had shot him by the wall of Mallow; and so in his hut they found but his weeping wife and his little child. She made a bed of soft heather and brown leaves for her guests, and there they slept till the morning sun was darting his red beams through the gnarled branches of the great forest trees. As they went upon their way again, deep in the dim recesses of the forest they heard a rushing and strange whirring sound behind them, and, looking round, beheld a dim spiral cloud whirling round and round, and seeming to arise from the path on which they came. The cloud faded away, and there, upon the path, was the white fawn, standing still and motionless, and looking upon them with her wild, sinister eyes. They hurried on; but the white fawn followed them, until Eileen, turning round, held up a golden Cross, the gift of her Gerald, which she wore around her neck, and bade the fairy fawn to be gone in the Holy Name. And the fawn vanished between the mossy trunks of the giant trees at the sight of the potent Cross, and they went upon their way again, till at length the gray, turret-like boulders of Carrig Cleena appeared before them.

They built a little hut of lithe branches, roofed with the forest grass and fern beside the river, and there, every midnight, Fair Eileen came forth with her maid, and wept long and bitterly, and demanded her brave bridegroom from the Fairy Queen Cleena. But Cleena was deaf to her supplications.

On the weird night of All Hallows, when the tapers were lit in honor of the holy saints and of the departed souls in many a castle window, when the little lamp burned in the lowly hut for the same purpose, when many a merry Munster youth and maid looked love from their bright eyes, around the crackling fire, and when the capricious people of Fairyland were abroad in vale and forest, holding their mysterious gambols, Fair Eileen came before the Rock, and demanded again and again, with many a tear and moan, her husband back from fairy thrall. Suddenly the stern lineaments of the rock began to fade, and there appeared before her wondering eyes a great and gorgeous palace, with its stately towers and illuminated windows. Long trains of nobles and fair ladies passed in and out through the great gate, at which a number of guards in silver armor were standing, with swords or battle-axes in their hands. Eileen stood up with a sudden resolution, and attempted to pass through the gate; but the guards crossed their arms before her, and told her that no mortal could enter there.

"O, let me in, brave warriors!" she cried; "and your great queen will have pity on a poor maid, and give her back her darling husband!"

But the guards still kept their arms crossed, and spoke never another word, till Eileen could bear her disappointment no longer, and fell at the gate lifeless in a swoon. When she awoke, she looked up for the gay palace; but nothing appeared before her eyes save the stern and silent rock.

The leaves were withered in the forest, the golden flowers of autumn were dead and gone, and the hill-tops were gray with the biting frosts; yet still, night by night, did Fair Eileen come forth from her little hut before the rock, and supplicate the Fairy Queen to give back her husband. And Christmas was drawing nigh, and the merry villagers were looking forward to those festive days with gleeful hearts; yet no joy found its way to the mournful breasts of poor Eileen and her faithful maid. At length, on Christmas Eve, when the blessed light was burning in many a rural cot, and the gleeful children thought, with happy hearts, upon the morrow, Eileen went forth again, and knelt down, in tears and sighs, at the base of the Fairy Rock. Suddenly the bright palace reared itself up before her, with the gay cavalcades moving in and out, and the tall guards standing at the gate. Eileen did not address herself to the guards, but burst forth in a wild lament, addressed to the Fairy Queen.

EILEEN'S LAMENT FOR GERALD.

By loud Avondhu,
While the sweet flowerets blew,
I've mourned for my Gerald the brown autumn through;
And winter frowns lone
On Kilmore's mountain zone,
But Cleena, still Cleena ne'er heedeth my moan!

How sweet fell the hours
By Kilmoodan's gray towers,
When we strayed, ever loving, through sweet dells and bowers!
Ah, the winter and May
Were one blissful day,
Ere my true love was stolen from his Eileen away.

With gems of red gold
Gleamed his mail in the wold,
As we sat where the lone Druid worshipped of old;
But the great Fairy Queen
Passed there one bright e'en,
And she looked on my Gerald, and loved him unseen.

On our sweet bridal night,
To this palace of light
She bore him away by the spells of her might;
And she keeps him in thrall
The high prince of her hall;
Thus Cleena, fair Cleena ne'er heedeth my call.

And thus I must weep
By Cleena's gray steep,
Joy faded, hope clouded, and sorrow more deep;
Yet firmer and true
To the one love I knew,
Till I die in my sorrow by loud Avondhu.

Scarcely had the mournful lament of Eileen ceased, when the great portal of the palace was thrown open, and a long, glittering, splendid train of lords and beautiful ladies appeared, issuing slowly out, with the Fairy Queen at their head. The glow of eternal beauty was fresh upon her face, and the light of the heavenly stars was in her eyes, as she moved outward beneath the gate to the spot where Eileen knelt. She took the tearful suppliant by the hand, and raised her.

"Come, thou faithful maid," said Queen Cleena, in low, dulcet voice; "follow me, and I will reward thee for thy constancy."

And she led Eileen by her side through the great portals of the fairy palace, and on, and on into the glorious hall, which was soon thronged by the courtiers in their gorgeous dresses. A clear and pleasant light filled the hall, which seemed to emanate from no particular spot, but to flow out from the crystal walls, and the roof, and the beautiful carved pillars. Two golden thrones, blazing all over with innumerable gems, were reared in the midst; and Eileen almost fainted with the joyous rapture of her heart, when she beheld her beloved Gerald seated upon one. But he knew her not, and Eileen set up a wild, wailing cry that rang through the glittering chambers of the palace, when she looked into his eyes, and found there no recognition of her presence. Then the Fairy Queen took a white wand from the throne, and touched him with it on the brow, and the intelligence of mortal life came into his eyes, and he sprang, with a glad bound, from the throne, and folded his beloved bride in his arms.

"And now," said Queen Cleena, "take thy choice, O faithful prince, between the glory and the eternal happiness of these bright halls, and the miseries and misfortunes, and short-lived joys, of the troublous earth."

"I will take the green earth," answered the Geraldine, "and the blithe forests and halls of my ancestral domains; and I will take my faithful and beautiful bride, and should misfortune come, her love will console me in my sorrows."

And the Desmond took his fair Eileen by the hand, and she, smiling between love, and joy, and fear, led him down the gorgeous hall, and out through the diamond-spangled gate, free from fairy thrall, into the world of mortals once more.

And the usurper gave up his claim when the rightful prince returned; and the Geraldine and his beautiful bride held revel again in their blithe and merry castles. Through the length and breadth of fair Munster, the Christmas revels were renewed, and the blithesome games played night after night, and the sounds of the gleeful harp and martial pipe arose in town and tower, all in joy at the return of the brave Desmond; and many an after year joy reigned through the land, for the Geraldine and his bride ruled with a mild sway, that brought security and peace to cot and castle, and happiness and plenty to all.

THE PEARL NECKLACE;

OR, THE BEAUTY OF THE BLOSSOM-GATE.

THE ancient town of Kilmallock had, once upon a time, as the story-tellers say, four gates. Of these two still remain, namely, the tall, square, castellated one, which defended the road leading towards Limerick, and the smaller and more compact structure, beneath whose rounded arch the way towards Charleville still passes. Why this latter building was called the Blossom-Gate we were never able to discover with any positive certainty. On examining it, however, a few summers ago, we were struck with the profusion of wall-flowers and other similar plants that decorated its roof, and every chink and cranny from battlement to base, and which, seen in their full glory, in each revolving season, by the inhabitants of the town for many successive generations, may, perhaps, have given origin to the name to which we have alluded.

Be the above supposition as it may, the Blossom-

Gate, from time almost immemorial, served successively as a place of habitation, free of rent, for certain individuals of the town and its vicinity, who, having lost their home and substance either by misfortune or extravagance, were sent thither, to make their dwelling, by the influence of one or more of the neighboring gentry. There was one brilliant and happy period in its existence, namely, while it was tenanted by old Arthur Segrave and his only daughter, Rosa, the handsomest girl in the county — so handsome, indeed, that by the universal voice of all her neighbors, she was called the Beauty of the Blossom-Gate.

Old Arthur Segrave, her father, had once been a rich and prosperous man, an extensive landholder, in fact, whose estate lay about four or five miles outside the town, and was now in the possession of a successful tallow merchant from the neighboring city. After a course of reckless extravagance, he had married, rather late in life, a young lady, who, besides her beauty and birth, had nothing else to recommend her as a wife, save that she was able to clear a five-barred gate with her hack as scientifically as the best fox-hunter in Ireland. This, however, was more than sufficient for Arthur Segrave. So he married her, and the bare amount of her pin-money went no small way in sinking him deeper and deeper in debt, till her death, which deplorable event happened about five years after the birth of Rosa, their only child. After this, it might have been expected that Segrave would have made some reformation in his mode of living. But no such thing happened. Instead of that, he mortgaged half his estate to the aforesaid tallow merchant, and on the proceeds lived as jovially as ever for a time. There is, however, an end to all things on this earth, and nothing becomes "small by degrees and beautifully less" with such demoniac speed as money. It was thus with Arthur Segrave, who, the moment the proceeds of his first mortgage were gone, had recourse to the greasy guineas of the fat tallow merchant, Peery Montgomery, once more, and sunk the remainder of his property; and that, after a few years, was finally reduced so low that he was forced to apply for the aforesaid residence in the Blossom-Gate.

Now, after saying a few words relative to old Peery Montgomery, the tallow merchant, and his grand-nephew and only surviving relative, Bob, we shall pass rapidly on, and let the incidents of our story follow in their natural course. Peery, after seizing in his talons the estate of poor Segrave, left the city, and came to live in Kilmallock, where he seemed to have nothing earthly to do but to ride out, and take a look over his ill-gotten lands, — he had come into possession of them not over-honestly, it was said, — and to lend money to his needy neighbors, and charge a most destructive interest thereon; for he was a usurer of the first water. His grand-nephew, Bob Montgomery, whom he hated mortally, but to whom he gave a support and a home for some reason, notwithstanding, was about twenty years of age, and as fine and handsome a specimen of a young man as could be found in the country. He and his uncle lived under the same roof, till events which shall be hereafter related separated them.

Beneath an ancient oak tree, that once grew upon the shore of Kilmallock Lake, and while the setting rays of a calm July sun was gilding tree and water, and steeping in fervid glory the venerable walls and castles of the aged town, Rosa Segrave sat with a bunch of wild flowers in her hands, the petals of which flowers she was listlessly pulling asunder, and strewing upon the grass beside her. She was evidently waiting for some one, for she occasionally raised her clear, brown eyes from the doomed blossoms, and cast an eager and inquiring glance down the paths that led up to the tree from a far-off grove, whose giant trunks shone in the descending sun like the red pillars of some aged and barbaric temple.

"Well," she muttered to herself, after committing destruction on an unusual quantity of the flowers, "he will never come. And what keeps him I cannot tell, for he promised to be here long before this. Perhaps," — and an indignant blush overspread her beautiful face, — "perhaps he is lingering with Jane Courtney. No, no," she continued, after a pause, during which she seemed casting up in her mind all the good qualities of him for whom she lingered there; "I have never found him to break his word or tell an untruth, and why should he do so now? He *will* come; and so, if it were till nightfall, I will wait."

With this praiseworthy and confiding resolution, she again sat down, and after another glance down the path, took up the bunch of flowers, whose total wealth of blossoms was soon strewn around her. Appearing at a loss for occupation during the delay, she drew from her bosom a folded paper, opened it, and as she cast her eyes over its contents, every appearance of mistrust and displeasure seemed banished from her countenance.

"Ah," she said, while her eyes sparkled with pleasure, "I am sure he loves but me. He cannot care for Jane Courtney, especially as he says that he likes no one but myself." She cast her eye again over the paper. "He would never send a song like this to Jane!" and in a low voice, and in the sweetest of tones, she read to herself the following effusion, from one who was certainly a lover, if not a poet:—

THE LINNET.

I've found a comrade, fond and gay,
  A linnet of the wild-wood tree;
We hold sweet converse day by day,
  My heart, my rambling soul, and he.
He sits upon the blossomed spray,
  Within the hollow, haunted dell;
And every song-note seems to say,
  That wild bird knows and loves me well!
Sweet linnet! Sing all merrily
  Beside the glittering streamlet's shore,
For love-bright dreams thou bring'st to me
  Of Rosaleen for evermore!

As I lie in my waking dreams,
  And dreamy thoughts successive rise,
Down from the blooming bough he seems
  To look on me with human eyes;
And then he sings — ah, such a song
  Will ne'er be heard while seasons roll,
Save thy dear voice, that all day long
  In memory charms my heart and soul.
Sweet linnet! Still sing merrily,
  Beside the haunted streamlet's shore;
For many a dream thou bring'st to me
  Of Rosaleen for evermore!

If souls e'er visit earth again,
  With one my little friend's possessed;
Each dulcet, wild, elysian strain
  Springs so divinely from his breast;
Those fairy songs, that earnest look,
  Some minstrel sprite it sure must be;
Anacreon's soul, or hers who took
The love-leap by the Grecian Sea!
Sweet linnet! Still sing merrily
  Beside the murmuring streamlet's shore,
For happy dreams thou bring'st to me
  Of Rosaleen for evermore!

Again she looked impatiently down the path, but there was no appearance of him whom she expected, and who evidently was the author of the song. She was about replacing the paper in her bosom, when a rustling in the thickets behind startled her, and she let it fall. She stood up, and looked eagerly in the direction from which the sound proceeded, and, with an expression of dislike and disappointment on her lovely face, beheld, not the object of her thoughts at that moment, but the old usurer, Peery Montgomery, approaching her from the thickets.

"A fine evening, Miss Segrave," said old Peery, in a cracked, harsh voice, as he came up to the tree; "a fine evening for enjoying one's self, especially here, where everything is so lovely, and the air so cool and pleasant."

"It is a pleasant evening, indeed," said she, feeling strangely embarrassed, for she felt the eyes of the old man bent upon her with a conscious look that showed he guessed for whom she was waiting.

"It would be a great deal pleasanter," resumed he, moving nearer, "if you had some one beside you, with whom you might converse about—about the weather, say, if no other topic should suggest itself;" and he smiled a half-sneering smile that made his presence still more unwelcome to Rosa. "However," he continued, moving from beside the tree, and standing within about a foot from where the paper that contained the song lay upon the grass, "there's a time for everything, Miss Segrave. Look how beautifully the sun shines upon the spire of the abbey beyond! The old stones seem as if they would take fire, they are so red and bright."

Rosa turned and looked. Her back was towards Peery, who in an instant stooped, picked up the paper, and put it nimbly and noiselessly in his pocket.

"I never saw the old town looking so bright," said she, turning round again, but not in time to perceive the act.

"It is getting late, Miss Segrave," he now resumed; "should you wish me to accompany you home, I shall feel most happy to do so."

"I do not," she answered, with involuntary ungraciousness. "I wish to wait here till — till — but the paper that I dropped this moment! Where is it, for it fell just here."

"What paper?" asked Peery, in a careless tone. "I saw nothing here when I came up."

"O, I am sure it cannot be lost; it is in my dress," she said, evasively. "I wish you a good evening, Mr. Montgomery!" and, with an almost unaccountable impulse of dislike for the old purloiner of the song, she turned, and was about to leave the spot.

"Stay, Miss Segrave!" said Peery, as she moved away; "I have a few words to say to you, which you never gave me an opportunity of saying before."

Rosa stopped and looked at him calmly, although she guessed what was to follow.

"Your father's property is now in my hands, Miss Segrave," continued Peery; "at least so deeply mortgaged to me that he can never get it back — that I can almost call it mine. Has it ever struck you what he is to do in his old age, he that was always used to such good living? And what are you to do, perhaps, when he dies and leaves you penniless? I am counted a hard man by the world, Miss Segrave, and I don't know that I am a wise one, when I tell you I am willing to arrange matters so that the property, at least part of it, could come into your father's hands again."

"It is very kind of you, sir," said Rosa, interrupting him, "but it is not with me you should settle that business; it is with my father."

"No," answered Peery, "it is with you, Miss Segrave. I am a plain man," he continued, "and one that never wasted many words on business, as I cannot help calling this interview. I shall not keep you long ignorant of my meaning. I am a lonely man, Miss Segrave, and have been thinking that I did wrong in not marrying long ago. However, better late than never. As I have at last got the opportunity, I ask you now, will you become my wife? and all that man can do to make you and your father comfortable, I shall not fail to do. What answer may I hope for?"

"That answer," returned Rosa, while her eyes flashed with indignation — "that answer, I have reason to know, you got from my father lately. I now tell you the same — that I will never become your wife, even though I had to beg my bread from door to door, and die for want of it in the end!"

"Wait till want comes," said Peery. "However, think over it, Miss Segrave," he continued, with a slight sneer; "and should you change your mind, as I trust in Heaven you will and must, I am easily to be found."

"I have thought over it," returned Rosa. "From me you shall always get the same answer. Again I wish you a good evening;" and she turned and fairly ran down the path, leaving Peery Montgomery leaning against the trunk of an aged tree, in no very amiable frame of mind.

That night Peery Montgomery sat in his sparely-furnished parlor, before a table on which lay two separate bundles of papers. His nephew sat beside him.

"Here, Bob, take that heap of papers opposite you, and tot up the amounts marked upon them," said the old man. "When that's done with each, call it out, and I will enter it in the ledger."

Bob, willing to please the old man, took up a pen and commenced his work at once. When he had got about half way down the pile of papers, he paused suddenly for a moment, and the keen rat-like eyes of the old man fixed themselves upon him with a sinister and contemptuous gaze. At length the blood rushed up to Bob's temples, an exclamation of astonishment and anger escaped him, and he started up from the table, holding an open sheet of paper in his hand.

"What's the matter?" said Peery, in a jocular but yet bitter tone.

"Nothing!" answered Bob, endeavoring to recover his composure; "nothing, sir. Let us go to work again!" and he crumpled the paper in his clinched hand and sat down.

"Why do you start so, then?" asked Peery. "Come, come, Bob, let us understand each other at least. You have turned poet, I see. You need not crumple that paper — I have read it, and got it by heart already. You didn't meet your linnet this evening, though, I'll go bail. However, I met her beneath the old oak tree at the lake; and to show you what she thinks of you, Bob, she laughed, and gave me that song you hold in your hand, and which you thought would win her like magic. You are young, Bob, you are young, and don't know the vagaries of girls, and the way they make fools of people!" and he laughed bitterly.

Poor Bob was wholly confounded. He knew not what to think. It all appeared like a dream to him, the troubles of which would cease with waking; but, alas, there, still clutched firmly in his hand, was the damning paper that told the falseness of her for whom he would have willingly died. He was roused from his stupor by the voice of his grand-uncle, who fiercely and suddenly seemed to change in his manner towards him.

"I can tell you what," said Peery, "if you do not attend to your learning — that is, useful learning — you shall pack, like a fool as you are, from my house. Leave that old crack-brained, fox-hunting ass and his daughter to me, or, if you don't, you shall never see a shilling of my money. Do you hear me, sir? Have nothing further to do with them, or, mark my words, I'll take means to knock the love out of you."

"I do hear you, sir," answered Bob, standing up opposite the old man. "I have seen enough to-night to convince me that I cannot place much faith in any one. As regards leaving your house, I am not the man to stay when I feel that my presence is a burden.

You shall not see me again!" and he moved towards the door.

This, however, did not serve old Peery's purpose. He knew that if Bob left him and continued in the town, as he was likely to do, Rose Segrave would find means to clear up the affair of the song. He adopted a better method of separating them.

"Stop!" he said, now in a kind tone, as Bob was in the act of opening the door — "stay, Bob. You know, as for Arthur Segrave and his daughter, they are both beggars, and one with your prospects, if you obey me, has no business with them. There, however, is Jane Courtney, who will have a good fortune. You have my free liberty to talk to her as you wish. So let us be friends once more."

Bob returned and sat down. He took the sheet of paper on which he had so carefully written his song for, as he thought, the faithless Rosa Segrave, tore it in fragments, and scattered them on the floor. But he said not a word, although Peery expected a stormy outburst of indignation.

"That's done like a sensible man," said Peery; and so they parted for the night.

Now, when two young hearts love truly, it is not very easy to tear them asunder; and this was well proved in the case of Rosa Segrave and Bob Montgomery. For a time they avoided each other, but after about a month, they accidentally came together, had a conversation, and the affair was explained by both satisfactorily. Then it was that the anger of old Peery burst forth in all its vindictive bitterness, as will be shown presently.

At the time of which we write, Limerick and the neighboring counties were in a state of civil commotion. Parties of armed men paraded the country at night, wreaking their vengeance upon many who, perhaps, little deserved it, and upon many also to whom it was strictly due. Torn-up crops, levelled fences, and houghed cattle marked their track, and even the terrible signs of their progress were frequently seen by the light of a blazing farmstead, a village, and sometimes by that of a town. Several of the more troublous districts were proclaimed, and it need scarcely be added that martial law was exercised unsparingly upon the heads of all who were caught rendering themselves amenable to its rigorous statutes. Many a solitary mound and desolate cairn by mountain side and lonely glen still marks the spot where some misguided peasant expiated on the gallows the deeds he was was driven to by the prevailing mismanagement and poverty of the time; and many a story of popular retribution on the heads of the local potentates, who then ruled these districts with an iron rod, is yet told by the descendants of those who took part in the civil commotions. But to proceed.

About a week subsequent to the reconciliation of Rose Segrave and her lover, two men were sitting in a small back room of an inn, situated in the diminutive suburb beyond the northern gate of Kilmallock. One of them was Peery Montgomery; the other was a thick-set, middle-aged man, with a swarthy, weather-beaten face, and a pair of deep-set gray eyes, whose fierce and determined expression would be likely to make his company not very agreeable to most men of peaceable dispositions. They were carrying on a conversation in an undertone, and it seemed by the manner of both that they at last began to understand each other properly.

"At all events," said Peery, "get him to join, and you'll get the money, Davy Saer,* every penny of what I promised."

"Yes," answered Davy; "an' if I got him to go on his *keepin'* † like myself, what would you say?"

"Just the same," returned Peery. "You'll get the money."

"An'," rejoined the other, with a grim smile, "suppose he should leave a mark on the mountains in the shape of a heap o' stones, to show that he left the world dancin' his last jig, or the *Skibbiach's* ‡ hornpipe from a thriangle, what would you do? You'd make a lamentation on the boy's death, I suppose!" and the ruffian laughed hoarsely, and then solaced himself with a glass of punch he held in his hand.

"No matter," returned Peery, with an ugly glitter in his eye, "you'll get the money, I say, and here is the first balance;" and he handed Davy the Mason half a dozen guineas across the table.

* David the Mason. † That is, to be outlawed.
‡ Skibbach, a hangman.

"'Tis a bargain," said Davy, clutching the money in his large, bony hand. "An' now I must be off, Mr. Montgomery. Never fear, afore long he'll be one of us, or my name isn't Davy!" and the villanous pair separated.

We shall not here detail the various traps laid for poor Bob Montgomery in order to induce him to become a Whiteboy. It is enough to say that in the end they succeeded.

There was a regulation in force amongst those unfortunate men at the time, that in whatever district a deed was to be done, no matter of what nature, the captain of that district should have sole command of all deputed for its accomplishment. It was thus that on a certain November morning Bob Montgomery found himself on the side of a hill that overhung a neighboring town, in the command of a body of men that, if not for its equipments, at least from its number, might well be called an army. Thousands sat resting themselves around him on the withered fern and damp heath that clothed the side of the hill. It seemed from their looks that some event of more than usual magnitude and importance was about to happen. A considerable number carried fire-arms of some kind or other in their hands; others had swords, which were probably taken in some skirmish with the yeomen; but by far the largest portion of that fierce and motley array was armed with scythe-blades, hay-forks, and pikes, which, as the thick masses of men sat along the hill, they held firmly in their hands pointing into the air. That air was thick with fog, which hung upon hill and hollow, a gray and almost palpable canopy that effectually obscured the arrangements of the wild Whiteboy army.

There was no standard; neither fife nor drum, to the martial notes of which they might march on to grapple with their foes; but there was that which was far more ominous of damage to their enemies. There was a quiet, settled, yet fierce expression on the face of each man, which showed that he was willing to die or carry out the purpose of his leader, which will be seen presently. Not a word was spoken amongst them. Bob Montgomery, with some of the leaders under him, sat in a hollow, waiting, apparently, for the arrival of the scout she had sent off about an hour previously.

At last a tall, nimble-footed young man came briskly up the hill, and, without looking to the right or left, or saying a word to those amongst whom he passed, strode into the hollow, and stood leaning upon his gun before his leader.

"Well, Jack," said Bob Montgomery, "what have you seen?"

"I'll tell you, captain," answered the scout. "There are nearly two hundred soldiers standing to their arms in the middle o' the town square. At one side o' them — the side next to us here — there is a regiment o' yeoman cavalthry, an' at their off side is another regiment o' yeoman foot. That's what I saw."

On this account it was resolved to begin the attack at once. We may state that what follows has little of the imaginative in its details. It is found substantially related in the county histories of the time. Bob had made his principal arrangements previously. He now gave the word to those under his command, who immediately left the hollow with him, and in ten minutes afterwards the whole array, in three divisions, were leaving the hill, and marching cautiously upon the town. At the side they were marching on, a road led up through a narrow street into the square, to the spot whereon the yeoman cavalry were stationed. A lane also opened, and gave passage from the north-east into the town opposite the front of the soldiers.

Everything seemed now quiet. Both soldiers and yeoman were quietly resting on their arms when they beheld, up both lane and street, a few immense loads of straw moving towards the square. This, of course, was no suspicious sight. The horses of the yeomen cavalry, on the contrary, champed their bits and neighed a welcome to the loads of provender; but no word of command yet rang along the ranks to warn the riders of what was approaching, under cover of the straw. Suddenly the loads increased their speed, and at length rolled simultaneously into the square. Then, from behind them, a shout arose that curdled the blood of the inhabitants of the town and of its defenders, and Bob Montgomery with his men came rushing up the street upon the cavalry, while at the same time his second in command dashed up the lane, and fell upon the regulars and yeoman foot.

It was a fight quickly begun and speedily ended. The regulars for a few moments held their ground firmly, but the yeoman cavalry were instantly broken and put to flight by the headlong charge of Bob Montgomery and his division. Several men were, of course, killed on both sides; but a worse disaster than a battle had befallen the town, for it was on fire in several places. The Whiteboys, expecting a stouter resistance from their foes, had adopted this extreme and terrible plan of aiding their attack. The town, in many parts, consisted of rows of thatched houses, the dry roofs of which easily caught the flame, and communicated it to the neighboring slated ones, till at last it was one roaring blaze throughout every quarter. Bob drew up the men that remained after the pursuit, and with these endeavored to extinguish the flames; but his efforts were of no avail, and all he could do was to help the inhabitants to escape, and aid them in saving their effects from the fire.

As he stood before a house fronting the square, with its door firmly barred and its roof of iron, he heard a shriek, as if from a girl who was struggling to escape from the inside. He looked up to one of the windows, through which a volume of smoke was issuing, and, with a pang of terror which made his heart leap, beheld Rosa Segrave standing inside, and vainly struggling to open the sashes, the lower panes of which were broken, probably by the heat or some stray bullet shots. Bob snatched a musket from one of his men, and in an instant dashed in the door with a blow of its heavy butt. Throwing the gun aside, he sprang up the stairs, and was just in time to save the life of Rosa, for the floor of the room had begun to ignite. The other inhabitants of the house had escaped by the back way, and Rosa, whose relatives they were, and with whom she happened to be on a visit of a few days, was forgotten in the fright. Bob caught her up in his arms from where she lay, half-smothered, beside the window, and bearing her quickly down stairs, and out into the garden at the rear of the house, deposited her amongst her friends, kissed her pale brow fondly, and was gone. He had a grave task before him in the street. It is hard to gather and lead off a large body of undisciplined men, especially after a battle in which they have proved victorious. This Bob accomplished, however. He sent his men safely to their homes, and in a few days afterwards took to the mountains, an outlaw, informed against by Davy the Mason, who, as a matter of course, obtained his promised reward from old Peery Montgomery.

There is a picture in which a young Royalist, of the time of Charles the First, is represented as hiding in a hollow tree, and receiving his food from the hands of a beautiful young girl, possibly his sister, but far more probably his lover. Such a fate was now that of Bob Montgomery. There was an old wood near Kilmallock. It was a lonely place, seldom visited except by a stray sportsman, and such only penetrated but a small distance into its outskirts. Beside a tangled path that led through its centre, and which showed, by the amount of brambles that grew over it, that it was very rarely trodden, grew an ancient beech tree, whose trunk had become hollowed in the lapse of ages. Within this hollow trunk Bob concealed himself; and were it not for the brave girl who loved him so well, and who never failed to bring him food every day, he would have died of starvation. How they escaped detection so long is a marvel; but they did, nevertheless, for several weeks, although the yeomen were every day scouring the country in hopes of capturing him. It may be asked why he did not leave Ireland at once. But love is wayward and strong, and the thought of living near Rosa, though in the utmost peril, was sweeter to Bob than the certainty of safety far away.

But an hour came, on which he was at last forced to bid her farewell. The merry Christmas time came and went, leaving many a heart in the old town glad at its memory. Rosa Segrave, however, had but little cause for happiness on that night of wassail and pleasant laughter. At the very moment that the glad jingling of the bells was echoing over the town, she was speeding through the snow towards the lonely wood where her lover lay concealed, her sad heart throbbing violently, and her mind filled with apprehension and misery. At length she reached the tree, and met the object of her mission, sitting moodily at its foot, awaiting her coming, for she had not been with him during the day.

"I thought you would never come, Rosa," he said, standing up and catching her hand fondly.

"Bob — Bob!" she answered, endeavoring to repress a cry; "I fear it is the last time we shall ever meet again. They have discovered you, and you must fly instantly for your life!" and she burst into tears.

"It can scarcely be," he said, incredulously. "Here I am now nearly a month, and not a single human being have I seen in the wood during that time save yourself."

"But I tell you they have discovered all," she resumed, trembling with terror. "Your grand-uncle watched me, and then set Davy the Mason to dog my steps. He has found you out, and this evening has informed the yeoman captain of it. I am sure they will be here instantly. So you must fly. No matter how I found it out. I did so, however, an hour ago. O God! that we must part so soon, never, I suppose, to see each other more! Good by — good by!" and she held out her trembling hand.

"Have you no keepsake?" he said, with strange calmness; "nothing to give me as a token when I am far away?"

"Here — here!" she answered, suddenly drawing off a small pearl necklace which she wore, and handing it to him; "take this and be gone, for even now I think I hear a party approaching the wood. Take

it — take it, Bob; and may God bless and guard you!
I want nothing by which to remember you!"

Bob took the trinket, and placed it in his bosom.

"Nor I," he said; "but still it will be pleasant to look upon it when I am far away."

As he whispered the fond words they heard a sound of footsteps approaching in the darkness.

"Go, Bob!" she whispered, scarcely knowing what she said. "Go! They are coming, too truly, indeed!" and Bob, throwing his arms around her, pressed her for an instant to his heart, and then, with a sorrowful "farewell," darted through the wood. Rosa had just time enough to glide in beneath the black shadows of the dense trees hard by, when a party of yeomen rushed up to the spot she had left, led by the treacherous Davy Sair. They were too late, for, after searching the hollow trunk and every part of the wood, they could nowhere find their intended victim.

Late next morning Bob reached Limerick, where he met a recruiting sergeant, and without a moment's delay enlisted. He was now safe, for there was a war, and the government wanted men badly. In a week afterwards the detachment to which he belonged embarked for India, the seat of war, where he fought in many a gallant battle.

Three years rolled away. In the interim old Peery Montgomery was more urgent than ever in his suit to Rosa; for a long time his cause seemed hopeless. Towards the close of the third year, Peery dressed

himself sprucely one day, and walked leisurely to the
Blossom-Gate, where he had an interview with Rosa
and her father. During that interview he showed
them a letter, — and it may as well be stated here
that the same document was forged by himself, —
which contained the account of Bob's death in some
Indian battle. It was terrible news to Rosa; but
she bore it bravely for the sake of her father, who
was at the time in extreme ill health. For his sake
also — for they were now in absolute want — she
consented, after another fortnight, to become 'old
Peery's wife. The wedding day at length came.
The ill-assorted pair stood before the clergymen who
was to make them one. Peery gave his affirmative
response in a piping and exultant tone, that would
have done credit to the lungs of a man of twenty.
Just as it came to Rosa's turn to give the answer that
was to decide her fate forever, there was a bustle
amongst the bystanders, and an old woman, a former
servant of her father's, walked quickly up and thrust
a small parcel into her hand. She opened it, and,
with a wild cry of anguish, found therein her necklace, with a single lock of her lover's hair. The sight
of both wrought a sudden and fatal change for Peery.
The clergyman put the decisive question.

"No," she said, in a trembling but distinct
voice, "I will never become his wife. I cannot. Let
me go home, or I shall die."

Peery cast his cold, flashing eye upon her for a
moment. The blood rushed up to his face and head,

and, after vainly endeavoring to recover himself, he fell forward on the floor in a fit. The clergyman who came to preside at his wedding had the melancholy duty to perform of preparing him for another world, for that day old Peery died — died suddenly, and left no will.

Again it is New Year's Eve. Rosa is sitting at her window in the Blossom-Gate, and looking out over the Charleville road, along which a regiment of soldiers, with a merry band playing before them, is marching into the town. As the first company approach the gate, her eyes rest, searchingly, for a moment upon the gallant-looking young officer who marches in front, and, with a scream of delight, she almost falls backward into the chamber; for in him she recognizes her long-lost lover, Bob Montgomery, who by his valor and intelligence had thus risen during the wars.

What need of more? Bob, as the only surviving relative, came in for his grand-uncle's property. He and the faithful girl who loved him so well were married soon after.

CREEVAN, THE BROWN-HAIRED;

OR, THE SEVENTH SON.*

ONCE upon a time, in the pleasant Munster clime, when this land was in its prime — by my soul! far better than 'tis now, when the poor must cringe and bow to lords that won't allow any *ceol*† at the patron or the fair, at the hurling — anywhere, but all is woe and care black as night; when the clansman held his land 'neath no foreign lord's command, and all was fresh and bland, fair and bright; when he reaped whate'er he sowed; when he dug, and thrashed, and mowed, till his healthy brown face glowed with delight; when he sat in peace, full merry, save when the noise and hurry of some rattling, roaring foray kept his hand in practice evermoe with the glaive and with the bow, so that devil a tyrant foe through the land could bully and could thieve, could wrack,

---

* This legend is known in Norway and in Germany. Two versions of it are given in Grimm's Popular Tales, but neither of them equal to the Irish one in wildness and originality.

† *Ceol*, fun, jollity.

and burn, and rieve, that he did not soon receive of
the brand, or the axe, or dart, enough, in many a battle
tough, from the clansman brave and rough, bold and
gay; when the fairies were in vogue, and each schem-
ing, wanton rogue whipped you off to Tir-n an-Oge
ere you could say "Jack Robinson" three times, and
they sang their merry rhymes, and played their pranks
and mimes, in meadows lone; when the giants ruled
in state in the mighty mountains great, and for power
and grandeur *bate* the world — mavrone! monstrous
giant, wanton fairy, with their revels great and merry,
from Dun Creevan's Mount to Kerry — all are flown!
In this olden time that I have said, where to the sky
tower old Cummeragh's mountains high a mighty
span, in the Fort of Coolnadun, where the merry
waters run, flashing, dancing in the sun, there dwelt
a man, and his name was Rory Fionn, a soldier of
renown, the boldest and the bravest of his clan.*

Now this Rory Fionn was very poor by reason of
the largeness of his family; for from the green and
pleasant summer-tide of his youth, till the snows of
life's winter began to turn his yellow locks to a silver
gray, there were born to him six sons and thirteen
blooming daughters. And now, when he had exhausted all the neighborhood for godfathers, and when
he awoke one summer morning, and found a seventh

* This prelude is in imitation of the rant frequently used by
the old Shanachies, or professional story-tellers, at the commencement of a tale.

son added to his numerous progeny, he arose and put his harness on his back, and, taking his brown-knotted spear in his hand, sallied forth, with a sour face and a sorrowful heart, from his native valley, in order to find among some distant clan a strange sponsor for his child.

After wandering for some time through the green, bosky forest that surrounded his native valley, he at length emerged from its outward skirts upon a flat, and desolate, and weird-looking moorland, extending away in lonely barrenness to the far-off horizon, and there shut in by a gigantic range of bluish mountains that shot up in many-pinnacled summits through the crystal air of the calm, summer morning. Through the midst of this great moorland, a broad, straight road stretched away towards the distant range; but he looked in vain for the dint of chariot wheel or track of living thing upon its dusty surface. All appeared strange, eery-looking, and melancholy to the eyes of Rory Fionn — to him who had ranged over forest, and hill, and dale a thousand times, but had never beheld this wild, and wonderful, and desert flat before.

"By my father's soul," he said, striking his spear-shaft upon the ground, "but I've come upon an enchanted land. However, there is the road straight before me; so here goes, whatever comes of it, and it will go hard with Rory Fionn if he do not take the right hand of the causeway from whomever he encounters this blessed morning."

With that he strode out upon the great road, and travelled on, thinking, in a morose and gloomy temper, of some plan for providing suitably for his great family. At length he raised his eyes from the dusty road, and, although a moment before not a living thing could be seen over its whole extent, a figure now stood a few yards before him upon the way. The new-comer was a man of spare proportions, tall, with a brown, crafty-looking face, and a pair of keen, sparkling, jet-black eyes, that seemed to pierce through the very marrow of Rory's bones as the latter suddenly halted, and advanced his brown-knotted spear-shaft towards the intruder.

"I am unarmed, Rory Fionn!" said the stranger, in a keen, thrilling voice; "so recover pike instantly, or you are not a true man and a soldier!"

"It is true," answered Rory, withdrawing his weapon; "but how know you my name?"

"No matter," returned the stranger. "I know also what you seek. Will you take me for a sponsor for your seventh son?"

"The first staff one meets with in the wood may be the best," thought Rory to himself; "but then it may be crooked and rotten;" and he paused and eyed the stranger sharply.

"Are you doubtful?" said the latter. "This morning, on leaving your home, you were not so dainty in the choice of a sponsor."

"Yes," answered Rory, "I must first know your name, before taking you for a gossip."

"I am one who was often beside you in the red tide of battle," returned the other. "I am he who made you kill your wife's cousin long ago through jealousy, and who steeled your heart in the foray of Glendarra, so that you burned the house over the heads of the widow of Keal and her six blooming daughters! Now do you know me?"

"I do, tempter," answered Rory. "I know you but too well; may the Lord forgive me for my acquaintance. Avaunt, demon! You shall be no gossip of mine; and here is to pay you the old scores remaining between us!" and with that he brought his pike to the charge, and dashed at the infernal king; but nothing met his thrust save a black and sulphury pillar of cloud, that gradually faded away in the crystal air of the moorland. Satan was gone, and Rory found himself alone and travelling once more along the weird causeway.

On gaining a spot about half way across the moorland, he saw something excessively bright and glorious moving towards him upon the road in the far distance. At first Rory thought it was a small cloud kindled into splendor by the morning sun; but, as it approached, he at length perceived that it was an angel. With soft wings folded, and glowing, and glistering with a thousand iridescent dyes, and yellow locks of golden light flowing down upon his fair shoulders, the angel now came up and accosted Rory in a voice far sweeter than the tone of the most dulcet harp-string that ever sounded within the four silver seas of holy Ireland.

"What seekest thou, Rory Fionn?" he asked, "and why art thou wandering thus lonely over the Plain of Life?"

"And is that the name of the great moorland?" asked Rory in return.

"It is," answered the angel. "First thou couldst not see. Now, look around thee right and left, and behold over the great plain its bright sparkling rivers and streams, its pleasant groves, its hamlets, and towns, and rich-gleaming cities. See, there are deserts too, and tartaric chasms, and abysses, where the wanderers betimes perish, and are lost for want of forethought."

Rory looked, and with wonder beheld the face of the whole plain changed; yet his eyes rested not upon pleasant grove or smiling valley, but wandered in admiration over the rich towns, with their shining battlements.

"By the blood of my body," he exclaimed, "but had I known this in the morning I would have brought the whole clan at my back, and such a foray was never seen before in old Ireland as we would make upon this fruitful plain."

"Wilt thou have me as a godfather for thy seventh son?" asked the angel, smiling sadly and pitifully at the avariciousness of Rory.

Now, the latter was nothing but a blunt and plain-spoken soldier, and had but small regard for the angel. Besides, his temper was soured, and his perceptions rendered somewhat dull, by his life of hard labor, and the stern vicissitudes of the wars in which he had served.

"No!" he answered, morosely. "I have rarely seen justice done by you or yours. The rich man revels and prospers; the villain, the murderer, and the oppressor, lead lives of ease and luxury, whilst the poor man has to delve, and toil, and sweat, till at length he goes down to the cold clay of the grave in the same penury in which he was born. I will have none of you. Begone!"

With a smile of ineffable sweetness and pity the angel passed on; and as Rory, after striding forward a few perches, turned round to have a farewell look at him, nothing met his gaze save a light, glittering, golden vapor that floated up and up, till at last it was lost in the gay effulgence of the blithe summer sun. The towns and the blooming scenery also, right and left, had faded from his sight, and the great plain wore the same barren and desolate aspect it had worn before.

At last Rory reached the foot of the mighty range of mountains that shut in the far verge of the plain; and, as he looked up the great road that wound still amidst its herbless and desert crags, he beheld a horseman mounted upon a milk-white steed, galloping downward with loud resounding clang, clad in a coat of glittering silver mail, with a plume snowy as the canavaun blossoms that shine along the brown bogs in autumn waving from his glittering helmet in the buxom breeze of the morning.

"Good morrow, brave Rory," said the horseman in a thundering voice, as he reined up his steed opposite the clansman.

"Hail to you, mighty warrior," returned Rory.

"Wilt thou have *me* for a sponsor for thy seventh son?" asked the horseman.

"Who are you?" returned Rory; "for I like the keen, piercing glance of your eye, and the gallant look of your stern face."

"My name is Death," answered the horseman, proudly.

"Yes," answered Rory; "I will have you, you mighty, just, and unconquerable king. With you, chief, and clansman, and beggar are equal, and fear or favor show you to none on earth. You and none else will I take as sponsor for my seventh son."

And thus it came to pass that Death attended at the clansman's christening feast, and stood godfather for his little son, whom they called Creevan the Brown-haired. And while the revel lasted the great warrior behaved with kindness to all, and with becoming gallantry to the ladies, especially to the fragile-looking and beautiful young girls with the pale golden hair, and the light blue eyes, and the bright hectic flushes upon their cheeks, like the sheen of the opening wood-roses in early summer. At the end of the christening feast, Death promised that he would give the godfather's gift to young Creevan the Brown-haired at the proper time, and then took his departure from Coolnadun.

Year then rolled after year in ever-varying succession of sorrow and gladness, till at length Creevan had grown up to man's estate in the light and joy of youthful health and comeliness. At last, on the youth's twenty-first birthday, Death strode into the Rath of Coolnadun, took him by the hand, and led him through forest and glen out upon the great wizard plain. The hamlets, the towns, the merry, glittering streams, the sunny groves, the green valleys, the torrid deserts, and the tartaric rifts and abysses were there again, as the angel had made them appear once before to Rory Fionn; and Death, still holding the young Creevan by the hand, led him into a gay meadow of emerald grass and blooming asphodel, in the midst of which grew a tree of surpassing loveliness.

"This is the Tree of Life, O Creevan," said Death. "Take a handful of its leaves, and squeeze their amber juice into this phial."

Creevan did as he was directed.

"And now, keep the phial as the godfather's gift," continued Death, "and I will endow thee with a knowledge that shall spread thy fame far and wide through thy native land. I make thee a great physician, with the power of knowing instantly who are mine and who they are that are permitted to walk farther a pace over the crooked paths of life. When thou visitest the sick, if thou shouldst see me, invisible to all save thyself, standing at the bed-foot, they are mine; if at the head, pour a drop of the phial into their mouths, and they shall arise immediately hale and strong. Return to this tree, and fill thy phial betimes; but never, as thou lovest thyself and honorest me, prove deceitful, or use craft or guile in thy dealings with me; for from the moment thou dost thou art mine also, and shall descend in darkness to my silent kingdom."

Creevan promised; and Death, taking him again by the hand, led him forth from the great plain back into his native valley, and then departed with loud clang upon his mighty snow-white steed.

And thus it was that Creevan the Brown-haired became the first physician in Ireland; for people said he had only to look upon the sick to tell instantly who was to live and who was to descend into the chill clay of the grave; and they came from far and near for his ministrations, and made him rich with their fees and presents.

And now the riches and glory of the world began to corrupt Creevan's heart. One day an easlach, or courier, upon his foaming steed came thundering into the fort of Coolnadun, with the intelligence that O'Phelan, Prince of Desies, lay upon his last bed of sickness; that a mighty reward was offered to the physician who should effect his recovery, and commanding Creevan the Brown-haired to come to his aid. So Creevan mounted his horse, and rode off with the swift easlach to the palace of O'Phelan, and when he entered the sick prince's chamber, saw Death standing grim and motionless at the bed-foot.

Anger, disappointment, and the lust of gain swelled
high in Creevan's heart at the sight; but the fear of
his godfather's displeasure restrained him for a moment, and he paced up and down the chamber
irresolutely. At length he paused, and, with an
appealing look, gazed into the stern and inexorable
eyes of Death; but beholding there no sign of re-
lenting pity, he strode suddenly to the bed, seized
the prince in his arms, and turned him round so that
his head rested where his feet had been before, and
then administered a few drops from the revivifying
phial. Death shook his mailed hand sternly at Creevan, and disappeared; but the Prince of Desies
immediately arose hale and strong, gave Creevan his
reward, and ere three days' time ordered the beacon
fires to be kindled on his mountain tops for the gathering of the clans, and led a rousing and uproarious
foray into Thomond to commemorate his recovery.

And now Creevan sat in Coolnadun in daily fear
of a visit from his mighty godfather. The silver horn
of the new moon began to wax brighter and brighter
till it filled into a round and refulgent globe of glory
in the blue heavens, and then waned and waned, till
at last it disappeared in a curved thread of snowy
light beyond the western sea; but still Death came
not, and Creevan's heart grew glad, and the black
cloud of fear faded away, and left him in peace once
more. But one day, as he sat at the door of his home
looking at the setting sun as it sank in glory beyond
the western slopes of the mountain, Death appeared,
and laid his heavy hand upon Creevan's shoulder.

"Thou art false to thy compact, O, Creevan!" he said, sternly; "and now thou art mine forever. Arise, and follow to my silent kingdom."

"Take me not in the flower of my days, great godfather," besought Creevan. "Give me time to enjoy this pleasant earth and the riches you have brought me."

"Didst thou not know that day in O'Phelan's palace that I have no mercy upon princes?" said Death; "that in the height of their power, and pomp, and tyranny, I come upon them, and strike them down as I strike the tattered and woe-worn beggar who starves while they feast in godless luxury?"

"I knew it," answered Creevan; "but, O king, spare me, even for my father's sake, and I shall offend no more!"

"Be it so," returned Death. "For his sake I spare thee; but beware how thou breakest our compact again;" and with that he disappeared, and left Creevan trembling in the dying twilight by Coolnadun.

For a time Creevan kept the compact faithfully, and, month by month, his wealth increased, and his fame spread, till his renown became the brightest in the land. One day, as he was returning from Dublin through Green Galien of the Spears, his path led him by the skirts of a great forest that stretched far away over many a brown hill and bosky valley. As he turned round a clump of trees, a forester's hut appeared before him. No cheery spiral of smoke ascended from its little chimney over the tops of the green trees, but from the door came a sound of lamentations that fell sadly upon Creevan's heart. He dismounted, and entered the lonely hut, and there beside the fireless hearth saw a young and beautiful girl, sitting and rocking herself to and fro, as she sang the heart-rending *caoine,* or death-song.

"What has happened, poor girl?" he asked, kindly. "I am Creevan, the physician. Perhaps I can help you in your hour of need."

"May the great God be glorified a thousand fold!" exclaimed the girl, starting to her feet. "The honeymoon is not yet over, and there lies my husband stricken down by fever, and in the last throes of death. O, Creevan, have pity upon us, and give him aid!"

Creevan looked to the other side of the apartment, and there saw the form of a young and handsome forester huddled up upon his hard pallet, his mouth and large blue eyes wide open, his hands twitching and picking at the coverlet, and Death bending over him at the bed-foot. Without attending to anything save the first benevolent impulse of his heart, Creevan darted to the bed, turned the sick man's head to the foot, and applied the phial, as before, and instantly the young forester arose sound and strong, and clasped his girlish wife in his loving arms. Then, with many a blessing from the youthful pair, Creevan departed; but, as he rode down a green and pleasant valley of the forest, he heard a loud clang of horse-hoofs behind him, and immediately Death came up

upon his great snow-white steed, and laid his hand
upon his shoulder.

"I forgive thee this time!" exclaimed the mighty
king, "because thou wert blinded by the impulse of
human pity. But know henceforth that neither the
pomp of princes, nor the pure and holy love of the
humble and lowly, has power to avert my blow.
Go thy way in peace, but beware forevermore of
breaking thy compact with me."

After this Creevan travelled beyond the seas into
a distant land, where the ancient feudalism of the
barbaric Teuton tribes ground the people into despair and misery; where the poor laborer could
scarce lift his head like a man, to look at the blue
heavens that God placed over him, for fear of the
prison, the thumb-screw, or the gibbet; where the
forlorn husbandman's hard-won gains were swept
into the coffers of his tyrant-masters, and where, if
he complained of his wrongs, either the sword of
the ruthless soldier came down upon his head, or the
law of the landlord swept him from the home and
green graves of his forefathers, and drove him across
the seas dispirited and broken-hearted, to seek a better
fate in a strange and far-distant clime. Here a man
arose from amongst the people, — a man of large
heart and bright brain teeming with noble thoughts,
— and, banding his brothers together, and bringing
them shoulder to shoulder in stern array, fell upon
the tyrants, and fought gallantly for freedom; but, in
a certain battle, he was stricken down, and now lay

concealed in a woody fastness, amid the hills, dying of his wounds. Him Creevan visited. Death stood at the bed-foot, but the great physician turned the patriot round, and made him hale and strong, as he did to the Prince of Desies and to the young forester. And now, Death overtook him as he went his way, but this time, instead of threatening, commended him, for —

"O Creevan," he said, "if there be one on earth that can prevail with me, it is the patriot who sacrifices and dares all for the welfare and the freedom of his oppressed and forlorn brothers."

Some time afterwards Creevan returned to his native land, and, breaking the compact, cured in the same lawless manner as before, Farran Grumach, the ancient and flinty-hearted miser of Dun Garman, for a large fee. Next morning, as he was kneeling at the matin prayer in the Fort of Coolnadun, Death appeared, and grasped him sternly by the shoulder.

"Come, thou recreant," he said, "arise and follow me, for the last grain of thy sand is run!"

"Wait, O pitiless godfather," returned Creevan, "till I say but one prayer before I die!"

"I grant thee that time only," answered Death; "but hurry thee, for the narrow home in my silent kingdom is prepared for thee at last."

"Then," exclaimed Creevan, "I defy you, for you cannot break your promise. I will never say prayer more!"

With an angry smile Death vanished, and Creevan

now began to use the phial in open defiance of his mighty godfather. One Sunday morning, as he was proceeding a second time to cure the Prince of Desies, his path led him across a green and flowery meadow, in the midst of which he saw a beautiful rosy-cheeked and golden-haired child sitting on the grass, and weeping with pitiful clamor. Creevan asked him the cause of his sorrow, and the child answered that he was going to the Abbey of Kil-an-Imidh to be examined in his catechism by Keeraun Keal, the Monk, and that he had not even the Lord's Prayer by heart for the examination. Forgetting at the moment his defiance of Death, Creevan, who had a tender heart, sat down beside the child, and commenced teaching him the Lord's Prayer. The moment the last word was finished, the child sprang to its feet, vanished, and in its place sat Death, smiling grimly, on his gigantic snow-white steed. In an instant he seized Creevan the Brown-haired, threw him across the pommel of his saddle, and, with a thundering clatter and clang, disappeared through a gorge in the neighboring mountains, showing that no man, be he ever so subtle and wise, can cheat Death the Inexorable.

THE FISHERMAN'S DAUGHTER.

A TALE OF RINDOWN CASTLE.

ONE of the largest, and at the same time most interesting ruins, with which the tourist will become acquainted as he voyages up the Shannon, is the ancient castle of Rindown, which stands upon a beautiful peninsula on the Roscommon side of Lough Ree, and about seven Irish miles to the north of Athlone.

The castle, with the peninsula on which it stands, was an important stronghold of the native Irish princes since a very remote period. In the ninth century, when Turgesius, the Danish king, anchored his fleet upon Lough Ree, he very probably occupied Rindown as one of his principal military stations. After the tragic death of that renowned Viking, it once more fell into the hands of the Irish, from whom it was wrested, towards the close of the twelfth century, by John de Courcy and a band of Anglo-Norman knights and men-at-arms, who took refuge there after their defeat in a pitched battle by Cathal Carragh O'Connor, son of Roderick, king of Connaught. From this period it became a regular object of contention between the forces of the Pale and the Irish troops, sometimes remaining for years in possession of the former, and again, at various intervals, falling into the hands of the latter, according as fortune favored their banners.

Between the Irish forces also Rindown became a frequent point of dispute during the destructive wars that raged in Connaught during the life, and for many years subsequent to the death, of the celebrated Cathal of the Red Hand. Under the year 1236, in the Annals of the Four Masters, is preserved the following record, which, giving as it does a minute and vivid picture of the military customs and mode of fighting practised at that period, we take the liberty of transcribing for the reader:—

"A. D. 1236. Felim, the son of Cathal the Red-Handed, returned to Connaught after his banishment, being invited thither by some of the Connacians, namely, by O'Kelly, O'Flynn, the son of Hugh, who was son of Cathal, the Red-Handed O'Connor, and the son of Art O'Melaghlin, all forming four equally strong battalions. They marched to Rinn-duin, where Brian, the son of Turlogh (O'Connor), Owen O'Heyne, Conor Boy, the son of Turlogh, and Mac-Costelloe had all the cows of the country; and Felim's people got over the enclosures of the island; and the leaders and sub-leaders of the army drove off each a proportionate number of the cows, as they found them on the way before them; and they then dispersed, carrying off their booty in different directions, and leaving only, of the four battalions, four horsemen with Felim. As Brian, the son of Turlogh, Owen O'Heyne, and their troops, perceived that Felim's army was scattered, they set out quickly and vigorously, with a small party of horse and many foot soldiers, to attack Felim and his few horsemen. Conor Boy, the son of Turlogh, came up with the son of Hugh, who was the son of Cathal the Red-Handed, and with his party; and mistaking them for his own people, he fell by Roderick, the son of Hugh, who was the son of Cathal the Red-Handed. Felim strained his voice, calling loudly after his army, and ordering them to return to oppose their enemies. Many of the host were killed by Felim upon the island; and outside the island were slain many bad subjects and perpetrators of evil, as they all were, excepting only Teige, son of Cormac, who was son of Tomaltagh M'Dermott."

The reader will remark that in the above record the peninsula of Rindown is called an island. At that time it was, in fact, an island, a huge fosse having been cut across the narrowest part, and filled by the waters of the lake. This fosse was further protected by a huge embattled wall, which ran across from one shore to the other, and the ruins of which can still be traced, together with the remains of the formidable barbican, or military gateway, in the centre. Near the draw-bridge are two ancient ecclesiastical ruins, one of which was a priory of the Knights Hospitallers, and was founded in the reign of King John. Passing over the various warlike events which must have occurred in and around it in remote times, we will come up to more modern days, and relate a short story of Rindown, which, we hope, will prove more interesting to our readers.

In that memorable year which the Scots call the "Forty-five," there stood beside the little cove, near the castle, a small hut, which was occupied by Owen Tierney and his wife and daughter. Owen was a fisherman, who, day after day, plied his avocation on the lake with such skill and industry that he was enabled to support himself and family in somewhat of a decent and respectable manner. Owen, however, was not merely dependent upon the rather capricious inhabitants of Lough Ree's waters for a maintenance. A small but fertile bit of land, attached to his cabin, was cultivated by him with great care and industry; in addition to which he had made, during the preceding years, several mysterious voyages to Limerick, after each return from which it was noticed that a far greater amount of tobacco than usual was consumed by his neighbors, and by the inhabitants of the surrounding villages. Be this as it may, in the spring of the year above mentioned, Owen Tierney was as happy and contented a man, to all appearance, as could be seen for many a mile around the lovely and romantic shores of Lough Ree.

Ellen Tierney, Owen's daughter, was a girl, as the phrase goes, well enough as to appearance — that is, in other words, she was not considered by her acquaintances as absolutely handsome, but at the same time there was a symmetry about her form, a kind tone in her voice, and a merry, guileless expression in her sun-embrowned face, that made her far more attractive than a girl of much greater beauty. At all events, she was the very apple of her father's eye, and the core of her mother's heart, and you may be sure she did not fail to reciprocate their affection with interest. At the time of which we speak, she had just turned her eighteenth year; and we must say, to her credit, that on account of her agreeable manners and pleasant temper, there was not a girl in all Roscommon that had a greater number of admirers. But she always contrived to repel the advances of these rustic beaux by either a pleasant good-natured denial, or a flat refusal, as the case might be — all save those of one, and that fortunate individual was no other than Brian Phelimy, or Brian Gow, as he was more commonly called from his trade, which was that of a blacksmith. Brian was a young man of scarcely twenty-five years, tall, well formed, and handsome; and a better hurler than he, a more expert hand at single-stick, or at any other athletic exercise, did not live from source to mouth of the lordly Shannon. His heart also was of the true, sterling stamp, kind and manly; and with all these attributes to recommend him, together with a flourishing trade at horse-shoeing and various other kinds of work, it was no wonder that the love he bore to young Ellen Tierney was returned by that simple-minded girl with an unusual amount of warmth, confidence, and affection. Brian's house and forge were about a stone's throw outside the village of Rindown, or St. John's, beyond the castle; and scarcely an evening passed over his head that he did not pay a visit to Owen Tierney's house beside the cove, there to talk on affairs of state with mother or father, or have a merry chat with his young sweetheart, who, if certain affairs which we are about to relate happened at the appointed time, was soon to become his wife.

It seems that, along with Owen Tierney's taking upon himself to supply the tobacco consumers of the district with a sufficiency of their favorite weed, Brian Phelimy, inheriting the philanthropical virtues of his father and grandfather, had carried out successfully, for a few years, his jovial resolution of adding to the enjoyments of the neighbors, and for that purpose occasionally put in operation a certain chemical apparatus, called a *still*, which lay concealed in a lonely chamber at the back of the forge, but the flue from which was ingeniously constructed, so as to communicate with the capacious chimney of the latter. In other words, Brian Gow, following the example of his ancestors of jolly memory, manufactured potheen; and better-tasted mountain-dew, as the poetic peasantry called it, could not be found within the four corners of Ireland. At the time to which we allude, the *still* was in full operation, and it was to the sale of a certain *run*, or plentiful distillation of whiskey, which was to take place at a stated time, and also to the success of Owen Tierney, who was about setting off on another of his voyages southward, in quest of an illicit cargo of tobacco, that he looked forward for an opportunity of being able to marry properly the daughter of the hardy fisherman, and to maintain her in suitable style, till another and similar smuggling adventure could be successfully entered upon.

With this purpose in view, Brian Gow eagerly watched the progress of his distilling operation, had a splendid *run*, and at length was in course of preparation for carrying about half a dozen firkins of the most glorious potheen to Athlone, where he could easily dispose of them, leaving the gauger altogether, of course, out of the transaction. Firkins, or butter casks, were the vehicles the sagacious Brian had chosen in which to convey his cargo to Athlone, because he knew by experience that they had the best chance of being borne through the town without suspicion.

At last the day came on which he was to set out for Athlone, and which also his intended father-in-law had settled upon for beginning his voyage to Limerick. About the same hour that Brian Phelimy had set out with a stout horse and cart, carrying his joy-inspiring load towards Athlone, the fisherman had spread his sail to the favoring wind, and was moving over the lake on his voyage southward.

"Well," said he to himself, as he steered his boat onward, and left the ruins of the huge castle towering upon its rock behind, as if guarding his little cot beneath, "if this turns out well wid me, they may all load their dudheens wid the gauger's tobacky ever after, for 'tis the last trip Owen Tierney will make for the neighbors' benefit an' his own. I'll then marry my daughter to Brian Phelimy, an' keep to the rod an' fishing-net for evermore."

It was a market day in Athlone, and the streets were crowded, as Brian Phelimy stopped his cart, and prepared to lodge it in a certain yard belonging to a public-house keeper of his acquaintance, to whom he usually sold his cargoes. A butter-buyer soon came in, and offered to make a bargain, but was told by Brian that the load was already disposed of. Another immediately followed, with his tasting instrument in hand, and was just about proceeding to regale his olfactory nerve by an experiment on one of the firkins, when he also was got rid of in the same manner. It was now evening, when a third butter-buyer came into the yard. This was a sharp, vicious-looking little man, whose name for probity in his dealings was not the best in the country, but who still, from his energy of character, contrived to make many a good bargain on market days.

"There's no mark on those firkins," said he, pointing to the load. "Will you sell?" continued he to

Brian, moving nearer to the suspicious-looking casks. "Prices are down now, an' you can't expect as much as was goin' durin' the mornin'."

"I'm determined to take it home," answered Brian, evasively. "I don't like the price, an' can afford to wait for better times."

"Let us look at the quality of id, at any rate," said the buyer, moving nearer.

"What's the use?" answered Brian, "as I'm not goin' to sell. You can't see the butter."

"I can smell id, howsomdever," returned the little tormentor, giving a sniff of his nose and a malignant wink: and with that he left the yard.

Another hour passed away, and the firkins of potheen would soon, under cover of the coming dusk, be stowed away in the cellars of the public house. Brian, who was not without his suspicions of the little butter-buyer's fidelity, was at last in the act of bearing one of the firkins into the cimmerian cellars of his customer, when a hand was laid upon his broad shoulder, and, turning round, he beheld, like a terrible apparition, the gauger and half a dozen soldiers standing right before him. The very same gauger was, on account of his stern character, his cruelty in various ways to those who came under the power of the law, and his implacable pursuits and persecutions of all and every one engaged in any kind of illicit trade, the detestation of the whole county, besides, up to this point of his career, having been the cause of the hanging of something near a half dozen countrymen. At the sight of him, the precious cask of potheen dropped from between Brian's sturdy arms, and smashed upon the pavement of the yard, its contents flowing away incontinently through the gutter. The soldiers then surrounded him, took him prisoner at the bidding of the gauger, and marched him along the now half deserted streets towards the jail, the gauger himself taking possession of the casks of potheen in the name of the king. The soldiers, who thought they had a being something after the nature of a lamb to deal with, were greatly surprised when, on approaching the door of the jail, Brian struck one of them a tremendous blow of his clinched fist upon the forehead, that tumbled him senseless against the wall, snatched a musket from another, and striking right and left with its butt, rushed round a corner, and away down a narrow street. It was a sudden surprise, but the soldiers as suddenly recovered, and rattled away in hot pursuit after him. The street, along which he was now darting at his topmost speed, led down to the river, without a single turn by which he could escape to either side. He knew there was no chance for him but the river, which was broad and deep before him; but his pursuers were now almost at his heels, shouting to one another exultantly, as they imagined he would have to turn back, and thus fall into their hands. But they had a man of no ordinary physical powers to deal with — one who, in conjunction with his activity and strength, was also rendered desperate.

As he approached the edge of the dark water, he cast another hasty glance behind, and to the amazement of his pursuers, instantly plunged in, and struck out for the middle of the river. The soldiers did not dare to fire without orders, else probably poor Brian Phelimy would then and there have ended his career. On he plunged, and being a practised swimmer, succeeded at last, in spite of his heavy clothes and shoes, in gaining the middle of the broad stream. The current here was very strong, and he was gradually yielding to its influence, and beginning to float rather helplessly downward, when he was hailed by a well-known voice from a dark object towards his right; and steadying himself for a moment, and looking over the obscure water, to his great joy he at last saw, a few perches away, Owen Tierney quietly resting on his oar, and keeping his craft steady for his reception. In another moment Brian Phelimy was in the boat; and after a few words of explanation and surprise, the pair were floating down the stream, and far beyond the reach of Randal Clinch, the gauger.

"Begor!" said Brian, as he divested himself of his coat, and began squeezing it, "we're done for, Owen. Put the boat into shore, and let me peg away to Rindown. If I don't, ould Clinch will be there afore me, and flitther *still* an' all to pieces."

"Never mind the *still*," said Owen, coolly. "If you go now, you'll sartinly be taken again by ould Randal an' the sojers. The *still* will be saized whether you go or not, an' 'tis better for you to keep out o' harm's way for a time. Come to Limerick with me, an' we'll bring back as much tobacky as will pay for all."

"'Twouldn't be a bad plan," answered Brian, reflectively. "Here, I'll go. Settle that sail, an' give me the oars, till I warm myself; an' if you have a drop o' the mountain-dew in the bottle, I'll take a taste of it also."

In about a week afterwards, they were on their return from Limerick with a cargo of tobacco, far larger than usual, stowed away in the boat. Meanwhile Ellen Tierney sat at her cottage door, beneath the castle, talking to her mother, and wondering at the absence of Brian Phelimy. It was the day after Brian's adventure in Athlone; and as she turned towards her mother, for the sixth time, to wonder why Brian did not pay his usual early morning visit, a tall, stern-looking man, of middle age, walked down from the castle, and accosted her.

"Is this Owen Tierney's house?" inquired the stranger, taking a sharp survey of the premises.

"It is, sir," answered Ellen, standing up with natural politeness, and moving her chair forward. "Won't you take a seat, sir? The mornin' is hot, an' perhaps you would like a drink of something after your walk."

"No, thank you," returned the other. "I merely want to ask you a question. Do you know one Brian Phelimy, who lives somewhere hereabouts?"

"Indeed, I ought, sir," answered Ellen, blushing. "He lives beyond there, near the village."

"Do you know where I might see him?" said the stranger again. "I have something to say to him that will be for his own advantage to hear."

"We were just talking about him," returned Ellen, "an' wondering why he did not come to see us this morning, for he comes often. I suppose you'll find him at his own house."

The stranger, seeing that Ellen could give him no information regarding the whereabouts of Brian, bade her a polite good morning, and took his departure. It was only in the evening, when she heard of the wrecking of Brian's house, and the capture of his *still*, that Ellen came to the knowledge that she had been conversing that morning with the dreaded gauger, Randal Clinch himself. Days passed away without the appearance of her lover, and many a sad hour poor Ellen Tierney spent upon the battlements of the old castle, looking out for she knew not what, over the bright, gleaming expanse of Lough Ree. It was the evening of the tenth day. The skies were of a lurid, copper-red hue, and the winds were howling savagely over the wide waste of waters, for there was a storm on Lough Ree, when Ellen, from where she sat in a sheltered nook on one of the ancient towers of the castle, beheld a sail far to the southward, struggling with the blast. A glance told her that it was her father's boat, and she waited eagerly, as the night gathered down, for his arrival, hoping

that he might bring some news of her lover. As for
the storm, Owen Tierney was the boldest boatman
on the lake, and his daughter had but little fear for
his safety.

The night came, and Ellen, who had now left her
perch upon the tower, was standing on a rock over
the lake, at one side of which was a little cove, where
her father usually landed his illicit cargo. At length
a boat drove swiftly into the cove, two men stepped
from it to the strand, and began ascending the rock;
and the next moment, to her great joy, her father
and her lover stood beside her. Scarcely was their
first greeting over, when they heard a rush in the
little cove beneath, and the quick tramp of men approaching them. In an instant Brian Phelimy and
Owen were seized in the king's name, and the first
man who spoke was the hated gauger, Randal Clinch,
who, with the help of a soldier, held Brian a firm
prisoner. Brian, however, was not a man to yield
easily. A blow from his ponderous fist prostrated
the gauger, and a terrible struggle then ensued between Brian and the soldier, from which the former
soon rose, leaving his antagonist senseless upon the
ground. Brian was now standing upon the edge of
the rock, when the gauger arose, and presented at
him one of the long holster pistols which he never
failed to carry with him on such errands. Ellen saw
the pistol presented, and the noble girl, rushing forward to shield her lover, just as she had succeeded in
standing between him and the guager, received the

bullet through her faithful heart, and instantly fell dead upon the extreme edge of the cliff. With a terrible bound, Brian Phelimy sprang upon the gauger, and tore him to the earth, and then both went rolling over and over, in mortal struggle, towards the verge of the rock. Poor Owen Tierney struggled hard to reach the body of his daughter, but three of the soldiers held him fast, while the rest ran to aid the gauger; but ere they had time to reach the combatants, the latter, still locked in their deadly embrace, rolled over the brink of the precipice, carrying with them, in their wild struggle, the body of poor Ellen Tierney into the black gulf of whirling and roaring waters beneath, where they were lost forever.

From the prosecution that followed, Owen Tierney escaped with a short imprisonment, and then returned to his cot beside the old castle of Rindown, where he never ceased lamenting his faithful daughter and her lover till his death.

THE BUILDING OF MOURNE.

ROME, according to the old aphorism, was not built in a day. Neither was the old town of Mourne, although it was destroyed in a day, and made fit almost for the sowing of salt upon its foundations, by the great lord of Thomond, Murrogh of the Ferns, when he gathered around it his rakehelly kernes, as Spenser in his spleen called them, and his fierce gallowglasses and roving hobbelers. But the present story has nought to do with the spoliation and burning of towns. Far different, indeed, was the founding of Mourne, to the story of the disastrous termination of its prosperity. You will look in vain to the histories for a succinct or circumstantial account of the building of this ancient town; but many a more famous city has its early annals involved in equal obscurity — Rome, for instance. What tangible fact can be laid hold of with regard to its early history, save the will-o'-the-wisp light emanating from the traditions of a more modern day? A cimmerian cloud of darkness overhangs its founding and youthful progress, through which the microscopic eyes of the historian are unable to penetrate with any degree of certainty. Mourne, however, though it cannot boast of a long-written history, possesses an oral one of remarkable perspicuity and certainty. The men are on the spot, who, with a mathematical precision worthy of Archimedes or Newton, will relate everything about it, from its foundation to its fall. The only darkness cast upon their most circumstantial history is the elysian cloud from their luxuriant dudheens, as they whiff away occasionally, and relate —

That there was long ago a certain Donal, a nobleman of the warlike race of Mac Caurha, who ruled over Duhallow, and the wild mountainous territories extending downward along the banks of the Blackwater. This nobleman, after a long rule of prosperity and peace, at length grew weary of inaction, and manufactured in his pugnacious brain some cause of mortal affront and complaint against a neighboring potentate, whose territory extended in a westerly direction on the opposite shore of the river. So he mustered his vassals with all imaginable speed, and prepared to set out for the domains of his foe on a foray of unusual ferocity and magnitude. Before departing from his castle, which stood some miles above Mallow, on the banks of the river, he held a long and confidential parley with his wife, in which he told her, if he were defeated or slain, and if the foe should cross the Blackwater to make reprisals, that she should hold out the fortress while one stone would stand upon another, and especially that she should guard their three young sons well, who, he doubted not, whatever might happen, would one day gain prosperity and renown. After this he set out on his expedition, at the head of a formidable array of turbulent kernes and marauding horsemen. But his neighbor was not a man to be caught sleeping, for at the crossing of a ford near Kanturk he attacked Donal, slew him in single combat, and put his followers to the sword, almost to a man. After this he crossed the Blackwater, laid waste the territories of the invader, and at length besieged the castle where the widowed lady and her three sons had taken refuge. For a long time she held her own bravely against her enemy, but in the end the castle was taken by assault, and she and her three young sons narrowly escaped with their lives out into the wild recesses of the forest.

After wandering about for some time, the poor lady built a little hut of brambles on the shore of the Clydagh, near the spot where stand the ruins of the preceptory of Mourne, or Ballinamona, as it is sometimes called. Here she dwelt with her children for a long time, in want and misery. Her sons grew up without receiving any of those accomplishments befitting their birth, and gained their subsistence, like the children of the common people around, by tilling a little plot of land before their hut, and by the products of the chase in the surrounding forest. One day as Diarmid, the eldest, with his bow and arrows ready for the chase, was crossing a narrow valley, he met a kerne, one of the followers of the great lord who had slain his father. Now, neither Diarmid nor his brothers recollected who had killed their father, nor the high estate from which they had fallen, for their mother kept them carefully in ignorance of all, fearing that they might become known, and that their enemies would kill them also. So the kerne and himself wended their way for some time together along the side of the valley. At length they started a deer from its bed in the green ferns. Each shot his arrow at the same moment, and each struck the deer, which ran downward for a short space, and at last fell dead beside the little stream in the bottom of the valley.

"The deer is mine!" said the strange kerne, as they stood over its body.

"No," answered Diarmid, "it is not. See! your arrow is only stickin' in the skin of his neck, an' mine is afther rattlin' into his heart, through an' through!"

"No matther," exclaimed the kerne, with a menacing look. "I don't care how he kem by his death, but the deer I must have, body an' bones, whatever comes of it! Do you think such a *sprissawn* as you could keep me from it, an' I wantin' its darlin' carkiss for the table o' my lord, the Mac Donogh?"

Now, Diarmid recollected that his mother and brothers were at the same time almost dying in their little hut for want of food. So, without further parley, he drew his long skian from its sheath.

"Very well," said he, "take it, if you're a man; but before it goes, my carkiss must lie stiff an' bloody in its place!"

The kerne drew his skian at the word, and there, over the body of the fallen deer, ensued a combat stern and fierce, which at last resulted in Diarmid's plunging his skian through and through the body of his foe into the gritty sand beneath them.

Diarmid then took the spear and other weapons of the dead kerne, put the deer upon his broad shoulders, and marching off in triumph, soon gained his mother's little hut. There, after eating a comfortable meal, and telling his adventure, Diarmid began to lay down his future plans.

"Mother," he said, "the time is come at last when this little cabin is too small for me. I'm a man now, an' able to meet a man, body to body, as I met him to-day; so I'll brighten up my weapons, an' set off on my adventures, that I may gain renown in the wars. Donogh here, too, has the four bones of a man," continued he, turning to his second brother; "so let him prepare, an' we'll thramp off together as soon as we can, an' perhaps afther all we'd have a castle of our own, where you could reign in glory, as big an' grand as Queen Cleena o' the Crag!"

"Well, then," answered his mother, "if you must go, before you leave me, you and your brothers must hunt in the forest for a month, and bring in as much food as will do me and Rory here for a year and a day."

"But," said Rory, the youngest, or Roreen Shouragh, or the Lively, as he was called, in consequence of the 'cute and merry temperament of his mind, — "But, Diarmid, you know I am now beyant fifteen years of age, an' so, if you go, I'll folly you to the worldt's end!"

"You presumptious little atomy of a barebones," answered his eldest brother, "if I only see the size of a thrush's ankle of you follyin' us on the road, I'll turn back an' bate that wiry an' freckled little carkiss o' yours into frog's jelly! So stay at home in pace an' quietness, an' perhaps when I come back I might give you a good purse o' goold to begin your forthin with."

"That for your mane an' ludiacrous purse o' goold!" exclaimed Roreen Shouragh, at the same time snapping his fingers in the face of his brother. "Arrah! do you hear him, mother? But never mind. Let us be off into the forest to-morrow, an' we'll see who'll bring home the most food before night!"

"Well," said his mother, "whether he stays at home or goes away, I fear he'll come to some bad end with that sharp tongue of his, and his wild capers."

"With all jonteel respect, mother," answered Shouragh again, "I mane to do no such thing. I think myself as good a hairo this minnit — because I have the sowl an' heart o' one — as King Dathi, who was killed in some furrin place that I don't recklect the jography of, or as Con o' the Hundhert Battles, or as the best man amongst them, Fion himself; an' I'll do as great actions as any o' them yet!"

This grandiloquent boast of Roreen Shouraghs' set his mother and brothers into a fit of laughter, from which they only recovered when it was time to retire to rest. In the morning the three brothers betook themselves to the forest, and at the fall of night returned with a great spoil of game. From morning till night they hunted thus every day for a month, at the end of which time Diarmid said that they had as much food stored in as would last his mother and Rory for a year and a day.

On a hot summer noon the two brothers left the little hut with their mother's blessing on their heads, and set off on their adventures. After crossing a few valleys, they came at length to the shore of the Blackwater, and sat down in the shade of a huge oak tree on the bank to rest themselves. Beneath them, in a clear, shady pool, a huge pike, with his voracious jaws ready for a plunge, was watching a merry little speckled trout, which in its turn was regarding with most affectionate eyes a bright blue fly, that was disporting overhead on the surface of the water. Suddenly the trout darted upwards into the air, catching the ill-starred fly, but in its return to the element beneath, unfortunately plumped itself into the Charybdis-like jaws of the villanous pike, and was from that in one moment quietly deposited in his stomach.

"Look at that!" said Diarmid to his brother. "That's the way with a man that works an' watches everything with a keen eye. He'll have all in the end, just as the pike has both fly and throut — an' just as I have both fly, an' throut, an' pike!" continued he, giving his spear a quick dart into the deep pool, and then landing the luckless pike, transfixed through and through, upon the green bank. "That's the way to manage, and the divvle a betther sign o' good luck we could have in the beginning of our journey, than to get a good male so aisy!"

"Hooray!" exclaimed a voice behind them. "That's the way to manage most galliantly. What a nate dinner the thurminjous monsther will make for the three of us!" and on turning round, the two brothers beheld Roreen Shouragh, accoutred like themselves, and dancing with most exuberant delight at the feat beside them on the grass.

"An' so you have follied us, afther all my warnin', you outrageous little vagabone," exclaimed Diarmid, making a wrathful dart at Roreen, who, however, eluding the grasp, ran and doubled hither and thither, with the swiftness of a hare, around the trunks of the huge oak trees on the shore. In vain Diarmid tried every ruse of the chase to catch him. Roreen Shouragh could not be captured. At length the elder brother, wearied out, returned to Donogh, who, during the chase, was tumbling about on the grass in convulsions of laughter.

" 'Tis no use, Donogh," he said; " we must only let him come with us. He'll never go back. Come here, you aggravatin' young robber," continued he, calling out to Roreen, who was still dancing in defiance beneath a tree some distance off. " Come here, an' you'll get your dinner, an' may folly us if you wish."

Roreen knew that he might depend on the word of his brother. " I towld ye both," said he, coming up to the spot, " that I'd folly ye to the worldt's end; so let us have pace, an' I may do ye some service yet. But may I supplicate to know where ye're preamblin' to at present? for if ye sit down that way in every umberageous coolin' spot, as the song says, the divvle a much ye'll have for yeer pains in the ind."

" I'll tell you then," answered Donogh, now recovered from his fit of laughing. " We're goin' off to Corrig Cleena to see the Queen o' the Fairies, an' to ask her advice what to do so as to win wealth an' renown."

" 'Tis aisier said than done," said Roreen, " to see Queen Cleena. But howsomdever, when we're afther devourin' this voriacious thief of a pike here, we'll peg off to the Corrig as swift as our gambadin'-sticks will carry us!"

After the meal the three brothers swam across the river, and proceeded on their way through the forest towards Corrig Cleena. On gaining the summit of a little height, a long, straight road extended before them.

On and on the straight road they went, till, turning up a narrow path in the forest, they beheld the great gray boulders of Corrig Cleena towering before them. They searched round its base several times for an entrance, but could find none. At length, as they were turning away in despair, they saw an extremely small, withered old atomy of a woman, clad all in sky blue, and sitting beside a clump of fairy thimbles, or foxgloves, that grew on a little knoll in front of the rock. They went up and accosted her.

"Could you tell us, owld woman," asked Diarmid, "how we can enter the Corrig? We want to speak to the queen."

"Ould woman, inagh!" answered the little atomy, in a towering passion. "How daar you call me an ould woman, you vagabone? Off wid you — thramp, I say, for if you sted there till your legs would root in the ground, you'd get no information from me!"

"Be aisy, mother," said Donogh, in a soothing voice. "Sure, if you can tell us, you may as well serve us so far, an' we'll throuble you no more."

"Ould woman an' mother, both!" screamed the little hag, starting up and shaking her crutch at the brothers; "this is worse than all. You dirty an' insultin' spalpeens, how daar ye again, I say, call me sich names. What for should I be decoratin' my fingers wid the red blossoms o' the Lusmore, if I was as ould as you say? Be off out o' this, or be this an' be that, I'll ruinate ye both wid a whack o' this wand o' mine!"

"Young leedy," said Roreen Shouragh, stepping up, cap in hand at this juncture, and making the old hag an elaborately polite bow, — "young, an' innocent, an' delightful creethur, p'r'aps you'd have the kindness to exercise that lily-white hand o' yours in pointin' out the way for us into Queen Cleena's palace!"

"Yes, young man," answered the crone, greatly mollified at the handsome address of Roreen. "For your sake, I'll point out the way. You, at laste know the respect that should be paid to youth an' beauty!"

"Allow me, my sweet youbg darlint," said Roreen at this, as he stepped up and offered her his arm, — "allow me to have the shuprame pleasure of conductin' you. I'm sure I must have the honor an' glory of ladin' on my arm one of the queen's maids of honor. May those enticin' cheeks o' yours forever keep the bloomin' an' ravishin' blush they have at the present minute, an' may those riglar ivory teeth o' yours, that are as white as the dhriven snow, never make their conjay from your purty an' delightful mouth!"

The "delightful young creethur" allowed herself, with many a gratified smirk, to be conducted downward by the gallant Roreen towards the rock, where, striking the naked wall with her crutch, or wand as she was pleased to call it, a door appeared before them, and the three brothers were immediately conducted into the presence of the fairy queen.

It would be long, but pleasant, to tell the gallant

compliments paid by Roreen to the queen, and the queen's polite and gracious acceptance of them; merry to relate the covert laughter of the lovely maids of honor, as Roreen occasionally showered down praises on the head of the "young leedy," who so readily gained him admittance to the palace, and who was no other than the vain old nurse of the queen; but despite all such frivolities, this history must have its course. At length the queen gave them a gentle hint that their audience had lasted the proper time, and as they were departing, she cast her bright but love-lorn eyes upon them with a kindly look.

"Young man," she said, "you ask my advice how to act, so as to gain wealth and renown. I could give you wealth, but will not, for wealth thus acquired rarely benefits the possessor. But I will give you the advice you seek. Always keep your senses sharp and bright, and your bodies strong by manly exercise. Look sharply round you, and avail yourselves honorably of every opportunity that presents itself. Be brave, and defend your rights justly; but above all, let your hearts be full of honor and kindness, and show that kindness ever in aiding the poor, the needy, and the defenceless. Do all this, and I doubt not but you will yet come to wealth, happiness, and renown. Farewell!"

And in a moment, they knew not how, they found themselves sitting in the front of the Rock of Cleena, upon the little knoll where Roreen had so flatteringly accosted the "young leedy." Away they went again down to the shore, swam back across the river, and wandered away over hill and dale, till they ascended Sliabh Luchra, and lost themselves in the depths of the great forest that clothed its broad back. Here they sat down in a green glade, and began to consider what they should further do with themselves. At length they agreed to build a little hut, and remain there for a few days, in order to look about the country.

To work they went, finished their hut beneath a spreading tree, and were soon regaling themselves on a young fawn they had killed as they descended the mountain. Next day they went out into the forest, killed a deer, brought him back to the hut, in order to prepare part of him for their dinner. Diarmid undertook the cooking for the first day, while his two younger brothers went out along the back of the mountain to kill more game. With the aid of a small pot which they had borrowed from a forester at the northern part of the mountain, and a ladle that accompanied it, Diarmid began to cook the dinner, stirring the pieces of venison round and round over the fire, in order to have some broth ready at the return of his brothers. As he was stirring and tasting alternately with great industry, he heard a light footstep behind him, and on looking round, beheld, sitting on one of the large mossy stones they used for a seat, a little crabbed-looking boy, with a red head almost the color of scarlet, a red jacket, and tight-fitting trousers of the same hue, which, reaching a little below the knees, left the fire-bedizened and equally rubicund legs and feet exposed in free luxury to the air. His face was handsomely formed, but brown and freckled, and he had a pair of dark, keen eyes, which seemed to pierce into the very soul of Diarmid as he sat gazing at him. There was a wild, elfish look about him altogether, as with a vivacious twinkle of his keen eye he saluted Diarmid politely, and asked him for a ladle full of the broth. Diarmid, however, in turning round from the pot, had spilt the contents of the ladle on his hand, burning it sorely, and was in consequence not in the most amiable humor.

"Give you a ladle of broth, indeed, you little weasel o' perdition!" exclaimed he. "Peg off out o' my house this minute, or I'll catch you by one o' them murtherin' red legs o' yours, an' bate your brains out against one o' the stones!"

"I am well acquainted with the cozy an' indestructible fact, that a man's house is his castle," said the little fellow, at the same time thrusting both his hands into his pockets, inclining his head slightly to one side, and looking up coolly at Diarmid; "but some o' that broth I must have, for three raisons. First, that all the wild game o' the forest are mine as well as yours; second, that I'm a sthranger, an' you know that hospitality is a varthue in ould Ireland; an' third, an' best, because you darn't refuse me! So, sit down there an' cool me a good rich ladle full, or, be the hole o' coat, there'll be wigs on the green bethune you an' me afore your much ouldher!"

"There's for your impidence, you gabblin' little riffin!" said Diarmid, making a furious kick at the imperturbable intruder, who, however, evaded it by a nimble jump to one side, and then leaping up suddenly, before his assailant was aware, hit him right and left two stunning blows with his hard and diminutive fists in the eyes. Round and round hopped Redhead, at each hop striking the luckless Diarmid right in the face, till at length with one finishing blow he brought him to the ground, stunned and senseless.

"There," he said, as he took a ladle full of broth and began to cool it deliberately, "that's the most scientific facer I ever planted on a man's forehead in my life. I think he'll not refuse me the next time I ask him."

With that he drank off the broth at a draught, laid the ladle carefully in the pot, stuck his hands in his pockets, and jovially whistling up, "The cricket's rambles through the hob," he left the hut, and strutted with a light and cheerful heart into the forest.

When Diarmid's brothers returned, they found him just recovering from his swoon, with two delightful black eyes, and a nose of unusual dimensions. He told them the cause of his mishap, at which they only laughed heartily, saying that he deserved it for allowing himself to be beaten by such an insignificant youngster. Next day, Diarmid and Rorcen went out to hunt, leaving Donogh within to cook the dinner. When they returned they found the ill-starred Donogh lying almost dead on the floor, with two black eyes far surpassing in beauty and magnitude those received on the preceding evening by his brother.

"Let me stay within to-morrow," said Roreen, "for 'tis my turn, an' if he has the perliteness o' payin' me a visit, I'll reward him for his condescension."

"Arrah!" said both his brothers, "is it a little traneen like you to be able for him, when he bate the two of us?"

"No matther," answered Roreen, "'tis my turn, an' stay I will, if my eyes were to be oblitherated in my purricranium!"

And so, when the morrow came, Diarmid and Donogh went out to hunt, and Roreen Shouragh staid within to cook the dinner. As the pot commenced boiling, Roreen kept a sharp eye around him for the expected visitor, whom he at length descried coming up the glade towards the door of the hut, whistling cheerfully as he came.

"Good morrow, youngster!" said the chap as he entered, and made a most hilarious bow; "you seem to have the odor o' charity from your handsome face here; at laste it comes most aromatically from the pot, anyhow."

"Ah, then! good morrow kindly, my blushin' little moss-rose!" said Roreen, answering the salutation with an equally ornamental inclination of his head. "Welcome to the hall o' my fathers. P'r'aps you'd do me the thurminjous honor o' satin' that blazin' little carkiss o' yours on the stone fornent me there."

"With all the pleasure in the univarse," answered

the other, seating himself; "but as the day is most obsthreporously hot an' disthressin' to the dissolute traveller, p'r'aps you'd have the exthrame kindness o' givin' me a ladle full o' broth to refresh myself."

"Well," said Roreen, "I was always counted a livin' respectacle o' the hospitality of ould Ireland. Yet, although the first law is not to ask the name of a guest, in regard to the unmerciful way you thrated my brothers, I must make bowld, before I grant your request, to have the honor an' glory of hearin your cognomon."

"With shuprame pleasure," answered the visitor. "My name, accordin' to the orthography o' Ogham characters, is Shaneen cus na Thinné, which, larnedly expounded, manes John with his Feet to the Fire. But the ferlosophers an' rantiquarians of ould Ireland, thracin' effect from cause, call me Fieryfoot; an' by that name I shall be proud to be addhressed by you at present."

"Well," rejoined Roreen, "it only shows their perfound knowlidge an' love for thruth, to be able to make out such a knotty ploberm in derivations; an' so, out o' compliment to their oceans o' larnin', you'll get the broth; but," continued he, as he took up a ladle full and held it to cool, "as there are a few questions now and then thrubblin' my ruminashins, p'r'aps you may be so perlite as to throw a flash o' lightnin' on them, while we're waitin'. One is in nathral histhory. I've heerd that of late the hares sleep with one eye shut an' th' other open. What on earth is the raison of it?"

"That," answered Fieryfoot, "is aisily solvoluted. 'Tis on account o' the increase o' weasels, and their love for suckin' the blood o' hares in their sleep. So the hares, in ordher to be on their guard, an' prevent it, sleep with only one eye at the time; an' when that's rested, an' has slep' enough, they open it, an' shut the other."

"The other," said Roreen, "is in asthronomy, an' thrubbles me most of all, sleepin' an' noddin', aitin' an' dhrinkin'. Why is it that the man in the moon always keeps a rapin'-hook in his hand, an' never uses it?"

"Because," answered Fieryfoot, getting somewhat impatient, — "because, you poor, benighted crathure, he's not a man at all, but the image of a man painted over the door of Brian Airach's shebeen there, where those that set off on a lunarian ramble go in to refresh themselves, as I want to refresh myself with that ladle o' broth you're delayin' in your hand."

"O, you'll get it fresh an' fastin'!" exclaimed Roreen; and with that he dashed the ladle full of scalding broth right into the face of Fieryfoot, who started up, with a wild cry, and rushed half blinded from the hut. Away went Roreen in hot pursuit after him, with the ladle in his hand, and calling out to him, with the most endearing names imaginable, to come back for another supply of broth; away down the glades, till at length, on the summit of a smooth, green little knoll, Fieryfoot suddenly disappeared. Roreen went to the spot, and found there a square

aperture just large enough to admit of his body. He
immediately went and cut a sapling with his knife,
stuck it by the side of the aperture, and placed his
cap on it for a mark, and then returned to the hut,
and found his brothers just after coming in. He related all that happened, and they agreed to go together to the knoll, after finishing their dinner.
When the dinner was over, the three brothers went
down to the knoll, and easily found out the aperture
through which Fieryfoot had disappeared.

"And now, what's to be done?" asked Diarmid.

"What's to be done — is it?" said Roreen; "why,
just to have me go down, as I'm the smallest, —
smallest in body I mane, — for, to spake shupernath-
rally, my sowl is larger than both of yours put together; an', in the mane time, to have ye build another
hut over the spot, an' live there till I return with a
power o' gold an' dimons, an' oceans o' renown an'
glory."

With that he crept into the aperture, while his
brothers busied themselves in drawing brambles and
sticks to the spot in order to build a hut as he had
directed. As Roreen descended, the passage began
to grow more broad and lightsome, and at length
he found himself on the verge of a delightful country, far more calm and beautiful than the one he had
left. Here he took the first way that presented itself, and travelled on till he came to the crossing of
three roads. He saw a large, dark-looking house, part
of which he knew to be a smith's forge, from the

smoke, and from the constant hammering that resounded from the inside. Roreen entered, and the first object that presented itself was Fieryfoot, as fresh and blooming as a trout, and roasting his red shins with the utmost luxuriance and happiness of heart before the blazing fire on the hob.

"Wisha, Roreen Shouragh," exclaimed Fieryfoot, starting from his seat, spitting on his hand for good luck, and then offering it with great cordiality, "you're as welcome as the flowers o' May! Allow me to offer you my congratulations, *ad infinitum*, for your superior cuteness in the art of circumwentin' your visitors. I prizhume you'll have no objection to be presented to the three workmen I keep in the house — the smith there, the carpenter, an' the mason. Roreen Shouragh, gentlemin, the only man in the world above that was able to circumwint your masther."

"A céad mille fáilté, young gintleman," said the three workmen, in a breath.

Roreen bowed politely in acknowledgment.

"Any news from the worldt above?" asked the smith, as he rested his ponderous hammer on the anvil.

"Things are morthially dull," answered Roreen, giving a sly wink at Fieryfoot. "I've heard that the Danes are making a divarshin in Ireland; that a shower of dimons fell in Dublin; that the moon is gettin' mowldy for want o' shinin', an' that there's a say in the west that is gradually becoming transmogrified into whiskey. I humbly hope that the latther intelligence is unthrue, for, if not, I'm afraid the whole worldt will become drunk in the twinklin' of a gooldfrinch's eye."

"Milé, milé gloiré," exclaimed the three workmen, "but that's great an' wondherful intirely! P'r'aps, master," continued they, addressing Fieryfoot, and smacking their lips at the thought of whiskey,— "p'r'aps you'd have the goodness o' givin' us a few days' lave of absence."

"Not at present," answered Fieryfoot; "industry is the soul o' pleasure, as the hawk said to the sparrow before he transported him to his stomach; so ye must now set to work, an' make a swoord, for I want to make my frind here a present as a compliment for his shuperior wisdom."

To work they went. The smith hammered out, tempered, and polished the blade; the carpenter fashioned the hilt, which the mason set with a brilliant row of diamonds; and the sword was finished instantly.

"An' now," said Fieryfoot, presenting the sword to Roreen, "let me have the immorthial pleasure o' presenting you with this. Take it, and set off on your thravels. Let valor and magnanimity be your guide, an' you'll come to glory without a horizontal bounds. In the mane time I'll wait here till you return."

"I accept it with the hottest gratitudinity an' gladness," said Roreen, taking the sword, and running his eye critically along hilt and blade. " 'Tis a darlin' handy swoord. 'Tis sharp, shinin', an' killin', as the sighin' lover said to his sweetheart's eyes, an' altogether 'tis the one that matches my experienced taste; for 'tis tough, an' light, and lumeniferous, as Nero said to his cimether, whin he was preparin' to daycapitate the univarsal worldt wid one blow."

Saying this, Roreen buckled the sword to his side, bade a ceremonious farewell to the polite Fieryfoot and his workmen, left the house, and proceeded on his adventures. He took the west and broader road that led by the forge, and travelled on gayly till night. For seven days he travelled thus, meeting various small adventures by the way, and getting through them with his usual light-heartedness, till at length he saw a huge dark castle before him, standing on a rock over a solitary lake. He accosted an old man by the wayside, who told him that a huge giant, of unusual size, strength, and ferocity, dwelt there, and that he had kept there in thrall, for the past year and a day, a beautiful princess, expecting that in the end she'd give her consent to marry him. The old peasant told him also that the giant had two brothers, who dwelt far away in their castles, and that they were the strangest objects ever seen by mortal eyes; one being a valiant dwarf, as broad as he was long, and the other longer than he was broad; for he was tall as the giant, but so slightly formed that he was designated, by the inhabitants of the country round, Snohad na Dhial, or the Devil's Needle. Roreen thanked the old man with great urbanity, and proceeded on his way towards the castle. When he came to the gate, he knocked, as bold as brass, and demanded admittance. He was quickly answered by a tremendous voice from the inside, which demanded what he wanted.

"Let me in, ould steeple," said Roreen; "I'm a poor disthressed boy that's grown wary o' the worldt on account o' my fatness, an' I'm come to offer myself as a volunthary male for your voriacious stomach."

At this the gate flew open with a loud clang, and Roreen found himself in the great court-yard of the castle, confronting the giant. The giant was licking his lips expectantly while opening the gate, but seemed now not a little disappointed as he looked upon the spare, wiry form standing before him.

"If you're engaged, ould cannibal," said Roreen again, "in calkalatin' a gasthernomical ploberm, as I'm aweer you are, by the way you're lookin' at me, allow me perlitely to help you in hallucidatin' it. In the first place, if you intend to put me in a pie, I must tell you that you'll not get much gravy from my carkiss; an', in the next, if you intend to ate me on the spot, raw, I must inform you that you'll find me as hard as a Kerry dimon, an' stickin' in your throat, before you're half acquainted with the politics of your abdominal kingdom."

As an answer to this the giant did precisely what Roreen Shouragh expected he would do. He stooped down, caught him up with his monstrous hand, intending to chop off his head with the first bite; but Roreen, the moment he approached his broad, hairy chest, pulled suddenly out the sword presented to him by Fieryfoot, and drew it across the giant's windpipe, with as scientific a cut as ever was given by any champion at the battle of Gaura, Clontarf, or of any other place on the face of the earth. The giant did not give the usual roar given by a giant in the act of being killed. How could he, when his windpipe was cut? He only fell down simply by the gate of his own castle, and died, without a groan. Roreen, by way of triumph, leaped upon his carcass, and, with a light heart, cut a few nimble capers thereon, and then proceeded on his explorations into the castle. There he found the beautiful princess sad and forlorn, whom he soon relieved from her apprehensions of further thraldom. She told him that she was not the only lady whose wrongs were unredressed in that strange country, for that the two remaining brothers of the giant, to wit, the dwarf and the Devil's Needle, had kept, during her time of thrall, her two younger sisters in an equally cruel bondage.

"An' now, my onrivalled daisy," said Roreen, after some conversation had passed between them, "allow me, while I'm in the humor for performin' deeds o' valior, to thramp off, an' set them free."

"But," said the princess, "am I to be left behind pining in this forlorn dungeon of a castle?"

"Refulgint leedy," answered Roreen, "a pair of eyes like yours, when purferrin' a request, are arrisistible, but this Kerry-dimon heart o' mine is, at present, onmovable; and in ferlosophy, when an arrisistible affeer conglomerates against an onmovable one, nothin' occurs; an' so I must have the exthrame bowldness of asking you to stay where you are till I come back, for 'tis always the maxim of an exparienced an' renowned gineral not to oncumber himself with too much baggage when settin' out on his advinthures."

And so the young princess consented to stay; and Roreen, with many bows and compliments, took his leave. For three days he travelled, till at length he espied the castle of the dwarf towering on the summit of a great hill. He climbed the hill as fast as his nimble legs could carry him, blew the horn at the gate, and defied the dwarf to single combat. To work they went. The skin of the dwarf was as hard and tough as that of a rhinoceros, but at length Roreen's sword found a passage through it, and the dwarf fell dead by his own gate. Roreen went in, brought the good news of her sister's liberation to the lady, and, after directing her to remain where she was till his return, set forward again. For three days more he travelled, till he came to the shore of a sea, where he saw the castle of Snohad na Dhial towering high above the waves. He climbed up the rock on which the castle stood, found the gate open, and, whistling the romantic pastoral of "The piper in the meadow straying," he jovially entered the first door he met. On he went, through room after room, and saw no one, till at last he came before an exceedingly lofty door, with a narrow and perpendicular slit in it, extending almost from threshold to lintel. He peeped in through the open slit, and beheld inside the most beautiful young lady his eyes ever rested upon. She was weeping, and seemed sorely troubled. Roreen opened the door, presented himself before her, and told her how he had liberated her sisters. In return she told him how that very day she was to be married to Snohad na Dhial, and wept, as she further related that it was out of the question to think of vanquishing him, for that he was as tall as the giant, yet so slight that the slit in the door served him always for an entrance; but then he was beyond all heroes strong, and usually killed his antagonist by knotting his long limbs around him, and squeezing him to death.

"No matther," said Roreen. "I'll sing a song afther my victory, as the gamecock said to the piper. An' now, most delightful an' bloomin' darlint o' the worldt, this purrilignious heart o' mine is melted at last with the conshumin' flame o' love. Say, then, the heart-sootherin' an' merlifluous word that you'll have me, an' your thrubbles are over in the twinklin'—"

"Not over so soon!" interrupted a loud, shrill voice behind them; and Roreen, turning round, beheld Snohad na Dhial entering at the slit, with deadly rage and jealousy in his fiery eyes. Snohad, however, in his haste to get in and fall upon Roreen, got his middle, in some way or other, entangled in the slit, and, in his struggles to free himself, his feet lilted upwards, and there he hung, for a few moments, inwards and outwards, like the swaying beam of a balance. For a few moments only, for Roreen, running over, with one blow of his faithful sword on the waist, cut him in two, and down fell both halves of Snohad na Dhial as dead as a door-nail. After this Roreen got the heart-sootherin' answer he so gallantly implored. He then bethought himself of returning. After a few weeks he found himself with the three sisters, and with a cavalcade of horses laden with the most precious diamonds, pearls, and other treasures belonging to the three castles, in front of the forge where he had met Fieryfoot, and talking merrily to that worthy.

"An' now," said Fieryfoot, after he had complimented the ladies on their beauty, and Roreen on his success and bravery, "I am about to give my three workmen lave of absence. But they must work seven days for you first. Then they may go on their peregrinations about ould Ireland. Farewell. Give my ondeniable love to the ladle, and remember me to your brothers balligerently."

With that the two friends embraced, on which Fieryfoot drew out a small whistle, and blew a tune, which set Roreen Shouragh and the three princesses into a pleasant sleep; on awakening from which they found themselves by the side of the little hut on the knoll, with the three workmen beneath them, holding the horses, and guarding their loads of treasure.

Roreen's two brothers had just returned from the chase, and were standing near them in mute wonderment at the spectacle. After some brief explanations, the whole cavalcade set out on their journey home, and travelled on till they came to the hut of the lonely widow on the banks of the Clydagh. It was nightfall when they reached the place. Roreen told the three workmen that he wanted to have a castle built on the meadow beside the hut, and then went in and embraced his mother. The workmen went to the meadow, and, when the next morning dawned, had a castle of unexampled strength and beauty built for Roreen and his intended bride. The two succeeding mornings saw two equally splendid castles built for the two brothers and their brides elect, for they were about to be married to the two elder princesses. By the next morning after that they had a castle finished for Roreen's mother. On the second morning afterwards they had a town built, and at length, on the seventh morning, when Roreen went out, he found both castles and town enclosed by a strong wall, with ramparts, gateways, and every other necessary appliance of defence. The three workmen then took their leave, and, by the loud smacking of their lips as they departed, Roreen knew that they were going off to the west in search of the "say" of whiskey. After this the three brothers got married to the three lovely princesses, mercenary soldiers flocked in from every quarter, and took service under their banners; the inhabitants of the surrounding country removed into the town, and matters went on gayly and prosperously. The name of Roreen's wife was Mourne Blanaid, or the Blooming, and on a great festival day got up for the purpose, he called the town Mourne, in honor of her. In a pitched battle they defeated and killed the slayer of their father, and drove his followers out of their patrimony; and after that they lived in glory and renown till their death.

For centuries after the town of Mourne flourished, still remaining in possession of the race of the Mac Carthys. At length the Normans came and laid their mail-clad hands upon it. In the reign of King John, Alexander de St. Helena founded a preceptory for Knight Templars near it, the ruins of which stand yet in forlorn and solitary grandeur beside the little river. Still the town flourished and throve, though many a battle was fought within it, and around its gray walls, till at length, according to Spenser, Murrogh na Ranagh, Prince of Thomond, burst out like a fiery flame from his fastnesses in Clare, overran all Munster, burnt almost every town in it that had fallen into the possession of the English, and, amongst the rest, Mourne, whose woful burning did not content him, for he destroyed it altogether, scarcely leaving one stone standing there upon another. And now, only a few mounds remain to show the spot where Roreen Shouragh got his town built, and where he ruled so jovially.

And so, gentle reader, if you look with me to the

history of Troy, Rome, the battle of Ventry Harbor, the Pyramids, or Tadmor in the Desert, I think you will say that there is none of them so clear, so circumstantial, and so trustworthy, as the early history of the old town of Mourne.

MADELINE'S VOW.

OUR town is an ancient one. I am not the only inhabitant who takes a pride in it, not, indeed in consequence of its present prosperity, for that is nothing to boast of, but on account of its former strength and splendor, and for its gallant conduct in the wars, and during the many sieges to which it was subjected by those who measured swords so often within the four seas of old Ireland. On the one side, we have a calm, winding, picturesque river, and on the other, a lake, which, according to popular tradition, is destined to overflow its flat, reedy shores, and submerge ourselves or our descendants beneath its glassy waves — a catastrophe which I earnestly hope may not occur until I, for one, am sleeping my last sleep beneath the shadows of the mighty elm trees that shelter our ancient burial-place. River and lake were not, however, considered sufficient defences against intruders by our belligerent ancestors. They, therefore, encircled the town with a tremendous fosse, supplied from the waters of both lake and river, and above and within the fosse constructed a ramparted wall, two thirds of the ruins of which still remain to attest its former strength and solidity. Four roads, from the four cardinal points, led into the town, over each of which, at the entrance, was built a massive barbican. Two of these formidable gateways may yet be seen, but our principal objects of attraction are the ancient houses that still line the streets, and the magnificent ecclesiastical ruins that throw their fantastic shadows across the river, and carry, even in their decay, the mind back to the far-gone years when the melodious bells tolled from their turrets, the burning censers swung before their altars, and their mighty roofs echoed daily to the solemn songs of monk and friar.

The traveller who passes down our main street will not fail to pause before the ruin of a huge stone mansion that stands some short distance from the North gate. It is built partly in the Elizabethan style, and partly after a style still more ancient, namely, the strong, massive, Norman mode, examples of which may be frequently seen in the ruins of those mighty castles that loom up, from their rocky foundations, in many a pass, and hill, and river throughout the land. Its ornate windows and massive door-ways are still in good preservation, and upon the figured stone mullions of the former may still be detected the remains of ancient gilding, which, with the fantastic and elaborately carved effigies on lintel, window-sill, and arch-way, picture before the beholder's eye the magnificence that must have once reigned within its now deserted chambers. At its rear, the antique garden that belonged to the mansion, with its flower-beds and labyrinths of walks, all now gone to decay, extends backwards to the town wall, the foot of which, at that point, is washed by the waters of the lake.

Within the memory of some of the oldest inhabitants of the town, this mansion, before it went to ruin, was inhabited by an old gentleman named George Lombard, and his only daughter, Madeline. George Lombard was descended from a long line of ancestors, who had made the mansion their town residence since perhaps the days of the Invasion, that stormy time when the De Courcys, De Rupes, Geraldines, and many other stout Normans, gained their footing in this land by the sword, to become, soon after their settlement, however, in the language of the old historian, "more Irish than the Irish themselves." About a mile outside the town George Lombard possessed another mansion, and a goodly estate; but, to all his possessions, Madeline, his daughter, was sole heiress. The father was a good type of the squire of those days,— a proud, hot-tempered, wayward man, sometimes overbearing, exacting, and stern towards his tenantry, and, on other occasions, as the humor swayed him, warm-hearted, indulgent, and humane, — a man who kept a pack of fox-hounds at his country mansion, and put his neck in jeopardy on their track several times a week, and who never retired to rest before himself and his friends had emptied an array of wine bottles (good claret and Burgundy) that would strike a modern toper with dismay, to the memory of their sylvan achievements on the track of bold Reynard, or to the reigning toasts of the country.

Madeline, also, who was scarcely twenty years of age at the time of the following events, was a good type of her class. She followed the hounds with her father, and took fence for fence with the best of them, not unfrequently distancing the whole hunt, and coming in at the death. As a natural consequence, she was the great favorite among the young fox-hunting gentlemen of the country, their theme in the song, and their toast at every revel; and in those reckless old times the latter were not few. She knew also all her father's tenants by name, went amongst them frequently, interceded for them in their difficulties with her father, on which occasions she seldom failed in being successful; and thus, if they did not raise her to the dignity of toast at their merry-makings, she had, at least, many an earnest prayer and good wish from them for her welfare and happiness. She was a beauty, too — a dark-haired, haughty-looking, splendid girl; but the proud look of her perfectly-chiselled face was relieved by a sweet, mild expression, which ever hovered upon her pretty lips, and by a pair of dark eyes, whose kindly glance never failed to win the hearts of rich and poor in her neighborhood.

From her infancy Madeline had been brought up with her cousin. The latter, whose name was Harry Godsall, was a young man of reckless and dissolute habits, and had gained the hatred of his uncle's tenants, even before he had grown up to man's estate, by many an act of oppression, and by his licentious conduct. Many a royal battle he had fought with his uncle on these occasions; but he always contrived to fight through them tolerably well, until an event occurred which separated them, as all the neighborhood thought, forever. Well had it been for both, indeed, had the latter been the case. Old George Lombard's principal tenant was a farmer named Brian Connell, an honest, industrious man, well to do in the world — in fact, with an amount of wealth that entitled him to give his children, of whom he had five (three sons and two daughters) a good education, and to expect for them what the country people called a good match, whenever they might take it into their heads to marry. Upon the youngest of Brian Connell's daughters, about two years previous to the events of our story, Harry Godsall had cast his eye. Harry was then about twenty-one years of age; and when he found his efforts at gaining the heart of Ellen Connell frustrated by the good sense and propriety of the latter, he resolved upon her abduction. With about a dozen accomplices, he attacked the house on a certain night, and carried off the daughter of Brian Connell; but he had scarcely proceeded a mile upon his way to the mountains, when he was overtaken by the brothers of his victim, with several of their neighbors. He fought hard for his prize, but, in the end, was overpowered, and received such a rough handling on the occasion, from Ellen's eldest brother, Dick, that he was confined to his bed for a full week afterwards. Before the end of that time, the whole transaction had come to the ears of his uncle, and that irascible old gentleman determined, then and there, to discard the worthless Harry Godsall forever. With this resolution, a few days afterwards, he rode out to his country mansion, and, after some search for the delinquent, at last found him in the stables, looking after a favorite hunter that belonged to him.

"Leave that horse," said the uncle, sternly; "for, as sure as my name is George Lombard, you shall never see him again. Leave him, sir, and quit my house, that you have disgraced by your debaucheries and other bad conduct!"

"I reared him myself," answered Harry Godsall; "and he is mine. If I go, he, at least, will go with me!"

"It is not enough that I adopted you," pursued the old gentleman, taking no notice of the answer of his nephew, "yes, adopted you when your parents died, and brought you up on an equality with my own daughter, but you must seek for the rights of a son in your relations towards me! You are my nephew, it is true, the child of my only sister; but I tell you, Harry Godsall, if you were my own son, after your villanous attempt the other night, I would discard you, and send you adrift upon the world, as I am determined to do this day. Begone, sir, and leave me, and never more set foot within my house! Perhaps, when you try to fight your battle with the world unaided, you will then think of the opportunities you wilfully lost, and upon the uncle who was willing to set you up like a gentleman, if you had conducted yourself."

"Very well, sir," answered Harry. "But think yourself of the wild life you led when you were young; and then, perhaps, you will find an excuse for me."

"If I think upon my own life," returned his uncle, "I can find nothing in it, wild as it was, that came up in baseness to this late act of yours. I bore with you long enough, and now I am resolved to put up with your profligacy and wickedness no longer."

"And I, too, have borne with your tyranny long enough," answered Harry Godsall, with a sinister look, now that he saw his uncle was determined on his expulsion. "Give me some money, and I promise you it will be many a long day ere I set foot within your house."

"I am after tearing up my will this morning," answered his uncle; "and in that parchment, which is now consumed to ashes, I had left you a good round sum. You have lost all by your own misconduct; but it will only make Madeline the richer. Here, however," added he, handing his nephew a purse, "here are two hundred guineas. Take the money, and leave my sight at once, or I shall be tempted to horsewhip you round the stable."

"I will take it," said Harry; "but I tell you, uncle, I am a man now, and will have none of the other ware, no matter from whom; so you had better put up your whip."

"Ha, ha!" retorted his uncle, bitterly; "you took a thrashing, however, quietly and meekly enough the other night from young Dick Connell."

It was horrible to gaze upon the vengeful expression that darkened the swarthy face of Harry Godsall, as he heard the name of the farmer's son pronounced.

"I tell you what it is, uncle," he said, as he led his horse, which was ready saddled and bridled, into the yard, "you and that damned young bog-trotter may yet live to rue the day that you have combined against Harry Godsall." With a spring, he was in the saddle. "Good by," he added, with a bitter sneer, as he rode away; "you see, after all, that I and the horse I reared are not determined to part company. Good by, and remember me to Ellen Connell. Tell her brother also, for his comfort, that I will have his life yet, as sure as there's blood in my body."

Away he rode; but he was scarcely gone a day when the old fox-hunter relented, began to speak of him as kindly as ever, and wish him back. But it was of no avail now, for Harry Godsall was away in the purlieus of the neighboring city, engaged in the pleasant task of spending his money as fast as possible. It was soon gone. He next sold his horse, the price of which soon followed the two hundred guineas. There was now no alternative for him but the usual one in such cases; and in a moment of desperation, Harry Godsall enlisted in a regiment of dragoons, which was then quartered in the city. The troop to which he belonged was ordered in a few days to the East Indies; and from that burning and unhealthy clime nothing was afterwards heard of him. In fact, all supposed that he was dead.

Two years after the departure of Harry Godsall, there was a fair held in our stout old town. The latter — I may say it safely, with pride — is situated in the midst of the finest and most fertile plain in Ireland, or in Europe, or perhaps I may go so far as to say, the whole world. It will easily be conceived, then, what a concourse of people, and what a number of cattle of every description, were packed into the streets on that day of business and uproar, fun and mischief. From early morning until noon, every salable commodity, living and inert, changed hands with astonishing celerity, for it was a prosperous time, and business was consequently brisk and flourishing. There was one part of our main street — and it happened to be that opposite to the mansion of old George Lombard — that was on fair days specially devoted to the tinkers and their faithful and hard-working companions, the donkeys. Here the noise of traffic was perfectly deafening during the morning, and enlivened also occasionally by several oratorical encounters between the fair partners of the workers in brass and tin; but by degrees, as the noonday sun smote hot upon the paving-stones, even that babel of voices began to subside into a murmuring and quiet roar, that, as the immortal Milton says of the rising of the demons in Pandemonium, was "like the sound of thunder heard remote."

By degrees, as the noon passed, the cattle disappeared, in a great measure, from the street, but the people remained. The great bulk of the latter also disappeared from the street, but they did not leave the town, like cattle. They were, in fact, quietly ensconced within the hostels and hilarious public houses, whose hospitable doors ornament our streets, and invite, with their quaint signs, the weary and thirsty passers-by to come in and refresh themselves. There they were, talking over their bargains, laughing, singing, and match-making to their hearts' content, and pouring upon the altar of friendship libations of whiskey-punch, plentiful enough to drown all their bickerings and faction grudges for a dozen years. Now, our town seems to be under a pugnacious spell since the day its first stone was laid. Since that never-to-be-forgotten day, it has stood at least a score of sieges, not taking into account the running engagements with sword and gun that took place along its streets, and around its well-battered walls. Along with this, we have four fairs yearly; and I can say it, both from report and observation, that the sun of each of those fair days never set without beholding a universal scrimmage, from end to end of the place, between the rival factions of the surrounding country. The day in question was, of course, not an exception to this general rule.

The tinkers always seemed to arrogate to themselves the initiative in these belligerent demonstrations. There was a little man amongst them who never failed to be present at each fair, who usually began the fight, and who, for the thirty previous years, seemed to every one who observed his looks never to grow a day older in appearance, according to the unquestionable authority of Jeremiah Macnamara Moloney, Philomath, the schoolmaster of the town, who usually celebrated each scrimmage, and the prominent heroes therein, in Greek, Hebrew, Latin, and Irish effusions, but never in English, the worthy professor of dead and dying tongues, according to his own deliberate expression, having a "shuprame, and sovereign, and immorthial contempt for the latter polyglottiferous and cacophonous language." On the evening of the aforesaid day, the little man alluded to rushed out with a ferocious "hurroo!" from a public house, cut a few warlike capers in the street, and then struck his own fair partner above the eye with his clinched fist, to which the incensed amazon replied promptly by a resounding hammer of her own flinty digits upon the little man's chest, that sent him sprawling against the adjacent wall, and doubled him up for the rest of the evening. The victorious matron then attacked her next neighbor, and he, after somewhat disabling her, attacked another; and thus the fight spread, the men and women rushing out into the street, and joining in the fray, till the whole tinkers' quarter was in a universal uproar. This was followed by a shout, some distance up the street, from an excited member of one of the factions; and ere a quarter of an hour had elapsed, a general battle raged supreme from the North to the South Gate of our pugnacious town.

Whilst this state of things lasted, a tall, dark young man, clad in the garb of a tinker, separated himself from the combatants, and, without being perceived by any one, glided under an old archway that led to the rear of George Lombard's mansion. He examined every wall and gable at the back of the house; and at length, as his gaze fell upon a long, leaden pipe that led by a certain window to the roof, there came an expression of demoniac exultation and malignity into his black eyes, which showed that his purpose was neither good nor honest. After another hasty but careful glance at the entrance to the garden, and towards the old town wall beyond, he immediately left the spot, glided out under the hoary arch by which he had entered, and, with a loud shout, joined the combatants once more.

Meanwhile the fight began to rage fiercer and fiercer up the street between the rival factions. There were then no police, and the few yeomen who lived in the town were, as a matter of course, quite incompetent to put a stop to the tumult. At this juncture, an old gentleman rode down the street, and with his horsewhip began to lay about him on the heads and broad shoulders of the combatants. It was old George Lombard, who, as the principal inhabitant of the town, usually adopted that novel method of quieting the frays that took place there upon each recurring fair day. Nor was he unsuccessful on the present occasion. In fact, like the fabled halcyon on a stormy sea, his presence seemed to quiet down the tumult wonderfully, as he rode along, distributing favors indiscriminately from his horsewhip on all sides, until he reached a certain part of the street, namely, the border land between the tinkers' quarter and that occupied by the factions. This, like all border lands, was a perfect maelstrom of contention, for the members of the factions were not only fighting there among themselves, but the tinkers, from some cause or other, had got mixed up in their fray, and all was in most horrible uproar as George Lombard came to the spot. In the midst of the roaring throng, two tall young men were engaged in an encounter with sticks. One of them, by his dress and appearance, looked a gentleman. It was Richard, or, as he was more commonly called, Dick Connell, son of George Lombard's tenant. The other, who wore the usual apparel of a tinker, was the same who had examined so minutely, some time before, the back premises of the old mansion. Towards this pair, as they fenced and struck fiercely at each other with their sticks, George Lombard rode, whip in hand, and, flourishing his pacific talisman, struck Dick Connell, who happened to be nearest to him at the moment, a sharp blow across the shoulders. At the same instant Dick floored his antagonist with a blow, and now turned upon George Lombard, his eyes flashing still with the fury of the combat.

"How dare you strike, sir?" he exclaimed, unable to overcome his rage, and catching the bridle of George Lombard's horse. "Mark me, Mr. Lombard," he added, as some of his companions caught him, and pulled him away; "mark me, sir; you will pay sorely for that blow, or my name is not Richard Connell."

He was pulled by his companions into a house hard by; and thus the faction fight came to an end. When George Lombard looked out for the other combatant, the latter was nowhere to be seen.

That night a most horrible and atrocious murder was committed in our town, and the victim was George Lombard. He was found upon his bed in the morning, with a deep, narrow wound, as if from a knife or small dagger, in the region of the heart. Very little blood appeared to have flowed from the wound. He must have bled internally. Of course this created a terrible uproar in our town, and throughout the surrounding country. Every search was made for the murderer, but not even a clew to anything connected with the fearful event could be found by the most diligent investigations. The ill-fated old gentleman was, in the mean time, buried, the inquest that had sat upon his body having given a verdict of wilful murder against some person unknown.

It is not to be wondered at that Madeline grieved sorely for her father's unhappy fate. For a week or two she was unable to understand anything with the excess of her sorrow; but at last she bestirred herself, and soon showed that she had a will and a spirit of her own, that enabled her to accomplish more in the search for her father's murderer than the most active magistrate in the vicinity. But it was all of no avail, and another week passed, scarcely adding a single fact to what was already known. At the end of that time, Madeline drove to the house of a magistrate, who lived outside the town, and who also had been her father's trusted friend and constant companion.

"I need not say, Madeline," said the old gentleman, who went by the name of Squire Waller, "that I have done everything in my power in this sad case, and yet, you see, it is all of no avail. The murderer must indeed have laid his plans well, to be able to baffle us in this manner."

"He must, indeed," answered Madeline. "But still I think we will find him out yet. Some one must be tempted by the largeness of the reward we have offered."

"I hope," said the cautious old magistrate, "that

no one will be tempted by its amount to swear away the life of some innocent person. Large as it is, however, you see that it has failed, as yet, to bring any one forward with a particle of information."

Now, old George Lombard had been somewhat eccentric in his habits and manners. Some of these eccentricities had descended to his daughter. It will not astonish any one, therefore, to learn what passed between Madeline and old Squire Waller. After going over the meagre array of facts that had been elicited by the inquest, and after arguing between them the feasibility of increasing the reward, Madeline resumed, —

"I have come at last to the conclusion," she said, "that something extraordinary must be done, and I will do it for the sake of my father. You know, Mr. Waller," continued she, blushing at what she was about to say, "the large number of bachelors, young and old, that have of late years sought my hand, some, perhaps, for my own sake, but a great many, I fear, for the sake of the fortune and estate to which I am heiress. There are others, too, who, I suppose, would wish to enter the lists, only that they are deterred by poverty. You may now circulate it amongst them all, rich and poor, that to the man who will be successful in bringing the murderer of my father to justice I will give my hand and fortune. This, before you, a magistrate of the county, I vow most solemnly and truly to perform."

Old Squire Waller endeavored, by every means in

his power, to dissuade her from keeping her vow; but it was all to no purpose. Madeline Lombard's resolve was taken, and the affair was soon spread through the country. As may be supposed, the search after the murderer became now more diligent and active, in a tenfold degree; but it was still fruitless. Madeline, since the death of her father, often thought of her absent cousin, Harry Godsall, and wished him at home; for she knew, bad as he was, that he would make himself more active than all the others in the search.

Her wish was strangely granted; for, about six weeks after the murder, Harry Godsall came home. He seemed much changed and darkened by the foreign clime; but he came like a gentleman, dressed well, and apparently with plenty of money. He said that he had purchased his discharge, and come home to lead thenceforth a steady life. Harry was soon established in the country mansion of the Lombards, and, of course, was most indefatigably engaged in the search for the murderer.

Now, our town is, and was always, remarkable for strange characters. Among the strangest of them all was old Peg Trassy, the fairy woman. She had a most astonishing knowledge of herbs and their properties, and was famed through the wide country round as a most successful doctress. Her home was in one of the deserted cloisters of the huge old abbey beside the river, and there she usually received her patients, with an amount of mystery that added not a little to her fame amongst the peasantry and townspeople.

One night, about a fortnight after the return of Harry Godsall, he and old Peg Trassy were holding secret counsel together in the ancient cloister. It was a long and mysterious consultation, and related to the murder.

"You saw him, then," said Harry Godsall, with a dark look of intelligence at the fairy woman, as he rose to depart; "you saw him coming out of the window with the knife in his hand, and climbing down the leaden pipe at the back of the house?"

"I did," answered Peg Trassy, with a sinister look in return.

"And you will swear to it?" said Harry.

"That will I," answered Peg, "as sure as there is a fairy in Lisbloom."

"Then," said Harry Godsall, as he moved to the door of the cloister, "the reward will be doubled, Peg — yes, and doubled again, not counting the sum I shall give you when all is settled. Good night, and remember!"

"Remember!" exclaimed Peg Trassy, when he was gone. "As sure as there's an angel in heaven, I will! I heard you talking to yourself," continued she, "when you thought there was no one near, the other night, under the town wall; an', *mo bron!* 'tis remember your words, an' the reward you were to give me! I'll not forget it, word for word, till the day o' my death!" And she poured out, from a small

earthen pot, a steaming jorum of tea, which was, in
those days, both a rarity and luxury among the poor,
and began to refresh herself. "Swear it, inyah!"
added she, as she finished her cup, walked over to
one of her secret closets, and brought forth a long
clasp-knife, all stained and incrusted with blood;
"faith I will! I can safely swear, aboveboard, that
I saw him coming out o' the window, in the dead o'
night, with this knife dripping red in his bloody
hand, and also how he dropped it in the weeds,
climbing over the garden wall, and couldn't find it.
But I found it, an' will keep it till the day o' trial.
Then those who think money and villany, can gain
the day will see truth stepping forrid, horse an' foot,
an' winning the battle!"

Next day half a troop of yeomen cavalry left our
town, under the command of Harry Godsall and old
Squire Waller, and proceeded in the direction of
Brian Connell's house. After an absence of about
two hours, they returned, with Richard Connell a
prisoner between them, and accused of the murder
of old George Lombard. The same evening a meeting of the surrounding magistrates was held in the
town. Several men, who had been in the faction
fight on the evening of the fair, were brought before
them by Harry Godsall. They proved to the manner in which Dick Connell had threatened old George
Lombard. After some other evidence brought forward by Harry Godsall, who said that other and
more important facts would be forthcoming at the

proper time, Dick Connell was there and then committed, by the over-zealous magistrates, for the wilful murder of George Lombard, Esquire, and was next day sent off, under the guardianship of the yeomen cavalry, to the county jail, there to await his trial.

Strange to say, notwithstanding all this, Madeline persisted in believing Dick Connell innocent of the terrible crime with which he was charged.

"Take care," she said to Harry Godsall, "that you are not acting over-hastily in the matter. I know them all well, and I am persuaded that Richard Connell would not injure a hair of my poor father's head."

"I thought, Madeline," answered her cousin, with something of a sneer on his lip, "that you would be the last person to hold back, after all that has occurred. When the day of the trial comes, you will see, to your surprise, that he is guilty, for I am now on the track of witnesses that will prove him so."

"May God defend the innocent, at all events," pursued Madeline. "I tell you, Harry, again to take care, however. You know the ill will you bear the Connells, and this may have led you to act too hastily towards them."

"As for me," answered her cousin, "that affair you allude to is past and gone, and you know I am a different man now. I bear them no ill will. But I want justice to be done on the head of the guilty. Meantime, Madeline, when all is over, and the murderer brought to justice for his crime, I shall then remind you of the promise you made before old Tom Waller."

"I have made my vow," answered Madeline, quietly, "and I will perform its conditions, come what may!"

"That is all I want," said Harry; and an hour afterwards he was riding out of the town, towards their country mansion, with a dream in his head of a fine estate, a splendid bride, and prosperity forevermore.

About a week before the assizes came on, Peg Trassy, the fairy woman, presented herself before the hall door of old Squire Waller, and demanded an audience of that wine-drinking and jovial dignitary.

"Well, Peg," said the squire, "what do you want? Is it going to lodge information against the fairies you are?"

"Wisha! faith it isn't," answered Peg; "but I want a small bit o' writing from your honor."

"Perhaps," said the squire, who was always jocose with Peg, "it is a lease of the old cloister, or the whole abbey, you want from me."

"It is not, then," returned Peg, doggedly. "It's only Brian Connell sent me to your honor for an order. He wants to see his son."

"And why did he not come himself?" asked the squire.

"Becaise, your honor," answered Peg, "after the disgrace an' burning shame that has been brought upon his family by his misfortunate son, he doesn't like his face to be seen by any o' the gentlemen that know him."

"Well," said the squire, "I suppose I must give it;" and he wrote an order to the governor of the county jail to admit its bearer to the cell of poor Dick Connell. Instead, however, of proceeding to the house of Brian Connell with the order, Peg Trassy immediately set off on foot for the city, and presented the order at the jail herself. She was admitted to Dick Connell's cell.

"Aren't you afraid of dying?" asked she of the prisoner, after she had greeted him with all due solemnity.

"I am not afraid of death," answered Dick Connell; "but still I am afraid of dying with the stain of murder on my name. I am innocent, Peg, and God will show it yet, perhaps when I am cold in my grave."

"I know it," said Peg; "an' it's only natural that you would fear dying with the stain of blood upon your name. What would you give to a person who would prove you innocent to judge, jury, an' the world, an' put the chain o' the law upon the guilty afore the eyes o' them all?"

"I have not much to give," answered Dick Connell, eagerly. "I have only the small farm allowed me by my father. That I will sell, and give the proceeds of it to the one who will do as you say."

"Richard Connell," said the fairy woman, solemnly, "do you remember one day, when you were but a little boy, that you found me lying by the road-side, in a burning fever? Do you remember how you ran and told your parents, an' how your father got a little hut built for me in the corner o' one o' his fields? and how, all through my raging sickness, you an' yours tended me, an' fed me as if I was their own blood-relation? I don't forget it, at any rate, an' I am now come to do you a good turn — to save your life, an' punish the guilty."

"Who is guilty of the deed?" asked Dick Connell, with wild eagerness.

"No matter," answered Peg. "I'll prove you innocent, anyhow; but you must first write me a letter to the young lady o' Castle Lombard, saying that you had no part in that deed, an' that God will raise you up a witness on the day o' trial that will put the felon's chain around the four bones o' the murderer. Here is pen, ink, an' paper;" and she produced the latter articles from the capacious sleeve of her red gown.

On the evening of next day, Madeline Lombard received from the hands of Peg Trassy the following short letter, written by Richard Connell, strictly according to the directions of the fairy woman: —

"MADAM: I pray you to excuse my boldness in addressing you. I am innocent of the murder of your father; but when the day of the trial comes on, with the help of God, I will undertake to bring to justice the real murderer; in which case it will be far from one in my humble position to remind you of the vow you made before Squire Waller.

"I have the honor to be,
 "Madam, with profound respect, yours,
  "RICHARD CONNELL."

The day of the trial at last came, and, as a matter of course, our county court was crowded by rich and poor from the whole country round. Richard Connell was placed in the dock, and his pale face showed the sufferings he had undergone, alone in his felon cell; but at the same time his eye was bright and his demeanor calm, so that the spectators could trace in his looks no sign of fear for the result of his trial. Madeline Lombard sat at the judge's right hand to witness the proceedings; and Harry Godsall, who had to aid in producing the witnesses, was stationed near the spot allotted to the latter while giving their evidence. The preliminary evidence, the threat uttered by Dick Connell at the faction fight, with other incidental things, were gone through, greatly, in the mind of judge and jury, to the prejudice of the prisoner, when, at last, the crier called out, in a loud voice, the name of Margaret Trassy, and ordered her to come forward and give her testimony. You might have heard a straw drop in the court, all were then so silent, for they knew that it was upon her testimony the final result of the trial depended.

"Here I am, my lord," said Peg, as she stepped

up to the witness table, and looked proudly on the judge.

After she had complied with the usual preliminaries, the judge asked her to go over her evidence. In a clear, distinct voice, she then told how, on the night of the murder, she had gone to gather a certain herb, which she could find nowhere but on the garden wall at the back of the Lombard mansion; how, as she stood beneath the shadow of the wall, she heard a noise at the back of the house, and, on looking up, beheld the murderer, in the moonlight, coming forth from a window, with a knife in his hand, both hand and knife apparently bloody; how he climbed down the leaden pipe that led by the window, and how he clambered over the garden wall, and disappeared, but not before she had seen his face; in fine, that she knew him well.

"Point him out," said the judge; and the rod was immediately put into her hand by one of the officials of the court.

The fairy woman paused a moment, looked at prisoner, judge, and crowded court, and then, stepping forward a pace, laid the rod upon the head of Harry Godsall!

"What insane trick is this?" said the judge, sternly, while the whole court rose in astonishment, and Harry Godsall fell back in his seat, shaking with terror. "Woman," continued his lordship, "you were brought into this court to give testimony to the truth. Beware, now, how you tamper with us!"

"I am giving true evidence, my lord," answered Peg Trassy. "I saw the murderer climb over the garden wall. In doing so, he let fall his knife, returned for it, but could not find it. But I found it, my lord, after he was gone, in a bunch of weeds, where I saw it drop. Here is the knife; you can look for yourself who is the owner of it;" and she handed the weapon to the judge. His lordship took it in his hand, and examined it carefully. It was still encrusted and stained with blood, and on its brass handle was the name of Harry Godsall, in large, plain capitals.

"It is enough!" exclaimed the judge. "Attach Harry Godsall for the murder of George Lombard, his uncle!"

Harry Godsall, more dead than alive, was taken, then and there, into custody, and immediately lodged securely in prison. His trial soon came on. He was convicted, and not long after underwent the penalty of his terrible crime. It came out on the trial how he had leagued himself with the tinkers, in order to come unobserved into our town, and how also he had deserted from his regiment, with various other particulars unnecessary to mention.

And Madeline Lombard — did she keep her vow? She did; and since the foundation stone of our town was laid, there was never seen such a wedding as took place on the occasion of her marriage with Dick Connell, a twelvemonth or so afterwards. On that day, from what cause I cannot explain, — perhaps some great doctor or optician might take the trouble of examining the matter,—I saw at least four brides and four bridegrooms at the ceremony, with innumerable repetitions of the same objects, as I walked hilariously along the street. I know it could not be the number of chickens I ate at the wedding breakfast that caused it. All I can say about the matter is, that I retired to bed in the evening, slept for a time soundly, woke again with a feeling of thirst and a slight headache, then fell asleep, and dreamed that our lake had at last arisen in its might and submerged the town, and that I was in the centre of the cool water, swilling away at it to my heart's content.

A LITTLE BIT OF SPORT.—No. I.

DUCKS AND DIVERS.

A STUDENT'S life is the pleasantest in the world, if he belong to a good "set." Ours was the liveliest "set" in college. The members of it, one and all, were possessed of an infinite amount of animal spirits, and were endowed also with that sanguine mental temperament that enabled them to see a silver lining to every cloud that gathered over their path during the college session. These clouds were numerous enough, Heaven knows; for between the reprimands and cautions of professors and deans of faculty on one side, and the grave verdicts of president, vice-president, and council in judgment assembled on the other, scarcely a day passed over our heads that some individual amongst us was not in trouble. It is wonderful what slight things will bring students to grief, and medical students in particular. Everybody seems down upon them. With one, the poor disciples of

Æsculapius are mad; with another, they are worse than mad — they are wicked; with a third, they are idle, dissipated, and quarrelsome; and a fourth wiseacre warns his acquaintances to avoid them as they would the fabled upas tree, because they are going straight to — Well, we shall not, in our indignant denial of his assertion, mention where; but a pair of tightly-pursed lips, a hypocritical sigh, and an ominous shake of the head from the wise propounder of the opinion, will sufficiently indicate the locality. But if their faults and virtues were put on opposite sides of the scale, it is our opinion, both private and public, and one which we would cheerfully put our "four bones" in jeopardy to uphold, that the good would weigh down the balance at a glorious rate.

But be the above as it may, it is wonderfully easy, nevertheless, to get a student into trouble. The slightest infringement of his college rules will bring upon him the frowns and reprimands of those in authority. One day, during a deep snow, about five score of us waylaid two mail-coaches that passed every afternoon by the college. Well, our ringleaders were forthwith called before the council, and severely admonished. And for what, think you? We stopped the coaches, sure enough, and on examination found that all the passengers were men, save one. Dick Sommerville, the dandy of the college, immediately handed down the individual of the gentle sex, and politely led her to a safe distance.

We then, taking pity upon the half-frozen looks of the remaining passengers, namely, twelve upon one vehicle and fourteen upon the other, in order to warm them, commenced a cannonade of snow-balls, which we never ceased for an instant until every living man of them, drivers and all, had been brought to the ground. One of the passengers, in his rage, discharged an old cavalry pistol amongst us. But his hand was so unsteady, that the bullet only passed through the mortar-board, i. e., the college cap, of dandy Sommerville, and then lodged victoriously in the haunch of a huge donkey, who was contemplating our onslaught from a field hard by, and which, the moment it felt the leaden messenger, immediately went prancing in terror round the field, his agonizing hee-haws at the same time echoing in startling tones through the halls and corridors of our Alma Mater! The remaining passengers, seeing the determination of their companion, showed fight; but we soon buried them in the snow, and then bundling them upon their seats once more, set the coaches in motion, and sent them off under a farewell discharge of snow-balls, and with a shout whose hilarious cadences brought a dozen or so of police upon us from an adjacent barrack. Then followed a new cannonade and a second victory, which resulted in the severe reprimand aforesaid from the college council.

But what has all this, you will say, to do with diver-chasing and duck-shooting? You will soon come to it, gentle reader. I only want to show you how the jovial spirits of my "set" usually passed their time in college till the final examination of the session approached. Then it was that, like the young foxes, who, after disporting themselves merrily in the noontide ray, seek their silent burrows on the approach of the storm, the jolly spirits of my "set," one and all, betook themselves to their rooms, trimmed their midnight lamps, and studied away incessantly to retrieve their lost time. This was not a good plan, you will say. It was not, I admit. But there was good stuff in some of us, nevertheless; and this the book-worms of the college often found out to their cost; for when the examinations came on, the coveted prizes were almost in every case borne off by the wild ones, who, if they had not the "genius for work," — at least for incessant work, — had usually a plentiful store of brains and intellect, that carried them through victoriously when the tug of war came on in the shape of the prize examinations.

Have any of you, dear readers, competed for a scholarship? If you have not, I have; and I should know what it is. The sessional examinations are over, and the prizes in the different departments are awarded, generally to the great dismay of the book-worms, and to the surprise and delight of some of the wild ones. We are all scattered at our several homes in the country to spend the summer vacation. The book-worms scarcely ever see a good gleam of sun-light. They are hard at work for the October trial, which is to decide the various scholarships.

The wild spirits are away over mountain and moor, in deep valley, by rushing stream or margent of lonely lake, fishing or shooting, according to time and season, little thinking on their hour of trial in their luxurious enjoyment of breeze and shower, and golden flood of sunlight flashing over hill, and plain, and joyous river. The golden trout and silver-scaled salmon are captured, the wary spaniel points on the heathery moorland, and the whizzing partridge or the brown goose falls beneath the unerring gun; and so the hours glide on.

Thus I spent my time during a certain summer vacation. The partridge season soon came on, and every morning, as it shone, saw me out in the breezy woodlands, gun in hand, and spaniel busily employed before me on the track of the wary birds. One morning it struck me that the time of the examinations was drawing alarmingly nigh. There was a scholarship to be competed for, the attainment of which would materially aid my success in college. So I threw by my gun, placed the dogs in durance vile, and commenced to study at the usual mad rate. The examination at length came off, but it was a sealed mystery to us all, the result — the names of the successful candidates for the several scholarships — nothing could be known until after the eagerly-expected meeting of the college council. O that weary time of incertitude and burning expectancy. Day after day flew by, and the members of my "set," many of whom, like myself, were in for scholarships, tried every plan to pass away the time till the sitting of the council. Our debating club, in which Ned Rivers held forth, a shining light, every evening was experimented on, and found wanting. Billiards, bagatelle, cards, football, and every species of game imaginable were tried, but all proved unsuccessful in calming our troubled minds. Spite of everything, the approaching council and its awards loomed up incessantly before our minds like a black cloud, and we were miserable.

In my despondency, the day before that on which the council was to sit, I strolled into the rooms of Ned Danvers, where there was always sure to be a good number of the boys sitting in conference upon some question or other. The physiognomies of the company were almost black with despair as I entered and sat myself upon a vacant chair by the fireside.

"What shall we do to please all?" exclaimed Ned Danvers, excitedly. "I'm sure, if you all wish to stay here, I shall be delighted to do the honors of my rooms. But what do you say to a night's duck-shooting in the marshes by the river?"

"The very thing! the very thing!" we all shouted.

"Well, then," rejoined Ned, "let all meet here by eight o'clock to-night, fully equipped, and I promise you, we will have some sport, for the weather will be favorable, and the ducks are numerous upon the marshes."

"And to-morrow," said Joe Dolphin, who had a passion for aquatic sports, "we will go down in my boat and have a diver-chase upon the river!"

The programme of operations was a good one. And so that night we all met according to our agreement in Ned Danvers's rooms. There were ten of us. Six were to proceed up the river banks to the shore of a little marshy lake — a favorite feeding-place of the birds during the night. The remaining four, of whom I made one, were to remain beside a solitary marsh about a mile nearer than the former. Together we proceeded up the shore, and I will venture to say that a more jovial company could not be seen that night from the Giant's Causeway to the Skellig Rocks.

It was a fine night. A strong breeze seemed to be blowing through the upper regions of the sky, for the light volumes of cloud flitted briskly across the moon, which at intervals shone down with pale radiance on hill, and moorland, and river. But all was calm beneath, and on we marched with our guns resting quietly under our arms, and our flasks of the *native* in our pockets, till we reached a solitary path that led across a wet moorland towards the marsh. Four of us immediately filed off, while the remaining six proceeded farther up the river, in order to reach the lake, which was to be the scene of their night's sport.

At last, after sinking several times to our knees in the succession of little quagmires that obstructed our path, we reached the marsh. At its southern side rose a low, ridgy hill, some distance up which was a ruined hovel, the desolate outlines of which we could see in the occasional glimpses of moonlight. Taking our course round the eastern boundary of the marsh, we ascended the hill towards the hovel, in which we intended to bivouac for some time, for we found that we had arrived upon the spot about an hour or so before that part of the night the ducks usually chose for visiting their banqueting-ground beneath. Part of the hovel still remained entire, namely, its single sleeping-room; and in this we were soon ensconced before a blazing fire of brambles and dry ferns we had gathered upon the hill outside. This dry fuel made but little smoke, and as we had taken the precaution of stopping the single and diminutive window of the ruined chamber with a bundle of grass and fern, there was but little fear of our fire-light disturbing the ducks, should they visit the marsh sooner than we expected.

After a few applications to the flask, the spirits of my companions began to ascend to a rather high degree of hilarity. Ned Danvers sang a song which set us all in a roar. Bill Shirket repeated the third act of a tragedy, which immortal production was to make its *début* during our usual winter theatricals. Unfortunately, however, it was never represented on any stage; and all I remember of it is a scene in which Solyman the Magnificent is represented in the act of relating to his queen how a Genius had given him a glimpse of the pre-Adamite world, from the summit of the Pyramid of Cheops. It was a grand scene, that in which Solyman, describing what he saw, stretches forth his hand majestically towards his consort, and says,—

"There lay Mylodon like a shattered hulk,
  And Megalonyx, the magnific might
 Of Megatherium, and the fleshless bulk
  Of Mammoth, like a ribbed sea-rock, and white
   Skulls of Mastodon; but the horrid light
From their fierce eyeballs, and the rolling breath
 Of their wide throats, were quenched and stilled in death!"

Why our poet had chosen the above measure for the greater part of his tragedy I know not, and very likely never will, for Bill Shirket is not the man to be questioned profanely on such subjects. Another song was sung, and at last it came to Tom O'Mahony's turn.

"Now," said Tom, "I will give you a fragment which I contrived to purloin one evening from the papers of a friend, which he evidently intended as a rival to Millikin's immortal 'Groves of Blarney;'" and in the mellowest of mellow voices he rolled forth the following, stretching out the notes occasionally to a tremendous length, in order to imitate the singing of the country people:—

"One morning sweet and glorious, when the wild birds sung their chorus,
 And all nature was uproarious in the charming month o' May;
And the lambs and trouts and horses, that knew not what remorse is,
 And the shark and whale and porpus, they gamboled in the say;

'Twas then I left Cork city, and sung a roaring ditty,
 And all in praise o' Kitty that I left in Cork behind —
'Twas then my manes were squandhered, and I in sadness
    pondhered,
 While far in grief I wandhered towards Leinster like
    the wind!

While I in grief relinted, a public house I inthered,
 Where my heart was circumvinted by a charmin' bloomin'
    maid.
Her form was stout and stately, and she smiled on me so
    nately,
 That she broke my heart complately, and left Kitty in the
    shade.
Her hair like goold or brass-sticks, her limbs were most
    elastic,
 And fit for all gymnastics, and for makin' punch and tay;
And 'twould be a crime most hainous, her comparisment with
    Vainus,
 Or Proserpine the janius, that *Plutarch* stole away!"

Just as Tom had ended this fragment from the papers of his witty and erudite friend, the faint reports of several double-barrels smote upon our ears from some distance up the river, and away we started, for we knew our comrades were at their work by the lake. The marsh, silent and desolate, lay spread beneath us in the moonlight. It was a broad network of sedgy banks, between which lay a number of muddy pools with margents surrounded by belts of tall reeds. After descending the hill, our stations were soon taken amid these reeds, each having a broad pool to himself. After lying crouched amid the reeds for about ten minutes, we suddenly heard a loud "quack! quack! quack!" from the direction of the lake farther up the river. Then followed a whir and whistle of wings, and we soon had the satisfaction of seeing a large flock of ducks wheeling over our head. Round and round they hovered warily, for the guns of our companions had made them suspicious of alighting. At length they seemed to think all safe beneath, and broke into several small flocks, which wheeled and whirred hither and thither, and at last went down with a sudden dash into the several pools, about a dozen or more alighting upon that on whose margin I was eagerly awaiting their arrival. I gave them no time to scatter, but fired the contents of my right barrel right into the midst of them. A splashing and a quacking followed, as the affrighted flock rose, that beggars description. Up they whirred, however, and through them went the contents of my left barrel, its report being followed by an almost simultaneous discharge from the guns of my companions. With eager eyes I gazed out upon the pool to see the result of my two shots, and had the satisfaction of seeing three birds floating helplessly on the water in their death-struggles. A peculiar rustling and trembling of the reeds at the other side told me that one or two others at least were wounded; and with this prospect before me I quickly reloaded, and crouched down carefully in my place again. I knew by the satisfied *sotto voce* remarks of my companions that they too were successful.

A deep silence once more fell upon the broad marsh, broken occasionally by the booming voice of the goureen-roe, or snipe, as it wheeled round and round in airy spirals through the moonlight sky overhead. As I lay snugly contemplating the dead birds which the night-breeze was gradually floating towards the margin of the pool, I heard a shrill and unearthly scream from the eastern border of the marsh. I knew it, although it floated through the air like the shriek of some lonely spirit of the hill. Again it was repeated, and in a few moments afterwards I saw a heron floating upwards, with its long legs hanging down, and head stretched forward, as if it came upon a reconnoitring excursion to the marsh.

"Don't fire!" exclaimed the voice of Ned Danvers, in a general admonition — "on your lives don't fire, for I hear another flock of duck coming over the hill!"

At the sound of his voice the heron emitted another unearthly and defiant scream, and flew directly over the pool where I was stationed. The temptation was too much for me; so I sat up, and suddenly let fly the contents of one barrel after him as he went. A scream, a flapping of wings helplessly, and down poor long-neck dropped dead into a bank of reeds hard by.

"You have spoiled our sport for two hours to come!" roared the enraged Ned Danvers across the marsh; and sure enough, the next instant we heard a distant "quack! quack!" from over the hill, and then the faint whizzing of wings, and at last a splendid flock of duck passed high over our heads, without deigning to pay us the shortest visit, and then faded away beyond our ken, through the dim, distant sky, to some unknown and more solitary region by river shore or ocean strand.

What a long penance we had to perform for that single shot! Not a duck, teal, or widgeon came near us for the next two hours, although we heard shots several times, during the interim, from the distant lake. How eagerly we crouched down in our damp hiding-places, after each of these shots, expecting some scattered flock to pay us a visit! But none such came, and we were forced to content ourselves with our own thoughts as the moments wore on. Ned Danvers and my other companions were, however, not disposed to remain always silent, for now and then they expressed their disapproval of the offender's conduct in deep and surly growls that echoed with weird effect across the still pools of the ghostly marsh.

At length a cannonade more prolonged than usual told us that our comrades were enjoying themselves to their hearts' content by the distant lake; and eagerly listening for the coming of the expected flock, we heard a sharper and more confused whirring and whistling of wings than before, and presently a numerous flight of mingled duck and widgeon passed high over our heads towards the east through the shadowy sky. Just as we expected that they would fade from our sorrowful gaze, they wheeled sharply round, and retraced their course again, this time somewhat nearer to the earth. On they came, wheeling in circles occasionally, and quacking with loud and eager voices, as if engaged in holding a consultation as to the whereabouts of their next banqueting-place. The gluttons! Despite the fright they had got at the lake, they now seemed disposed to try a meal upon the marsh, and with that intent wheeled round and round it a dozen times overhead with an incessant "quack, quack!" and a loud whistling of wings. Just as they were preparing to alight, something beneath aroused their suspicions, and away they went again in a straight and onward course through the blue. Again they stopped, and seemed deliberating, while we, from our hiding-places, held our breath, fearing to make the slightest noise. At length a single mallard, separating from the flock, flew back directly over the marsh, inspecting every part of it minutely as he circled overhead on his strong pinions. A satisfactory call from this fine bird announced to the flock that he imagined all safe; and back they came again over our heads, making the same manœuvres as before. At last they separated and came down, some in pairs and some in small flocks, with a dash upon the smooth surface of the pools. No sooner were they down, when bang! bang! went the fatal barrels, right and left; and with resounding screams and flutterings the affrighted flock arose and darted confusedly away through the far sky, leaving several of their companions killed and wounded behind them. It was an exciting scene. Eagerly I peered forth over the surface of the pool, and found an addition to my trophies in the shape of a widgeon and a fine mallard, both of which lay in their last throes upon the water.

Thus the night passed. A few hours' sleep and we were up again, guns ready, and shot-pouches on shoulders, and planning our course of action for the day. That evening at six o'clock the council were to meet to award the scholarships, and of course we were all in a high fever of excitement. Joe Dolphin had a large four-oared boat, and in this sturdy vessel eight of us were soon sweeping down the river. The day came on dry and windy, the white breakers broke in foam over the bows of our swift boat as we swept downwards. At length we reached a broad expanse of the river half a dozen miles below the city. This was to be our hunting-field. Here the surface of the water was unbroken, save by the light waves that coursed each other from shore to shore, making the whole expanse of the broad lake like a green meadow swaying before the light winds of an April day.

Several black objects might be seen dotting the surface of the windy lake; they were divers seeking their voracious meals of small fish. Occasionally we could see one of them, after capturing its prey, raise itself half out of the water with erected head and flapping wings, and swallowing the luckless inhabitant of the water it had taken. Now and then, also, one of them would rise and fly windward some distance, then drop down upon the water and float before the wind, diving and fluttering its black wings as the fish passed in its way. Our object was to wound a bird, and then have a chase upon the lake; but for a long time we were unsuccessful. At length, one fellow, that had floated to the far shore, arose and took his course windward, directly in a line for our boat. On it came close overhead, seemingly reckless of our proximity. As it passed, Joe Dolphin took up his gun and prepared to fire.

"Don't shoot him through the head, Joe!" cried we. "Wing him, and then he will give us a glorious chase!"

Bang! went the gun, but, unfortunately, the aim was too true, and down came the bird, with a whack, upon the surface of the water — dead. A storm of execrations saluted poor Joe, as he recovered his gun; but there was no help for it, and so we allowed the dead bird to float by, and rowed hither and thither, awaiting another opportunity. Not a bird was now to be seen over the broad expanse. At the report of the gun they all dived, and for a long time scarcely showed one of their black bills above the water. But new arrivals at length began to appear from the windings of the river farther down. Again a bird came in a straight course for our boat, this time so high that he was out of the range of a common fowling-piece. We had taken the precaution of bringing a long duck-gun with us. This I took possession of, and awaited the coming of the diver in the bow of the boat. I allowed him to pass several lengths overhead, and then fired. The smoke cleared away instantly, and I had the satisfaction of seeing the bird hover confusedly for a time in the air, and then drop down wounded into the water. The moment he reached the surface he disappeared, and then the sport commenced. On went the boat, propelled by the sturdy oars, towards the spot where the bird had dived. When we reached it we saw his black bill appearing above the water about thirty yards distant. Bang! bang! went the guns, and down again popped the black-bill. Now it rose at a considerable distance away, and again it would appear sometimes within a few arms' length of the boat, in which case it was saluted by the contents of a few barrels, or by a slash from one of the oars, for the rowers were determined to have their share of the sport, and I believe in my heart it was the best.

After about an hour's chase, during which, notwithstanding the coldness of the season, we had all got into a glow of heat, the black bill and nearly half the body of the diver appeared almost at the side of the boat. A shout and a slashing of oars followed, and down went the unfortunate bird again. In the last evolution, Joe Dolphin, who had put by his gun and taken a spare oar in hand, in his eagerness to salute the bird with a finishing blow, overstretched himself, and out he went over the side of the boat, with a splash, into the water. Joe Dolphin, however, like his aquatic namesake, was quite at home in the watery element, and by means of the oar which he still held in his hand, kept himself gallantly above the surface. He was two boats' length behind us before we could turn to his rescue. As we did so, the diver happened to rise within two feet of his chin. It was amusing to see the vengeful grab he made at the bird, which, however, dived again, and eluded him.

"Don't mind me, boys!" called out Joe, gallantly, at this. "The bird is getting weary. Follow him, and leave me to shift for myself a few moments!"

We knew Joe would have his way; so we rested on our oars for a minute or so, waiting for the bird to appear. The poor diver was evidently getting weak, and about to give in, for he now popped up his bill right in front of us, about two or three yards away. This time we did not dare to fire, for Joe was only about a perch beyond the bird; but the oars went down plash! plash! at the poor black-bill, Joe at the same time striking out with the celerity of a practised swimmer for the spot. Down went the bird; but he was no sooner down than up again right opposite Joe Dolphin's face. A quick dart of the nervous arm, and the fluttering bird was instantly held over the surface of the water by the bold swimmer. A loud shout welcomed the deft feat, and the next moment the dying bird and its exultant captor were pulled safely into the boat. Knowing that some such accident was likely to occur, we had stowed away a spare suit of clothes in our provision hamper. In these Joe Dolphin was soon arrayed, and after a few applications to the brandy flask, was as merry as the best of us.

Three other hunts followed. They were all something like the first, but they were not the less exciting to us at the same time. After dining like true sportsmen in our boat, we left the lake, and proceeding up the river, reached the city about half past five o'clock. We hid our guns under one of the dark porches of the college, and literally frying with impatience, awaited the news. At last it came. Hurrah! The wild spirits had beaten the book-worms. I was a scholar, Ned Danvers was a scholar, and others of our "set" too numerous to mention were equally fortunate.

A BIT OF SPORT. — No. II.

HUNTING DOWN THE WALRUS.

CHILDHOOD and boyhood passed tranquilly away in my pleasant home by the Shannon side; but, as manhood approached, a host of undefined dreams and wild longings after adventure thronged my heart and brain, and exercised such an influence over me, that, though I struggled manfully against them for a time, I was at length conquered. I soon gratified my passion for adventure after a somewhat singular manner. Near us there lived an old gentleman by the name of Dick Blennerhasset, who, in his youth, had been an officer in the navy. Captain Dick, as we used to call him, was an old and tried friend of my father's, and, during his visits to our house, the stories he was in the habit of telling me about his adventures had no small share in exciting my imagination. With him I was an especial favorite, for I was strong, active, and courageous; and, in our frequent boating excursions together on the Shannon, I showed such an aptitude for everything nautical, that he was wont to declare, with several asseverations which shall be nameless here, that I was born to be a sailor. And a sailor I was determined to be in good earnest.

In vain did I beseech Captain Dick and my father to let me go on one of these voyages. They were both inexorable. But, nevertheless, I was determined to be off by some means or other. It was May eve, and Captain Dick had come over to bid my father good by, for the Kathleen was to sail next morning, should the winds permit. Again I made the modest request of which I have spoken; again I was flatly refused, this time with a stern threat from my father. Heaven forgive me, his harsh tone only rendered me more obstinate in my determination; so I left them to finish their punch, and stole quietly to my bed-room. There I packed up all my warmest clothing in a bundle, and with it cautiously decamped from the house, and made my way to the shore, opposite which the Kathleen was lying quietly at anchor, with no one to watch her, for the crew were all away at their different homes, bidding their friends farewell. I took a small punt which lay by the shore, rowed it outward, and in fine, after letting it drift quietly down the river, found myself upon the deck of the Kathleen.

The first object almost that my eyes lighted on was a tub of biscuits lying against the ship's side. From this I took an ample supply, and, after abstracting a jar of water from several that lay near, I took my treasure down to the hold. As well as I could judge, it was about daybreak when Captain Dick and his crew came on board. By their cheery voices I knew that the weather was favorable. At length the Kathleen was in full sail down the river, and, after about three hours, I knew by the sound of waves from outside, and the bounding motions of the vessel, that she was rounding Loop Head, and dancing out into the open sea. O, how I longed to be on deck! but the certainty of being sent back ignominiously by Captain Dick kept me quiet in my dark and narrow lodging.

On the morning of the fourth day, my biscuits and water being gone, I resolved, come what would, to brave the anger of Captain Dick. He was standing near his cabin door as I walked boldly on deck. A cry of surprise from some of the men who observed me first, made him turn round. There I stood, pale and worn, confronting him, however, with a bold face. I shall never forget the look he gave me. Had a thunderbolt fallen and shivered the deck of his beloved vessel, he could not appear more astonished and confounded. After a roaring volley of nautical oaths, his next impulse was to seize a rope's end.

"You young lubber," said he, pausing, — for he saw that I was not to be trifled with, — "what will you do, when an hour hence I'll put you in on the shore of Donegal, and send you home to your father?"

"I'll never go home alive!" answered I, boldly.

There was a kind light in the old hero's eye at my determined manner, which was not lost upon me, for I knew his every mood. "Captain Dick," I continued, following up my attack, "you often said I was born to be a sailor. Let me go with you this once, and I promise I shall never offend either you or my father again."

"Egad," said he, shaking his head, "I suppose it must be so now. Into the cabin with you, and get your breakfast," continued he, severely; "and I'll see about a letter to your father, telling him what you have done, and all about you."

Into the cabin I went, followed by the now somewhat appeased Captain Dick. After breakfast, during which I explained to him my mode of living in the hold, he sat down, and wrote a letter to my father, promising the latter to bring me back safe from my Arctic adventures. We were now passing Tory Island, and I began wondering as to the fate of the letter, when our commander ordered the course of the Kathleen to be changed so as to run in towards the shore of Donegal. From a village there the letter was forwarded to the next post town, and, in course of time, as I learned afterwards, it arrived safely at the Shannon side, and quieted the apprehensions of my father with regard to my disappearance.

We sailed again for the far north. The wind was still fair, and on the morning of the fifth day we saw the sun rising from between the Western Scottish Isles. The gigantic crags of St. Kilda towered upon our left about midday, and, as night fell, we came in sight of the rocky mass of Suliker, looming before us in solitary grandeur over the desolate waste of waters. Here the wind, after veering round, blew almost a gale from the westward; and we were forced to change our course; for, instead of holding on straight for the Faroe Islands, as intended, the Kathleen ran before the wind to the Shetlands. Towards morning the wind abated, and when the sun rose we were in the little bay of Lerwick, the capital of those islands. From this we took our departure in the evening with a fair wind, which happily continued till, on the 24th of May, after passing Rost, one of the Loffoden Islands, we sailed into the Folden Fiord, and cast anchor opposite Rorstad — a small Norwegian village.

In sailing into the Folden Fiord, the scenery is inconceivably grand and terrible. On the left are the Loffoden Islands, with their tremendous precipices, some detached rocks of them rising, like naked and jagged spears, thousands of feet over the waters of that wild sea; others stretching in gigantic barriers between the eye and the horizon, while, from some of the islands, such as East and West Vaage, white pyramidal mountains shot up, far beyond the line of perpetual snow, their pointed summits glittering in the sun, and making doubly blacker by the contrast the sombre precipices beneath, and the gloomy waters that forever dash and roar through the perilous channels which intersect them. Right before you, as you enter the Fiord, towers up into the silent sky the stupendous mass of Sulitelma, the highest mountain in Europe beyond the Arctic Circle, with its successive forest zones of fir, pine, and birch, its naked and shaggy rocks frowning grim above them in another desolate belt, along which no living thing, plant, or bird, exists, save a few alpine plants, and the *emberiza nivalis*, a small bird, a species of bunting, which occasionally enlivens the steeps with its solitary note; while, high above all, forest, cliff, chasm, and girdle of rolling clouds, the mighty peak of the mountain itself throws up its many-tinted glaciers, white with eternal snow.

The Folden Fiord has no strand. It runs inland for a length of about seventy miles, and seems to have been channelled in the lapse of ages by the action of the furious sea that forever dashes against the Scandinavian peninsula. The naked and beetling crags, at either side, rise hundreds of feet sheer from the water's edge, except opposite Rorstad, where there is a break in the sable line of precipices, and where vessels of light burden can anchor with safety. At Rorstad we remained for a week, making various arrangements, for here it was that Captain Dick Blennerhasset usually hired his harpooners before finally setting out for the shores of Spitzbergen. It was now, however, too early in the season for sailing northward. The ice had not yet completely broken up, and so the captain settled the point by proposing that we should spend a fortnight or so capturing salmon and other fish that swarm in the sounds between the Loffoden Isles. For this purpose he hired a small Norwegian vessel, and, leaving the Kathleen with part of her crew anchored before Rorstad, sailed away for Mosken and Varroe, two islands that lie respectively north and south of the reputed Maelstrom. The dire yarns which fishermen and northern voyagers relate of this celebrated spot seem to have rather an insecure foundation, for beyond the fact that the waters there are in a perpetual state of unrest and frenzy in consequence of the rocks, hidden and visible, that surround it, I saw no other indication of its being a whirlpool such as Jonas Ramus, Kircher, and other writers describe with such horrifying minuteness of detail. It is a perilous spot nevertheless, for when the tide is coming in, and the wind blows hard from the west, the waters rush with headlong fury over the rocks, so that the largest ship that comes within the action of the current runs a chance of being dashed to atoms against those treacherous crags.

After spending a week in the neighborhood of the Maelstrom, around which there are excellent fishing-grounds, we were joined by a numerous fleet of small craft, belonging to Norwegian and Loffoden fishermen, who were bound for the shores of West Vaage, to intercept the shoals of herrings that at this season swarm around the islands. Captain Dick, according to his usual custom, joined them, and the day after our arrival on the grounds was one which I shall never forget, for it very nearly put an end to my voyages and my life at the same time.

It was a calm evening, and the fishermen were industriously plying their nets, when we heard sounds, like the confused bellowings of cattle, to the westward. We were in front of the wild inlet that indents the outward shore of West Vaage, and, as we looked out, we beheld a vast flock of the round-headed porpoise, tumbling inward, in pursuit of a shoal of herrings. Their appearance was like a regular signal of war. The fishermen instantly drew in their nets, and divided the boats into two fleets, so as to leave a free passage for the porpoises towards the shallow inlet. On they came, tumbling and gambolling about, sometimes bellowing with delight, as a more plentiful supply than usual of the doomed herring shoal rewarded their pursuit, till at last they dashed in helter-skelter between the boats, the fishermen in high glee, standing prepared, oar in hand, to follow them into the inlet. The quantity of oil obtained from this species of cetacea is both abundant and valuable. The command of the attack seemed, by common consent, to devolve upon Captain Dick, whom these wild fishermen knew and trusted wonderfully. At last he gave the word. The two fleets of small craft again joined, and away we went, as fast as oars could carry us, in pursuit of the round-heads. A huge old bull porpoise seemed to be their leader in their headlong foray after the herrings. But he proved a bad general, for, in the excess of his voracity, he stranded himself upon a shallow part of the inlet. When the leader of a flock of this species of porpoise runs upon the beach, the rest are sure to follow. And so it turned out in this instance, for the whole flock was stranded in a moment.

An onslaught equal to that which followed I never witnessed. The whole fleet swept in after the shoal, and for a full half-hour it was all mist, and spray, and thunder, for the unwieldy porpoises, in their fright, fury, and agony, as the wild islanders fell upon them with their oars and every weapon next to hand, bellowed and snorted, lashing the salt brine into white flakes and cataracts of blinding vapor yards over our heads. How some of the boats escaped being staved to pieces I know not, for the islanders, in their eagerness to slay as many as possible of the affrighted round-heads, pulled at once into the midst of the shoal with their oars, occasionally tumbling into the shallow water amidst the writhing bodies of their victims. It happened, whether by Captain Dick's skilful management I cannot say, that the boat in which we both were came, in the midst of the uproar and confusion, alongside the unwary old bull, the author of the whole catastrophe. How he roared in terror, and churned the water, as the keel went with a dig into his side! Captain Dick drew forth a heavy double-barrelled pistol, and fired both the bullets into the animal's head, greatly to the admiration of the excited combatants near us, while I, with one of the oars, thrashed away at its huge body, till at length it sprang almost completely out of the water, and then lay immovable, and apparently dead, right before us.

The fight was over. The greater part of the immense flock of course escaped; but, as we looked around us, we found that about thirty porpoises had fallen victims to our sudden attack. Captain Dick was so overjoyed at the successful issue of the affair, that he insisted on making the whole company of fishermen go on shore to regale themselves with the contents of a keg of Hollands, which he carried in the boat. After securing their prizes to the sides of their craft with ropes, they all followed the jovial captain on shore, and began to dispose of the Hollands with loud vociferations and many a shout of laughter. I, however, after drinking a small measure, remained behind in order to fasten the defunct old bull more securely, in which operation I was assisted by one of the fishermen, who, after running a long rope through the tail of the animal, and fastening it to the bow-end of the boat, followed his comrades.

The tide was coming in. I sat down in the boat, and, after the day's fatigue, readily fell asleep. How long I remained so I cannot well remember; but at all events, I dreamed that I had just been elected, by the unanimous voice of the people, king of Norway, and that I was seated in the state carriage ready to drive off to Christiana to be crowned. What a bound forward the six horses gave as the grandly-dressed coachman cracked his whip! I awoke at the start, and found that, instead of being placed in a regal carriage, with innumerable admiring courtiers around me, and a crown in perspective, I was sitting in the boat at the mouth of Vagen Fiord, with what I first imagined to be some marine demon dragging me out to sea. It was no such thing. It was the old porpoise again apparently alive and well. These animals are very tenacious of life, and when the tide came in sufficiently high to float his huge body, it seems he recovered from the swoon, which we all imagined to be his last, and was now, in the fast gathering shades of twilight, carrying me and the boat right out to sea, at the furious rate of seven or eight miles an hour. I stood up in the boat, and for a moment knew not what to do. I turned, and shouted back to my companions, but my voice died unheeded upon the darkening waste of waters. I now plunged my hand to my side for the knife I wore, in order to cut the rope; but I had lost it in the struggle within the inlet. The oar was now my only resource. I took it, and commenced hammering away at the rope, but could not make the slightest impression upon its strong, tarry fibres. The noise I made only made the desperate and enraged animal go the faster. I threw it from me, and fell upon the rope with the hope of chewing it asunder; but every jerk the porpoise gave, as he dashed along, nearly tore the teeth from my jaws, and so I was forced at last to sit down quietly, and submit to my fate, thankful that my tormentor did not take a dive, and carry me to the bottom at once.

The giant crags of West Vaage became dimmer and dimmer as I was borne along. I turned round in despair, and kept my eyes fixed wistfully upon their receding and ghostly pinnacles. In a few moments I was startled by a loud, hollow fit of bellowing from the huge porpoise. A frantic plunge, and another short and savage bellow that almost curdled the blood in my veins, and then the boat stopped. I turned, and looked forward, scarcely knowing what I did, and beheld the body of the terrible animal turned upside down, and lying helplessly on the water. While he dragged me along I thought a storm blew in my face. Now that the motion was stopped, I found only a slight breeze. This, however, with the fresh tide, and the oars which I handled with a will, was sufficient to drive me back to Vaage Fiord, at the entrance of which I met Captain Dick and the whole fleet of fishermen rowing outward to my rescue. The porpoise, however, anticipated them. He died in the nick of time, and thus I escaped from the prank he played in his last struggle.

Another week passed away, during which we fished the sounds and fiords of Southern Loffoden, besides landing every day upon one or other of the islands, in order to look out for the numerous foxes that inhabit their wild valleys, or for a stray bear making its way over from the main land. The captain and I shot a few foxes, but we found their fur not as valuable as we expected. No bear rewarded our search, and we sailed away for Rorstad, where we found the four harpooners on board the Kathleen, which was in good order, and ready to set sail at last, and bear us on our adventures to the Frozen Sea.

On the 12th of June, we bade farewell to Rorstad, and shaped our course towards the Moskoe-strom, in order to coast the Isles of Loffoden as we went north. As we sailed out through the Strom, a shoal of dolphins appeared in our wake, and accompanied us, with wild and playful gambollings.

On the 20th of June we doubled North Cape, and bore away for Spitzbergen. It was early in the season. The ice had just broken, and, though there was danger from the bergs, still Captain Dick kept boldly onward, saying that the earlier we began sport the better. It was true for him. After beating about, on account of contrary winds, for some time, we came in sight of the frozen headlands of Spitzbergen on the 1st of July; and here our sport commenced at last, and in right good earnest. As we hove in sight of a small sheltered bay, formed in the side of a vast ice-field that had not yet broken up, we found it literally crammed with walruses. The old males of this species of *Pinnipedia* are exceedingly fierce and quarrelsome, often contesting the dominion of a herd in single combat, just as two stags amid the forest will fight for the sovereignty of a herd of deer. Something like this appeared to be going on as we came in sight of the little bay, for two immense bulls were on the ice, tearing and bellowing at each other, their companions squatted thickly around, looking on stolidly at the struggle. So intent were they all on the issue of the combat, that they took no notice of us, as we lowered and manned the three small boats carried by the Kathleen. The harpooners stood ready, weapons in hand, as we bore in upon them. At last they perceived us, and, with a loud snorting and roaring, scrambled into the water, all except the two royal combatants, who seemed determined to finish their battle before turning their attention to our approach.

The captain and I fired at the same time, of course taking different animals. The wounds they received only maddened them the more, each imagining his own inflicted by the long tusks of his antagonist; and so to it they went again far more fiercely than ever, giving us time to reload and approach them nearer. A second bullet through the head of each confounded them somewhat; but it was only when they had received our fire four times that they tumbled over in their dying struggles upon the ice.

We had now leisure to see how matters proceeded in the bay. One of the harpooners had pierced a young calf with his weapon, and the doleful cries made by the luckless animal, as it vainly endeavored to escape, instead of dispersing the herd, only drew them in infuriated crowds round the boat, for they are excessively attached to their offspring. Leaving the bodies of the two bulls stretched upon the ice, Captain Dick and I rushed down to the water's edge, sprang into the boat, and put off instantly for the scene of conflict. Three full-grown walruses were struck and fixed by the remaining harpooners. Splashing and snorting with rage, they plunged out to sea, endeavoring to escape, bearing the boats in mad career after them. Two of them were attached to one of the boats, and by their tremendous plunging went very near sinking her, till, as they passed,— and one of them sprang almost out of the water,— Captain Dick let fly both barrels of his rifle, sending the bullets most probably into the animal's brain, for it was soon quiet enough. The other, after a terrible struggle, was at length secured.

We pushed for the boat to which the calf and its mother were attached, many of the herd still roaring and splashing around them, and endeavoring, with frantic efforts, to drag them away, in which they nearly staved the boat against a half-sunken block of ice. The boatmen and harpooners did their work well, the former, as the opportunity offered, plying their oars like flails upon every animal that came within striking distance, and the latter attending with cool judgment to the letting out or drawing in of the ropes, to which their barbed weapons were attached, according as their victims dived, plunged forward, or rushed back at the boat in their fury, while Captain Dick and I, as fast as we could load, banged away into the midst of the raging herd, till the troubled waters around us became crimson with their fast-flowing blood. In an unlucky moment, however, I shot the young calf through the head, and stilled its cries. In half an hour afterwards there was not a single walrus to be seen, save the bodies of the belligerent bulls upon the ice, and those we had captured in the little bay. It was a good day's work, notwithstanding, and Captain Dick expressed himself mightily pleased at the conclusion, as we both sat down to dinner in the warm cabin of the Kathleen.

As we coasted northward next day, we beheld on the far horizon line a jet of water projected to a surprising height into the air. It was a Greenland whale (*Balæna mysticetus*), expelling the water through his blow-holes, in order to drain his enormous jaws, probably after ingulfing half a shoal of herrings into their labyrinths. We set off immediately in pursuit, but the gigantic monster was too wary for us, and soon gave us the slip. Towards evening we fell in with an iceberg crowded with walruses, and had another exciting hunt, in which we captured four. I still continue to refer to the different hours of the day, for so it was our custom to jot down the log of the Kathleen, although, in point of fact, the sun never set, but wheeled continually in his ascending spiral through the sky, so that of course there was no night.

On the 6th of July we came in sight of the body

of a beluga, or white whale, which floated from behind an immense iceberg on our lee. Upon it was a white object, scarcely distinguishable at first from the huge body of the dead animal; but, as we drew near, we found it to be a white, or polar, bear, regaling himself with a meal of blubber. He soon perceived us, and, instead of taking to the water, sat up on his hind legs, like a huge ogre, to observe us better, and then, with a savage and contemptuous growl, began to gorge himself again upon the carcass. Captain Dick, after loading the long swivel gun with a charge of small bullets and shot, let fly at him. A tremendous roar from the bear followed the report of the gun. He raised himself up, shook his shaggy sides in pain, and then plunged into the water, endeavoring to make his way to a neighboring iceberg. We lowered a boat, into which I and Captain Dick at once sprang, and set forward in pursuit. The bear reached the iceberg, but, as he attempted to climb its slippery sides, we both fired and killed him. In an hour afterwards his skin was hanging from the yard-arm of the Kathleen, drying in the sun and breeze.

Until the 2d of August, we continued our forays after the walruses, and took a great many. During that time, besides two other bears and some black and white foxes, we killed half a dozen narwhals, or sea-unicorns. The 10th of August was a grand day with us. We came across an immense herd of walruses in one of the wild fiords of Spitzbergen, and, after a two hours' onslaught, killed twelve of them.

This was our last day off that desolate island. Getting ready our cargo, we sailed southward, and towards the end of August entered once more the Folden Fiord, and came to anchor opposite Rorstad. Here we remained for some time, preparing our cargo of tusks, blubber, and skins, during which Captain Dick and I made several excursions into the pine forests of Sulitelma, in search of the reindeer and the brown bear.

On the 7th of September, all things being prepared on board the Kathleen, we set sail from Rorstad, and, on the 1st of October, doubled Loop Head again, and sailed up the Shannon before a stiff breeze, which carried us safely home, where we were received with many expressions of wonder and satisfaction by my father. And thus I ended my first voyage.

A BIT OF SPORT, No. III.

OTTER-HUNTING ON THE BLACKWATER.

IN the interim, while the dogs are disposing of their early breakfast, a short sketch of the natural history of the animal whose haunts we are about to disturb, may serve to while away the time profitably. The otter is a carnivorous animal, belonging to the family *Mustelidæ*. Two forms of the animal are met with in these countries, namely, the river-otter, or *Lutra* of Storr; and the sea-otter, or *Enhydra* of Fleming. The structure of the latter resembles that of the seal (*Phoca Vitulina*), particularly in the formation of the cranial bones. It inhabits our sea-coasts, and is extremely numerous on the shores of the Scottish isles, and along the basaltic crags that tower over the wild sea-waves on the shores of Antrim. From the inaccessible caves and fissures that everywhere yawn around that iron-bound coast, it issues forth, chiefly by night, and commits dreadful havoc among the shoals of fish, particularly salmon, that swarm outside river mouths and bays; and for this reason it is looked upon with no small amount of hostility by the fishermen, who frequently band together and make vengeful raids upon its wild haunts. But with such excursions we have nothing to do at the present, and shall therefore return to the history of the river-otter.

The river-otter (*Mustela Lutra* of Linnæus) is generally from about two feet and a half to four feet in length. It is of a brown color, which verges into gray or yellowish-white on the breast and neck. Its body is long and cylindrical, and terminated by a tail, which, thick at first and compressed horizontally, tapers to a graceful point. The circumference of its neck is very little less than that of the body; and its head, which appears somewhat small in consequence of the thickness of the neck, is depressed and flattened in a horizontal direction, like the tail. It will be easily seen from the foregoing particulars that it is eminently adapted for the life it leads, which is principally aquatic. Its legs are short, but the articulations of the latter are so flexible, that when it swims swiftly the four limbs may be seen drawn up in a line with the body, and acting after the manner of fins. The foot of the otter is armed with five sharp-clawed toes, connected, for almost three fourths of their extent, by webbed membranes, like the feet of waterfowl. Its fur is short and glossy, and was formerly accounted of considerable value.

The food of this animal is principally fish, which it

destroys often in great numbers, but nothing comes amiss to its voracious stomach; for it not only feeds upon earth-worms, snails, and such like, but will sometimes pay a visit to the farm-yard, and prey upon poultry, young pigs, and lambs. It is seldom, however, that it resorts to the latter expedient for obtaining food, and probably, if the stories of such depredations were diligently investigated by the naturalist, the damage, almost in every instance, would be found to lie at the door of our craftiest beast of prey, namely, old Reynard.

The eyes of the otter are so placed that whether in front of, beside, or above, or below, it can keep its prey in sight by the slightest turn of its head. Its teeth are also well fitted for seizing fish, generally so slippery and difficult of capture. The tubercles on the molar or jaw-teeth, particularly in those towards the front of the mouth, are exceedingly sharp and pointed, so that when once a fish comes in contact with them, it has but little chance of escape. The moment the otter seizes its prey, it makes for the nearest secure spot on the shore, and there commences its voracious meal by taking a luxurious bite out of the shoulder of the luckless fish. It then proceeds downwards towards the tail, which, along with the head and neck, it leaves upon the bank, and plunges in once more, making sad and wanton havoc amongst the finny tribes of the river.

The otter makes its home beneath the fragments of rock that compose fish weirs, and between the gnarled roots of the trees that throw their cool shadows over the limpid waters, by burrowing in soft, sandy banks, and often within the fissures of those romantic crags that tower so gracefully over the green shores of our beautiful rivers. It seems to be very generally distributed over the world. It is an inhabitant of the northern parts of Asia, and formerly its fur formed an important article of commerce between the Russians and Chinese. Captain Cook, in one of his voyages, drew the attention of the English to the immense numbers of otters that infested Nootka Sound, and the coasts in its vicinity. Since that date the trade in otter skins was carried on briskly in Canada, and other parts of North America, up to some years ago, when it declined.

Otters, when taken young, can be easily domesticated. In India and China they are trained to hunt fish by the natives, and in South America they are also tamed and kept as household pets. In the latter country the otter (*Lutra Brasiliensis*) is of a bright ruddy-yellow color, and seems more gregarious than in other regions, for it assembles in packs, and thus scours the rivers in search of prey. It inhabits lakes, marshes, and broad streams in Paraguay and Brazil, where its shrill, sinister barking and whistling may be heard at night echoing over many a wild and deserted shore, amid the primeval forests which clothe those tropical regions. In Ireland, and in England and Scotland, it is also frequently domesticated. In Scotland there is a spotted variety, which the peasantry call the "king of the otters." They believe it to be enchanted, and that its death is the sure forerunner of some sudden calamity in the neighborhood — the destruction of some house or village by flood or fire, or tempest; or the violent death of one or more of the inhabitants. Its skin is accounted a powerful antidote against every misfortune, from the effects of a love potion up to poisoning and wounds, pestilence and shipwreck.

Otter-hunting was formerly a favorite sport in these countries. At present, however, the excitement of a fox-chase is more relished by our country Nimrods. But I question whether the wild ride over hedge, ditch, valley, and moorland, after the switching tail of Reynard, is one whit more exciting than an otter hunt upon one of our winding rivers, with all its accompaniments of ludicrous accidents, fury, fun, and uproar. It is still kept up by a few of our country squires, among whom Bob Barry, of C——, stands preëminent, a gentleman as distinguished for his antiquarian and literary acquirements as for his numerous sylvan exploits by well-stocked river and by merry greenwood side.

With Bob Barry, during a college vacation, I was on a visit. After exploring every object of historical and antiquarian interest in the neighborhood for miles round, we then took to fishing, coursing, rabbit-shooting, and dog-training, and at last, growing tired of them all, resolved to enliven our remaining days together by a few otter hunts on the Blackwater. This we were enabled to do in fine style, for Bob Barry, besides keeping some specimens of almost every species of dog on the face of the earth, had also a pack of otter hounds, twelve in number, and the like of which, for spirit and endurance, could not, I will venture to say, be found in Ireland or the sister countries.

It was a beautiful autumn morning. The dogs, after partaking of their noisy breakfast, were brought forth from the kennel, testifying their joy at the expected hunt by a variety of rough antics upon the lawn. The pack was accompanied by three terriers of pure Irish breed, whose duty it was to follow the otter to his burrow beneath the rocks, and start him for the hounds. The oldest of these terriers went by the familiar cognomen of "Darby," and was as queer and ugly-looking a specimen of the dog species as could be seen from Brandon Hill to the Giant's Causeway. His head was half bald, and marked all over with scars — relics of his numerous encounters with the otters in their fastnesses; his right fore leg was crooked, from the effect of a fracture he had received in one of his early battles; his left ear had also been bitten off; but a comfortable coat of shaggy gray hair still clothed his hard, compact body; and, as he limped on in front of the pack, and showed his teeth occasionally, when one of his younger comrades took some undue liberty with him, he looked more than a match for the stoutest otter from Youghal harbor to the far-off springs of the Avonmore.

Innumerable were the stories the old huntsman

could tell of Darby. Whenever any considerable length of time passed away without a hunt, it was the custom of the latter to steal away several times, during the interval, to the river, about a mile distant, and there refresh himself with a foray upon his aquatic foes. On such excursions Darby was usually accompanied by the oldest hound of the pack — a huge, powerful, and cunning dog, from which, when once fair upon their track, very few otters were ever known to escape. It was probably from an intimate knowledge of this old hound's excellence in the chase that Darby always selected him as his companion on a foray to the river. Whenever they could make their escape from the kennel, they were sure to keep out of the huntsman's way until evening, at which time they scampered away across the country to a certain sweep of the Blackwater, where the otters were numerous, and there hunted and fought until morning, when they returned together invariably.

"Begor, sir!" said old Tom Reilly, the huntsman, as we went along, "if you were to know them, you never saw in the whole coorse o' your life such two comrades as Darby and the ould Squire." (The Squire, by the way, was the usual appellation of the old hound.) "Two ould vetherans from Watherloo were nothing to them."

"It seems so," said I; for Darby and the Squire were now pacing side by side with wonderful dignity in front of the pack.

"Nothing at all to them, sir," resumed the

huntsman. "One night, they stole away, but didn't come back in the morning. I kept their breakfast waiting till near twelve o'clock; and the devil resave the bit of either o' them could be seen next or nigh the kennel at that late hour. At last, when I was tired o' waitin', I saw the Squire runnin', as fast as his legs could carry him, up the lawn towards where I stood. I thought Darby would next appear, but not a trace of him could I see. Well, up comes the Squire, an' afther standin' forenint me for nearly five minutes looking into my face as cute as a fox, he trotted over and caught me by the skirt o' the coat, and then began pullin' me down the lawn. I knew in a minute what he was about. I guessed that ould Darby was in thrubble of some kind or other; and so, callin' two or three o' the boys, and tellin' them to bring spades and shovels with them, we marched off towards the river with the Squire before us, ladin' the way. At last we came down upon a point o' the shore where a big white-thorn bush grew by itself on the bank near the wather. When the Squire came forenint the tree, he sat down and looked into a hole between its roots, and then, raisin' his head up towards the sky, he broke out into a loud *ulla-gone* of a lamentin' cry, that brought the tears a'most into my eyes, and that was ten times more sorrowful than the weepin' o' the best keener in the land. Now it was aisy to tell where Darby was; so we commenced with our spades and shovels to root up the burrow. Afther nearly half a day's work, we at last came to the end, and there found Darby stretched in a faint upon the dead body o' the largest otter that was ever seen in ould Ireland, I believe. Well, up I took the poor fellow in my arms as tinderly as I would a child, and carried him down to the wather; there I sprinkled and sprinkled away, but 'twas nearly a full half hour afore he recovered, or, at least, came to life, for he was nearly a week afther lyin' sick an' sore on his bed o' pain in the kennel afore he got entirely well. I could tell hundherts o' stories about the pair, but, by the enchanted fox o' Corrin Thierna, there they are down to the river, side by side, on the trail of an otter!"

It was true enough. We were descending an upland that sloped down to the river, and along its declivity Darby and the Squire were now dashing downwards, obliquely towards the bank, with their noses on the trail, followed by the remainder of the pack. We had with us three men, besides the huntsman. They were armed with spades and shovels, Bob Barry and I having supplied ourselves with a weapon each, much resembling in its construction a New Hollander's lance, only that our instruments of warfare, besides being barbed, were much heavier. Down we ran after the pack, and soon gained the river bank. Here Darby and the other terriers, after examining the entrances of various burrows, and finding them untenanted, at last came to one which promised sport. One of the younger terriers pushed himself in, in order to enter this burrow; but Darby caught him quietly by the back, flung him to one side, and deliberately entered himself. We were now sure of an otter of some kind, young or old; so, keeping the hounds back in order to give him an opportunity for a fair plunge in the water, we stood awaiting his coming on the bank.

At last we heard a confused thumping noise under our feet, then a rushing and tearing, then a clatter on the gravel, and a splash, and, amidst a wild shout from the boys and a glad yell from the pack, out went a fine otter into the river, with the persevering and relentless Darby close at his tail. Splash! splash! splash! went the hounds into the water, some above and some below the point the otter had chosen for his launching-place; and now the sport commenced in earnest.

The river at this point was still narrow and deep, and with low banks. Above, however, at about a furlong's distance, the valley of the stream assumed a different character — huge, caverned limestone crags rising in many a fantastic shape above the water, while about the same distance below where we stood, the river ran with extreme rapidity down a narrow, sandy shallow, for the length of about half a mile, and then ended in a deep, whirling pool, beneath another tier of limestone rock.

The otter was now after reaching the middle of the river, and had got a good start of all the dogs save Darby.

"Run!" said Bob Barry to one of the boys; " up

with you to the rock, and bring down Paddy Regan's boat. Quick! quick! or I fear the otter will have time to cross the river ere one of us gets to the other side!"

Away went the young man at the command of his master; and after some short time he appeared round the rock, paddling down the river.

"Now," exclaimed Bob, once more turning to me, "cross the river with Jack, and have an eye to the beast, should he think of taking shelter beneath those white-thorns at the opposite side!"

In a few moments I was sitting in the boat beneath those white-thorns, whose gnarled roots my friend dreaded so much. The otter was now after diving. Jack had stepped to the bank above to watch, and I was sitting in the boat cheering the dogs and waiting for the otter to rise. At length up popped his dark-brown nose within a yard of my small and rather shaky bark. In the excitement of the moment, I poised my spear, and made a lunge, Indian fashion, at him; but, instead of striking him, the weapon passed down to the handle through the water, and I, losing my balance, fell over the side of the boat amidst the dogs. The only consolation I got on my immersion was a rousing cheer, as I came to the surface of the water, from Bob Barry, who was quite used to such accidents. It was well, however, that I had divested myself of my coat and a pair of heavy boots I wore, after I had entered the boat. With them I would have had an unpleasant scramble in the water, but without them, being a good swimmer, I was soon enabled to regain my seat in the boat. I was, of course, wet through; but what did I care when I looked upon the stirring scene before me? It was also a warm morning; so, comforting myself with a pull from a brandy flask I had carried into the boat, I now sat quietly, spear in hand, and looked on.

The otter was again in the middle of the river, this time with the hounds swimming on every side of him. Again he dived, and went straight for the other bank, intending, I suppose, to take refuge in some secure burrow. But Bob Barry met him with his spear as he rose, and slightly wounded him in the neck. Down he went once more, and for a long time we saw nothing of him, till at length the sharp and experienced eye of old Tom Reilly detected a slight disturbance of the water amongst some weeds and sedges near the bank. This was enough to betray his whereabouts; and the hounds, which during his dive had kept themselves quietly on the surface of the water, now, directed by the voice and gestures of Tom, swam towards the bank. Four or five of the youngest of them left the water, and took a refreshing scamper upon the shore; but the elder dogs, headed by the Squire and Darby, rushed in among the reeds, and then followed a scrambling, splashing, and tearing, a barking, biting, and gnashing of teeth, the equal of which I had never before witnessed, and I had seen many a splendid hunt. I soon paddled alongside, and found nearly the whole pack before me, tearing at the otter, which was gallantly fighting for his existence.

"For your life don't touch him with the spear!" exclaimed Bob Barry, who was almost dancing with delight upon the bank; "leave him to Darby and the Squire, and let the young dogs learn how to kill an otter."

At the word I sat quietly in the little boat and looked on. It was an unequal struggle, for although the otter buried his white teeth occasionally in the neck or flank of one of the dogs, he soon began to give in; and at last, by the united exertions of old Darby and the Squire, he was torn from amidst the furious pack in to the shore, and there killed after another short scramble.

"Bring him up to the bank," said my excited friend to the huntsman. "And now let us go up to Donal's Cave. Paddy Regan told me yesterday that it is inhabited by the largest otter in the river."

The hounds were now marching up the shore, behind the huntsman and their master; and I, after paddling my boat along the calm surface of the river, at length came opposite a tall rock, that rose like an ancient castle above the water. At the base of this crag was a narrow aperture, leading into a large, gloomy chamber, which the country people call "Donal's Cave," from a celebrated outlaw who once made it his home, and which was unapproachable except by a boat. Into this cave Darby and his attendant imps, the two young terriers, were directed by Tom Reilly, the hounds remaining by the side of the rock on the bank, ready for the otter should he think fit to make his appearance.

After about a quarter of an hour's anxious watch, we at last heard a confused yelling from the cave; then a wild cry, something between a bark and a scream; and then out came a huge, dark-brown otter, with Darby, as before, closely behind, only one of the young terriers, however, following. Out went the hounds, with a dash, into the deep water, and the chase commenced.

"Fern's leg is sartinly broken!" exclaimed the huntsman, alluding to the young terrier that remained inside. "Would you put the boat in, sir?" continued he, addressing me, "and thry what's the matther with the poor crathur?"

I brought the boat to the mouth of the cave, and with great difficulty entered. The huntsman's conjecture was but too true; for I found poor Fern inside almost strangled, and with one of her legs broken by the terrible jaws of the otter. As quick as I could I brought her out, got into the boat, and gave her to the care of one of the boys; then, paddling down the stream, I followed the hunt. The otter we had now driven from his home was a far more experienced fellow than the first. He took his course in long, alternate dives, obliquely across the river, gained the bank of the opposite side, ran some distance downwards, and then took shelter in a burrow under a steep bank. From this, however, he was soon driven by the indefatigable Darby, and again dived away, now straight down the river, passing the place where we had killed the first otter. The hounds ran, yelling cheerily, down the shore at either side; and the chase went on so swiftly that I had to work hard at the short oars in order to keep up with it.

And now we were leaving the deep water and approaching the rapid above mentioned. Into it the otter plunged, after a sharp chase, and dived away with the swiftness of an arrow, the hounds following almost as swiftly, while I, in the excitement of the moment, regardless of my own safety and that of the boat, brought the latter into the rapid current, and swept downward for a time gloriously upon their track. It was only for a short time, however, that I went on so merrily, for the water, in consequence of its great rapidity, was in some places very shallow. Just as I had come up with the dogs, the keel of the little boat struck against the rough bottom, with a shock that almost tumbled me into the water. In a moment the boat got free, and began whirling giddily, yet steadily, down the current. Another shock, and another succession of gyrations, and the boat was swept rapidly onwards, Bob Barry all the time running down the bank, and laughing as if his heart would break at my predicament. And now I was coming to the end of the rapid, and beginning to think myself quite safe, when, just at the commencement of the deep pool, in which the hounds and otter were diving and scrambling, the boat struck against a small rock that lay right before it. In an instant its fragments were floating in a general wreck around, and I was struggling with the water almost in the very centre of the pack of otter-hounds. But here my rather extensive experience in swimming stood to me, and I soon gained the bank above the rock, up which I was assisted by my merry friend, Bob Barry. My coat and boots were recovered by one of the boys at the foot of the rock, but the flask was gone forever, with its contents. An application to my friend's flask, however, soon restored my warmth; and I now stood on the rock looking at the hunt.

It was soon over. Large and fierce as the otter was, he was no match for the simultaneous attack of Darby and his friend the Squire, and some of the otter-hounds; so he soon gave in, and was killed. It was now getting somewhat late in the morning, and our appetites — for we had eaten but little ere we set out — were getting rather keen. Leaving Tom Reilly and the boys to lead back the hounds, I and my friend walked briskly across the fields, and soon, after I had changed my suit for a dry one, had the satisfaction of sitting down to a jovial breakfast, in the comfortable parlor of C—— House, to which repast, I must add, that we both did ample justice after our morning's exertions. And thus ended my first otter hunt on the Blackwater.

A BIT OF SPORT. — No. IV.

THE ENCHANTED FOX OF DARRA.

FROM the notes of explorers in the fields of natural history, it would appear that before a colony of foxes determines on settling in a neighborhood, they send forward a pioneer, which, after accurately examining all the points, bearings, and facilities of the place, returns with his report ready drawn up, on hearing which, if it be favorable, the whole family throw the dust off their feet at the enemies they have made, leave the spot which, mayhap, they have rendered too warm by their nefarious practices, and stealing away under cover of night, quietly settle down upon the fresh lands they have chosen, and there commence a new and systematic career of depredation, most fearfully inimical to the game preserves and poultry yards around. If this be the case, the original founder of the fox colony in the valley of Darra must have been a patriarch of great judgment and foresight. In fact, he must have employed, in the selection of this fastness, some of the same description of skill under whose ministrations arose many a stern feudal stronghold by the river shores of North and South Britain, by the far banks of the storied Rhine, and by the craggy margins of our own glorious Irish streams — castles from which, in the mediæval times, the steel-clad and marauding barons were wont to issue forth at the head of their armed retainers, and levy black-mail from the surrounding plains, towns, and hamlets.

The judgment attributed to the fox in the above sentence is no untenable assertion. We challenge any historian, of ancient or modern times, to produce a greater mass of evidence in support of the possession of extraordinary genius by one of his heroes, than can be brought forwurd to prove that the fox, from the very earliest ages, was a personage of wonderful accomplishments in all the arts and sciences, from the picking of a bone in the most approved gastronomical method, to the selection of a safe citadel wherein to allow digestion to take its course after the best epicurean fashion, and from that to the highest examples of strategy and worldly craft. Have we not the works of the immortal Æsop to refer to, in which that facetious and sparkling little descendant of Ham seems never tired of relating incidents illustrative of the cuteness, the wisdom, the experience, the hair-breadth escapes, the funny exploits, and bold deeds of Reynard? Take a run through the literature of any country in the world; ere you have gone through half a volume of any poet, fabulist, or historian, you will find similes, tales, and allusions to no end, all bearing testimony to the brightness of Reynard's brains. But putting all these stray witnesses out of the question, have we not an epic to attest his greatness?—yes, an epic that shall remain green and blooming in the memories of mankind when Homer is forgotten, Virgil unread, and Milton, as the Kerry schoolmaster said, shadowed under the curtain of oblivion—an epic whose incidents we gloat over in childhood, and remember fondly as we advance in years, namely, the immortal "History of Reynard the Fox" himself; and we ask triumphantly, without fear of denial or a single reservation in the response, Is there a man, woman, or child unacquainted with its soul-stirring and enrapturing contents, from where the constellation of the Southern Cross sheds its light upon the banquets of Austral cannibals, to where the stunted Esquimaux gorge themselves with whale blubbers, by the icy shores of the Boreal Sea?

Even tradition itself is ever garrulous and eloquent in Reynard's praise. According to that everlasting authority, there was once upon a time a fox that could tell fortunes by the shore of Lough Ree, on the Shannon, and another at the foot of Croagh Patrick, which attended on an ancient hermit who dwelt there, as his gillie, or servant. This individual knew his business so well that he not only gathered firewood for his master's abode, but brought in daily a supply of berries, water-cresses, and game sufficient to appease the appetite of the old hermit. Not content with this, he generally superintended the making of the fire, roasted the wild fowl to a turn, and laid the table with a degree of taste and elegance that would set the best French cook out of his wits to emulate. There was another fox, which dwelt in a certain wood in the south of Ireland, between whom and the gamekeeper a tacit treaty existed, the nature of which was, that as long as he lived unmolested by the gamekeeper, the poultry and geese of the latter were to remain intact. Now, on a certain day, a number of gentlemen came with a splendid pack of hounds to the wood, unearthed Reynard, and chased him, neck or nothing, over many a rough mile of hill and valley. In the end, however, he escaped; but that night the best goose of the flock disappeared from the paddock of the gamekeeper. It seems that the fox, after his terrible run, being too exhausted to go on his usual rounds in search of prey, was forced by the pangs of hunger to catch the goose for his supper. The gamekeeper, of course, vowed vengeance for this infringement of the treaty, and next morning was proceeding, gun in hand, to inflict condign punishment on the offender, when, from the brow of a little hill near his home, he saw a sight which convinced him that a fox, of all animals in the world, has the tenderest conscience and the truest appreciation of the point of honor. In a field beneath was his friend of the wood, making his way, in a deliberate run, for the desecrated paddock, with a live geese thrown over his back. After gaining an adjacent field, he left his burden by a fence, and then returned for another goose, which he had left in some field behind, and which he bore into an enclosure at a distance beyond that in which he had deposited the first. Returning again, he bore the first some distance farther; and thus carrying both alternately, he at last deposited them with the flock in the gamekeeper's paddock—an ample payment for the robbery hunger had forced him to perpetrate on the preceding evening. Merely making allusion to the luxurious fox that at present is said to smoke his pipe every evening after dinner on Dawson's Table, near Gaultymore, we shall end our paragraph with the above exemplary individual, and pass once more to the valley of Darra, the scene of the hunt whose incidents we are about to relate.

The valley of Darra lies in the midst of a range of mountains, from whose summits no finer, more extensive, or more varied prospect can be seen in Ireland. It stretches from west to east, and was formerly clothed from end to end by an ancient and luxuriant forest of oak, mountain ash, and pine. At its western extremity rises a small, green hill, on the summit of which stand the ruins of an old church and round tower. Some distance from this hill, beneath a gigantic crag, rises one of the streams celebrated by Spenser in his Faërie Queene, namely,—

"Molana, daughter of old father Mole,"

which, after flowing downward with an infinite number of meanderings through the whole extent of the valley, discharges itself through a savage and romantic pass into the plain of Cork, where its waters soon join those of the pastoral Funcheon. Abutting into the valley at its south-western side rises the most elevated summit of the range, a steep, conical hill, with a mighty cairn of stones upon its crest. Along the left flank and foot of this hill stretches a dense and solitary wood, partly the remains of the ancient forest that once clothed the whole district. This wood, from time immemorial, has been infested with such a number of foxes, that no poultry-yard, however well fortified, can be considered safe for miles around its vicinity.

If you take a ramble through the old church-yard mentioned above, your attention cannot fail to be attracted by an ancient, half-defaced tombstone, which stands beside the dilapidated wall that fences in the dwellings of the dead from the green pasture land outside. Upon this tombstone can still be traced various quaint figures of hounds, horsemen, and a fox in full career, which circumstance will at once tell you that some mighty hunter sleeps beneath. And such is the case; for the spot marked by that old tombstone, with its fantastic figures, is the last resting-place of Tom Geelaher, the most celebrated huntsman that ever wound horn or set foot in stirrup amid the green woods of Munster. We are, however, somewhat over-hasty in calling the spot Tom's last resting-place. It may be so by day; but it is the firm belief of the inhabitants of the valley that he haunts Kyleglass, or the Green Wood, that sylvan expanse which we have mentioned as stretching along the foot and side of the hill. Often will the peasant tell you, after returning belated from bog or high pasture land, that he has heard the lonely hollows of the wood echoing the weird sounds of Tom Geelaher's hunting-horn, and the wild yells of the spectral pack as they swept madly over glen and glade; and so minute is the description, that you will most probably be treated to an account of the peculiar creaking noise made by the new saddle which Tom had used on the day of his tragic death, and with which he still revisits "the glimpses of the moon," when going on his nightly fox-hunt. Innumerable are the stories related of Tom's appearance in that wild and solitary wood.

On one occasion Paddy Shanahan, one of the best pipers that ever twirled a chanter, was coming late at night down the mountain path that led by the southern skirt of the wood. All at once he beheld a red-coated horseman riding up the path, with a splendid pack of fox-hounds behind him.

"Arrah, Paddy Shanahan!" said the horseman, as he came up, "a cead mille failte to Kyleglass."

"The same to you, sir," said Paddy, not a whit frightened, for he knew by the hearty and kind tone of the horseman that he intended no harm.

"Sit down, Paddy," said the cavalier again, "and

play us up the Maddhereen Roe. I haven't heerd it this month o' Sundays, and 'tis your father's son that ought to be able to finger the chanter in style and glory."

"Wisha, begor, sir!" answered Paddy, "never say it twice, and you're welcome to the best tune in my pipes;" and with that he sat down on a bank, and began to put his instrument in order.

"The Maddhereen Roe is the best tune," said the horseman; "an' I haven't heerd it now since the day your father played it over my grave, the day I was buried on the hill of Ardpatrick;" and in a sweet but unearthly voice he began to hum one of the verses of that soul-stirring Irish opera, of which Reynard is the hero, and from which Moore has taken one of the finest airs to his Melodies: —

> 'Good morrow, fox.' 'Good morrow, sir.'
> 'What is that you're aitin'?'
> 'A fine fat goose I stole from you—
> Come, taste it while you're waitin'.'

Yoicks, yoicks! tally ho! Strike up the tune, Paddy Shanahan, for I haven't long to delay; and bethune ourselves, the hounds aren't to be depinded on."

"Never fear, sir," answered Paddy; for he had just succeeded in setting his pipes in tune. "Here goes for the honor and glory of ould Darra, an' the blue skies above id."

With that he struck up the Maddhereen Roe in a style that would stir the heart of a stone; and at every skirl of the pipes, the hounds yelled joyously, and the huntsman holloaed or wound his horn, till the deep recesses of the wood resounded with the uproar. At last, as Paddy came to that portion of the piece of music which represents the hounds and horsemen rattling away in full chase over bush, brake, and glen, a huge fox, which appeared to be gray with age, darted out from the wood, and with his neck stretched out, and his long tail sweeping the ground, darted swiftly along the hill-side.

"Yoicks, yoicks! tally ho! Towler, Nelly, and Ringwood — there he goes! — tally ho-o-o!" shouted the horseman; and striking the spurs into the flanks of his spectral steed, away he went with his yelling pack on the track of the fox over the hill, in a weird and fearful chase, leaving Paddy Shanahan still skirling his chanter upon the green bank beside the haunted wood.

But now for old Tom Geelaher's death, burial, and our fox-hunt. One day old Captain O——, to whom Tom was huntsman, sent intimation to the various gentlemen around, that on the Monday following, he was about to have a tremendous fox-hunt in the valley of Darra. At this time there was great rivalry between the gentlemen of the county Cork and those of Limerick, with regard to their equestrian feats after the switching brush of Reynard. So you may be sure that, when the morning of the hunt came, there was a large attendance of sportsmen from both counties. Old Squire Pringle, whose legs had been broken five several times in the chase, was there from the banks of the Blackwater; but though his legs were quite crooked, and he was scarcely able to walk he was so lame, let him once get into the saddle, and he was the best and most daring rider of his county. On the other hand, pitted against him by the gentlemen of Limerick, was old Major Weston, from Ballinacurra-Weston, who, with an iron hook in place of his bridle-hand, — half the limb had been shot off by a chain-ball at the storming of Seringapatam, — was still the boldest and most expert rider from Gaultymore to the Shannon. Others were there also who were determined on that day to emulate the exploits of their leaders; and even the very huntsmen of the rival fox-hound clubs looked upon one another with no friendly eyes, as they proceeded to the covert of Easmore, in order thence to start the largest, most cunning, and most renowned fox in the country, which was said to make that wild glen his usual place of abode.

Sure enough, they found him there, and the delighted eyes of the red-coats, of whom there were about a hundred and fifty on the ground that morning, testified to the size and wind of the fox of Easmore when at last he broke cover. He was a fine animal. Patches of gray hair on his head and tail showed that he had attained a great age; but his lithe motions and long stretches over the side of the hill as he came into view proved that age had not done away with his activity, and the vigor of his muscular frame. Away over bottom and rushy moorland, and up again across the highland valleys and slopes, he led the dogs and red-coats in a mad chase for nearly two mortal hours, at the end of which it became apparent that the county Limerick gentlemen were getting the worst of it, for their rivals from Cork county were getting far ahead, and not a rider, save old Tom Geelaher, seemed capable of retrieving the honor of the red-coats of the Darra Hunt. Old Tom, however, was still in the van, side by side with the redoubtable Squire Pringle. The fox was now approaching the Glen of the Black Crow, which runs down through the centre of the wood of Kyleglass. At a certain point this glen narrows, forming a deep chasm, over which Tom Geelaher had once sprung his horse some years before. Here was an opportunity of retrieving the lost honors of the Limerick fox-hunters, and poor Tom was not slow in availing himself of it. Calling out to old Squire Pringle to follow, he dashed his horse at the terrible chasm; but the hither bank unfortunately gave way, and Tom Geelaher and his steed, going headlong to the bottom, were both killed upon the rough fragments of rock that lay strewn beneath. This dreadful catastrophe put an end to the hunt for that day.

Old Tom Geelaher had often expressed a wish to his master, that when he died, the gentlemen of the Darra Club, with all their paraphernalia of hounds, horns, and red coats, should attend his funeral. On this sad occasion, old Captain O—— attended most

religiously to the wish of his faithful huntsman, and
for that purpose invited all the gentlemen then present to wait for the mournful obsequies. Another
wish of the eccentric old huntsman was, that when
the last sod was laid upon his grave, the best piper in
the country should be brought to play the Maddhereen Roe over him as a requiem. The day of the
funeral came, and the gentlemen in their red coats,
with Captain O——'s pack of fox-hounds following,
attended in long array behind poor Tom's coffin, as it
was borne slowly along the winding road that led to
the old church-yard of Ardpatrick, on the top of the
green hill. The grave was made, the coffin lowered,
the earth thrown in, and the green sods smoothed
above; and then old Paddy Shanahan, the elder, sat
down upon the fresh mound, tuned his pipes, and
struck up the Maddhereen Roe in tones that drew
tears from the eyes of the assembled multitude.

Just as Paddy had come to the lament, in which the
fox is represented sitting on the summit of a green,
lonely hill, after a hard chase, mournfully giving vent
to his outraged feelings in a heart-rending strain of
melody, a young hound, which had contrived to steal
away from the pack, suddenly gave a wild and savage cry within the ruins of the ancient church, and
the next moment out bounded the identical old fox
that had lured poor Tom Geelaher to his doom, and,
clearing the church-yard wall, swept away across the
adjacent glen, and right down into the valley, with
the single hound behind him.

"Yoicks, yoicks, yoicks!" resounded from the attendant throng of red-coats.

"Tally ho! tally ho! tally ho-o-o!" and the next instant the whole meet, with the eager pack in front, swept from the church-yard, crossed the glen, and rattled away down the valley on the trail of the cunning old fox. Squire Pringle and old Major Weston rode abreast in front, and never on any occasion was such prowess shown in crossing dangerous quagmire, scrambling over scroggy fence, and flying headlong over deep trench and stone wall. Away, away down the bottom of the valley, by rolling stream, leafy wildwood, and fair dell; on and on with unslackened and desperate speed, now close upon the brush of old Reynard, and now far behind. Crag and wildwood tree seemed to fly past as the headlong chase swept on, till they reached the eastern extremity of the great valley, where the Molana rushes outward into the plain, from the pass of the Spirit's Ford. Before entering the pass, the Molana receives a tributary from the northern range of hills, and the confluence of the two streams was at that time crossed by a solitary one-arched bridge, and surrounded by a dense wood, no traces of which now remain. In this wood the fox for some time contrived to elude the eager pack. At last a peasant, who was fishing by the river, happening to look beneath the old bridge, saw Reynard quietly sitting upon a stone beneath the shadow of the arch, and deliberately licking himself after a few refreshing ablutions in the cool water.

The peasant immediately gave the alarm, and away went the fox once more back again up the valley, with the hounds and horsemen after him more madly than ever. It was a wild and dangerous chase, for none but the best and boldest horsemen could run the length of that rough and craggy valley without a headlong fall, or perhaps a broken neck. Before it was over, old Squire Pringle broke his leg for the sixth time, and the veteran Major Weston lost his iron bridle-hook. But what of that? He was now close behind his victim's brush, as that wary individual, after doubling again around the foot of Ardpatrick Hill, swept away once more towards the terrible chasm in which poor Tom Geelaher had met his woful doom. As Reynard approached the edge of the chasm, however, with the intention, perhaps, of luring a few more of the horsemen to their fate, a wild and jovial cry broke from Major Weston, who was still far in front, for Blue Nelly, the mother of the pack, seized her flying foe, at last, by the steaming flank; and thus ended the renowned fox-hunt of Darra.

THE BUCCANEERS' CASTLE.

"TO the right, wheel!" said the colonel.

The regiment, at the word, turned sharply, their scabbards jingling, their swords flashing, and a rolling cloud of dust overhead, as they thundered along the level strand.

"Halt!"

The dust-cloud ascended slowly into the air, disclosing beneath four long lines of horsemen, as they now sat their steeds like statues, facing the straight verge of the sunny sea, which scarcely rippled on the gray sand.

On rode the colonel with his orderly behind him, casting many a sharp look on the appointments and accoutrements of the men as he proceeded. The strand upon which glittered his long lines of horsemen stretched away along the estuary of a broad and navigable river in the south of Ireland. At its northeastern extremity lay the town, a busy and flourishing seaport, many of the inhabitants of which were now congregated upon the green, sloping shore above, to witness the review of that splendid cavalry regiment before its embarkation for the Low Countries.

He halted, as he came to the extreme left of the line, right in front of a young lieutenant, who sat his horse as though he were part and parcel of the animal. This young officer was a fine-looking man in every sense of the word, tall and strongly built, and with that exquisite proportion of limb that betokens a combination of strength and agility. His age might have been twenty-four, or thereabouts; but there was that in the expression of his bronzed face and piercing black eyes which showed that he had seen more of the " ups and downs " and vicissitudes of the world than many of his seniors in the regiment, into which he had exchanged about a week previously. His name was Bernard Neville.

Now, what was it that made Bernard Neville's brown cheek wax pale, and his coal-black eyes burn with an ominous and sinister light as the colonel halted opposite him? It will be seen presently.

"Sir," said the colonel, "why is it that you have not put on your new gorget, in obedience to my general order to the regiment to-day?"

Neville's eyes only sparkled brighter, but he answered not a word.

"Speak, sir," resumed the colonel, angrily. "And since we are in the humor for questions, why is it that you have mounted that light hunter, instead of the regimental troop-horse?"

"Because I was better employed," answered Neville, with a strange sneer.

"What!" exclaimed the colonel, endeavoring to keep down his rising anger. "You had better weigh your words, Mr. Neville, ere you speak thus to your commander. How were you employed, pray, that you were prevented from obeying the order?"

"I was talking to an old man, who was formerly my father's servant, and who is now a disabled soldier in the town."

"What has that to do with the present case, Mr. Neville? You had better answer clearly, or you shall march back to the barracks under arrest!"

"It has everything to do with the question," answered Neville, making his horse pace forward to within about half a perch from his colonel, — "everything, and I *will* answer clearly, according to the order. Do you remember," continued he, in a low, husky, but fierce tone, "that at Amsterdam, twenty years ago, you shot an officer unfairly in a duel? I am that officer's son, but I knew not how my father died till an hour ago, when his servant, the poor soldier, told me. I am that officer's son, but I knew not till to-day that you were his murderer. I am his son, base villain, and I thank my stars I have lived to be his avenger!"

With that he suddenly drew one of his pistols, which he had ready in the holster for the terrible occasion, levelled it at his commander, and fired. The ball passed right through the old colonel's breast, and he fell heavily from his horse, mortally wounded, on the sand. A strong gust of wind at the same instant blew over the waters, and rolled the waves noisily on the shore. The dragoons and a few officers, who were near, sprang from their horses and surrounded the dying man; but so confused were all at the suddenness of the deed, that they made no attempt to secure the vengeful lieutenant till the latter, giving spur and bridle to his swift horse, was sweeping up the height where stood the townspeople, trembling witnesses of the dreadful scene.

"After him!" exclaimed the expiring colonel, with his hand upon his breast, vainly endeavoring to keep back the blood. "Right about — pursue! pursue! pursue!"

Then it was that, as their colonel dropped back in his last sleep, the whole regiment, as if by a common impulse, turned, levelled their carbines, and fired after the wild fugitive as he topped the height. But he escaped the volley; and now, as he shaped his mad course along the shore, that splendid body of horse at last thundered after him in pursuit.

The shore along which Bernard Neville now urged his horse at its topmost speed, at first sloped gently down to the water, but about half a mile beyond, became more precipitous, and at last ended apparently on the far horizon in a jagged promontory, beyond which, however, it extended far away between the melancholy sea at one side, and at the other a wide waste of bog and rolling moorland, without a single human habitation to relieve its black, barren, and stern aspect of loneliness and desolation. Keeping still close to the edge of the sea, he swept on, never for a moment even looking back upon his pursuers, till he approached the craggy ascent of the aforesaid promontory. As his horse toiled up this rugged height, he turned in the saddle, and beheld the dragoons in scattered troops rattling away upon his track along the low shore behind, pointing towards him with their swords, and calling to each other to increase their speed.

"Now," muttered Neville to himself, "I happen to know this shore; and however swiftly they ride, I hope to elude them, for the night is coming on. "Quick! quick!" continued he, addressing his noble steed, that bravely bore him up that toilsome ascent — "quick, boy. They think they will have me soon, but you will save me yet!"

At length he gained the summit of the promontory, and looking back once more, beheld his pursuers toiling upward, their arms and helmets glittering in the ruddy light of the setting sun, and their scattered array appearing like a red flame driven on its devouring course by the autumn wind up the side of a dry, heathery mountain.

"Away, away!" resumed he to his horse, as he swept down the descent at the other side. "When they top the hill they will find their prey not such a laggard as they think!"

The gust of wind that had arisen at the moment

the old colonel fell from his horse had been followed by another of greater strength and longer duration; and now a continuous gale blew towards the shore, raising the heretofore tranquil water into white waves, and dashing them upon the rocks with a hollow and melancholy murmur, the hoarse and dreary sound of which upon that coast was the sure presage of an approaching storm. Beyond the dark summits of a distant range of hills the blood-red sun was sinking amid two masses of driving cloud that threatened soon to blot out its light altogether, and right in front of the fugitive the ruddy and fitful beams were reflected by a narrow arm of the sea that stretched several miles inland. This shallow inlet, about a furlong inside its mouth, was partly fordable at low water; but now the tide was rapidly coming in, and where, during the greater part of the day, a flat sandy strip stretched almost entirely across, Bernard Neville, as he looked eagerly forward, beheld a long line of white form careering inward, followed at regular intervals by others swifter and higher, till at length, as he approached the place, the whole shallow appeared one unbroken expanse of water.

The dragoons, instead of keeping right behind him, now struck upward across the desolate moorland, in order to intercept him, should he, as they imagined he would, turn by the shore in order to get round the inlet. But they had to do with a desperate and courageous man; for instead of endeavoring by increased speed to get beyond them, as they expected, Neville now brought his horse to a sober canter as he approached the edge of the water, and taking a solitary crag on the other side as a landmark, at once dashed in, and then floundered onward bravely for some moments. His pursuers, with a simultaneous shout as they observed this, turned sharply to the left, and came rushing on over the waste, with the hope of reaching the beginning of the shallow ere he had got out of the range of their short carbines. The water, as he went on, was scarcely beyond a foot in depth: but as he gained a point near the middle of the inlet, it gradually began to get deeper, and at last lay before him in a narrow channel, up which the tide swept like the current of a swift river, the wavy but shallow water at either side appearing much calmer in comparison. And now the water was up to his horse's knees, and began rapidly rising, till it reached the saddle girths.

"No matter," muttered Neville to himself, as with set teeth and rigid face he prepared to commit himself and his brave horse to the mercy of the strong mid-current,—"no matter. There is certain death behind, but there is still a chance before."

The next moment the waters rose around him as if he had fallen into a deep gulf, and he knew by the swaying motions of his horse that the noble beast had at last lost foothold beneath, and was swimming. At last the dragoons, on arriving at the shore, after extending themselves into a long line in as advanced a position as they dared, amid the rising water, unslung their carbines, and at the word of their commander sent a volley after the struggling fugitive.

"Ha, ha!" shouted Neville, in a wild kind of frenzy, as the bullets whistled, and hissed, and splashed round him; "a chance yet! Yes, poor fellow,"—and he bent forward and patted his horse upon the shoulder, —"you will save me yet! On! on!"

Darker and thicker floated the shadows down upon the wild and terrible scene, and the water began now to rise so high that the captain of the troop was forced to order his men to retire some distance.

"It is useless to hit a dying man," he muttered to himself. "By my soul, but he is a brave fellow. And yet he has now no chance of escape, even without our firing a shot."

Another detachment had now arrived at the shore, and was riding forward through the water to deliver their fire. As they formed into a line, and looked forward over the gloomy inlet, Neville and his horse appeared like a black speck upon the steel-gray water. They thought he was still swimming, but by an amount of coolness, judgment, and strength almost superhuman, he had contrived to get across the deep channel, and was once more struggling onward with a solid footing for his horse underneath. Again the wide waste of billows was lit by the red flashes of the carbines, and Neville, as with renewed hope he guided his steed in the direction of the rock he had first taken as a landmark, was thrown suddenly into the water: his horse was shot; but the dying animal employed his remaining strength in trying to gain the firm shore, which his instinct taught him to expect in front. The wind was blowing furiously over the water, and the night had set in, so that the dragoons, as they looked forward in the indistinct light, could barely see the body of the horse, after the poor animal had snorted out its last breath, floating helplessly with the rolling waves. Their work was done, and as they wheeled round and splashed back to the shore, a loud shout told their companions who were awaiting them that they had taken full vengeance for the death of their colonel.

But Bernard Neville was living for all that. With a desperate grasp he still clutched the bridle of his dead horse, and thus kept himself above the water, that had at last risen more than a fathom upon the flat shallow. Louder and more furious grew the wind, piping with deafening clamor over the turbulent expanse; but he still held on, looking occasionally with wistful eyes upon the black waste that stretched to the left as he was swept up the roaring inlet, into which, somewhat less than a furlong in front of him, a low tongue of the moorland extended itself right in the course in which he was driven.

"You will save me yet," he muttered hoarsely, as he rose from a boiling wave that had submerged him for a moment. "My curse upon the hand that fired that shot: but no matter, you will save me yet!"

and he grasped the loose bridle with a firmer and bolder hand. The roar of the waves, rushing over the flat shore beyond, became momently louder; but their sound was not unpleasant to his ears, for he knew they would soon cast him upon firm land. At last one immense billow, that seemed to spread across the whole inlet, arose behind him, and came thundering on with increased speed as it approached. Clutching the bridle with both hands, he held his breath, awaiting its coming. At length, with a deafening roar it overtook him, and when it retired again with a shock against the next that followed, he found himself stretched by the dripping body of his horse upon firm land. Another wave was coming on, and to avoid it as well as the weak state he was in would allow, he crawled forward, and stood tottering and scarcely knowing what he did, gazing back upon the turbulent waste of waters from which he had so wonderfully escaped.

He now turned, chill and weary, and leaving the foam-covered strand, walked on till he reached the precipitous coast, along which he pursued his way with stern and unflinching resolution, although the rain was still pouring down in blinding torrents, and the commingled wind and sea roaring with a deafening clangor that might well appall even a stouter heart than his. At length, beside a naked crag that crowned the ridge of a steep promontory, he rested for a while, intending not to pursue his way farther till the rain had ceased and the storm had somewhat abated its fury. An hour after, the storm ceased, and the moon shone out between the driving clouds.

Beneath him, at the side of the promontory, a small rocky haven, up which the waves still careered madly, stretched inward; and here a sight met Neville's eyes that made his heart bound with uncertain hopes. It was a large boat, like one of those belonging to a man-of-war, moored at the sheltry side of a projecting rock at the upper extremity of the little haven.

"Surely," said he to himself, "that boat must belong to some ship, which I know cannot be far away."

He now swept the horizon sharply with his eye, and at last discovered a solitary mast-head dipping under the far-off waves, and rising over them, alternately. As he turned his gaze inland once more, his eyes rested on a huge black mass, which at first he took to be a detached rock, but which, on closer inspection, he discovered was the ruin of a large building. It was situated upon a barren knoll, scarcely half a furlong inside the rock beneath which the boat was moored. Nothing could be wilder, more forbidding, or more desolate than the appearance of this ancient structure, as it loomed up from its bare and solitary knoll in the ghastly moonlight. Fit appendage to such an object, a mighty tree stood at its front on the very verge of the slope, throwing its gnarled and sapless branches abroad over what was once the court-yard, without a single leaf or green spray to shelter it from the biting winds, and looking as if it had been blasted and stricken dead by some sudden lightning stroke. In fact, the whole scene appeared as though a curse had fallen upon it in some by-gone age, and that it had remained ever since deserted by bird, and beast, and man.

But Neville knew that by man at least it was still often tenanted, for he remembered strange stories told, in connection with it, of smugglers and pirates who had made its vaults the hiding-places for their ill-gotten treasures.

"And," muttered he to himself, as he stood up, and began descending the side of the promontory, "there must be some one there to-night. No matter who or what they may be; I must at all events seek their company, and take shelter with them, at least till morning."

After getting round the little haven, he at last stood upon the edge of the rock, looking down upon the boat. It was a large and strong one, with six oars at each side. On examining it, he became more firmly convinced than ever that it belonged to some large ship, most likely that whose mast he had seen dipping in the offing. He now turned up towards the ruined castle, and, as he did so, loosened his sword in its scabbard, for he guessed rightly that he was about to come in contact with men, if possible, more desperate than himself. At last he entered beneath the ruined porch, and gained a hall, from which a broad stone stairway wound upward. Upon a pedestal in the midst of this hall, he saw, in the dim moonlight, a statue, in black marble, of a warrior, whose demoniac and sinister face looked upward to a point in the wall, to which also was directed a long spear held in its threatening hand.

Passing this terrible figure, he ascended the stairway, and at length paused before an arched door, through the chinks of which streamed a light outward upon the black walls around him.

Neville stood irresolute, but at last intruded his head beyond the edge of the door, and looked in. At the upper end of a huge vaulted chamber, before a blazing fire of wood, which burned beneath an arched fireplace, sat about a dozen men around a rude board which seemed formed from the planks of wrecked ships, and which was supported on four large blocks of stone, that served the purpose of legs. These men seemed of different nations. One was clad in the dress, and wore the broad sombrero, of a Spaniard; another squat and burly figure was habited in the ample trousers, and hose, and short, wide jacket of a Dutchman; another swarthy fellow sat luxuriously back with a huge bowl of Schiedam in his hand, and dressed in the picturesque habiliments of a Portuguese; a fourth, by his dress, appeared to be an Englishman; and so on to the end, not a man of the whole crew appearing to belong to the same nation with one of his fellows. Swords, guns, pistols, and boarding-pikes lay in wild confusion around them on the black oaken floor, or rested against the equally black walls, reflecting the gleams of the red fire, as it blazed and crackled beneath its capacious chimney-arch.

The countenances of these men were mostly fierce and warlike; but Neville marked one scarred face amongst them, which, by its expression, indicated a character of unusual energy and ferocity. It belonged to a middle-aged man, of low stature, but herculean bulk, who sat at the head of the board, near the fire, and who seemed, by the authoritative manner in which he delivered himself when he spoke, to be the commander of the motley gang of desperadoes. From one side of his belt hung a large, heavy cutlass and a dagger, the other side being ornamented with two long-barrelled pistols, which showed by their brightness the nice and continual care bestowed upon them by their owner. As this burly personage was now in the act of raising a cup of hollands to his lips, his eyes, after a seeming observation of the vaulted roof above, at last wandered towards the door, and met those of Bernard Neville, who was at the moment regarding him intently. Neville, the instant he caught the look of the other, stepped boldly into the apartment. A yell of surprise and anger greeted his entrance, as the eyes of the whole gang now marked his uniform. All started to their feet, thinking that a detachment of the intruder's comrades were about to follow; and three of them, who sat farthest from the fire, immediately rushed over, and began barricading the ancient and ponderous door. At the same time a number of pistols were presented at Neville's person, under which, however, he stood unflinchingly, gazing back calmly at the crew, as they regarded him over the iron tubes with knit brows and flashing eyes.

"Stop!" exclaimed Neville. "You do not mean to shoot me for claiming your hospitality!"

"Where are your comrades?" thundered the burly leader, with his pistol still pointed at Neville's head.

"I have no comrades," answered the latter. "I'm alone, and a desperate man, like yourselves. Will you give me shelter for the night?"

The pistols were now lowered.

"Look at me," resumed Neville. "I am after doing a deed whose guerdon is certain death — I am an outlaw. Think you, if I came to attack you in this place, that I would thus enter the room alone and unarmed? You see I have nothing but my sword — a poor defence against your ready pistols."

"Ay, ay!" said one of them. "That may be all very good, but, comrades, if you take Jack Bolton's judgment on the matter, you will regard this man as a spy."

"Vera goot," put in the Dutchman. "Himmel! but when old Mynheer van Schulkenwold commanded us on de Spanish Main, de same thing happened. Listen, and I vill tell you de story. Der teufel, but I vill!—"

"Shut that tough jaw of yours!" interrupted the commander from the head of the board, at the same moment raising his pistol again, the whole fierce crew following his example. "This is no time for yarns, Dirk Slagendyke, when a company of soldiers may, for all we know, be surrounding the old castle outside. Give a better account of yourself, sir," continued he, turning to Neville, "or, by the blood of my body, you will have a dozen bullets through your head in another instant!"

"I can give none better," answered Neville. "Send one of your men down to the porch, and, if he find a single soldier following me, then use your weapons as you threaten. I tell you that I come merely to claim shelter from you for the night, and your protection, perchance, in the morning, for I have now more enemies than yourselves, if you are what I take you to be."

This seemed a fair proposition to the leader.

"Dirk Slagendyke," said he, turning his fierce eye on the Dutchman, "away with you and Jack Bolton down to the porch, and out upon the slope. Look sharply around you, and if you see a single land-shark, then you may send our untimely visitor to Davy's locker as soon as you wish."

After about five minutes, the pair returned with a favorable report for Neville.

"Now," said the commander, throwing himself once more upon his seat, and pointing to a rude bench near the fire, "plant yourself upon that, Mr. Stranger. Tell us why you have come to these moorings, and, if you want it, you may have no reason to complain of the aid that a roving buccaneer and his men can give you."

Neville, without more ado, seated himself upon the bench; and the heat of the fire, aided by a rousing stoup of fiery hollands, tendered to him by the commander, soon succeeded in restoring the bodily warmth he was so much in need of. He then explained, as far as he thought prudent, the reason of his untimely visit, and ended by requesting his entertainer to give him a passage across the sea to some foreign shore.

"That we will, my lad," said the commander, his sympathy excited by the knowledge of the daring deed Neville had just done. "But the land is no place for a gallant youth like you. I warrant me, once you set your foot on the deck of the Flying Hawk, by which I mean our ship, whose mast you may have seen in the offing as you came along, that you will be tempted to become a rover of the Main, like ourselves. However, let that stand by. We have enough to attend to, ere we leave this, without recruiting for the Flying Hawk."

"What brought you to these shores?" asked Neville, after refreshing himself with another cup of hollands.

The brows of his auditors contracted darkly at this question, and some of them regarded Neville once more with looks of renewed suspicion.

"If you consent on the spot to become one of ourselves, — in other words, a stout buccaneer, — I may answer your question," said the commander. "Otherwise, I may not, and will not, inform you."

Neville paused, his lowering brows becoming

darker as the moments wore on without his giving a reply. It was a terrible life to run. He knew, however, that he had nothing better to hope for now, and thus made up his mind with little further delay.

"Yes," he said, vainly endeavoring to repress a sigh over his fate; "my career seems run on shore at last. Take me as you will on board the Flying Hawk, and whenever you have the doing of a bold deed, place me in front, and I think you will find me doing the part of a man with the best of you; henceforward such a life seems to be my destiny."

A murmur of approval from his auditors echoed round the vaulted apartment.

"Well," resumed the commander, "in that case I will tell what brought us here. Fifteen year ago, the commander of the Flying Hawk was Captain Bernardo, the boldest and bravest buccaneer leader that ever sailed the seas —"

"Except Von Schulkenwold," interrupted the Dutchman, "Donner wetter, but he was as goot a man, vich I vill maintain against de best foremast man on board, vit sword, pistol, or dagger. Himmel, but I vill!" and his huge clinched fist went down upon the rude board with a resounding thump.

"Silence!" said the commander, with a grim smile. "Von Schulkenwold was never as good a man as Captain Bernardo."

Bernard Neville started, as the thought struck him, that, one day or other, he might become a buccaneer captain of the same name.

"Never half as good," resumed the commander. "Well, sir, about that time our captain died, and I was elected by our brave crew to fill his place. Before his death he bade me sail to Barbadoes, and marry his daughter, who lived there in a certain village by the coast with her mother, a Creole; and he also told me that I would find in their possession a little iron coffer, which I was not to open till I visited this old castle on the Irish shore, in which he and his crew, after being half wrecked by a storm, lived for nearly a month, and to which he brought those strange figures you must have seen on the stairs from beyond the seas. I obeyed his dying command, and found everything as he told me. But as to sailing over to Ireland at that time, it was out of the question. Business was then too good on the Spanish Main. So, year by year, I neglected it, during which many a brave man's blood has dyed the planks of the Flying Hawk. At last I sailed over, as you see, and found the castle according to the points and bearings he had given for its discovery. We opened the coffer in this hall to-night, and found therein a bit of parchment; but may the fiend seize me if one of us could read a word of the outlandish gibberish that was written on it. And so, you see, we have had our cruise for nothing: but no matter; we will make it a dear one to the fat merchantmen on our return."

"Perhaps," said Jack Bolton, "our new comrade can read it."

"True," said the commander. "Bring over the coffer."

The little iron box was now brought, and placed in Bernard Neville's hands. He opened it, and took out the parchment.

"Why," said he, after casting his eyes curiously over it, "this is Latin!"

"Latin!" exclaimed the commander. "Well, that settles my opinion, at all events. When I looked over it, I said it was written in the New Zealand lingo, or something of the kind. Pierre Aubanelle, over there, said it was old French; but then Don Pedro,"—and he nodded to a tall, grave-looking man at the other side of the table, — "Pedro claimed it for Spanish; and between them both they went near settling the question with their hangers, till we pacified them before you came in. Can you read it?"

"My God! what is this?" exclaimed their new comrade, heedless of the question, and at the same time starting up and laying the parchment on the table. "Did none of you see this?" and he pointed his finger to the name "Bernard Neville," written in a bold hand at the end of the document. "This is also my name."

"It *is* strange," said the commander; "but, as we couldn't make out the first few lines, we did not mind the end."

"Was Captain Bernardo a Spaniard?" asked Neville, a strange suspicion crossing his mind.

"I have reason to think he was not," answered the

commander, "although he spoke the Spanish language fluently, and adopted the dress of that nation. He had been in his early days in the Spanish navy, but was outlawed by that government in consequence of a mutiny in which he was one of the ringleaders."

"That man must have been my uncle," said Neville. "Everything happened to him as you say; but then his friends thought that he was shot after the mutiny, which took place, if I recollect rightly, on the coast of San Domingo."

"It is true," said the commander. "And now, lads, that we are about to have some of the blood of our old captain on the decks of the Flying Hawk once more, let us welcome the brave heart that brings it!" and with that he raised a hoarse shout of welcome, which was responded to by the whole wild gang, till the vaulted chambers of the old ruin rang again and again with the wild clamor.

"But now for the reading of the parchment," said the commander, after he and his companions had shaken hands with Neville all round. "Can you do it?"

"I think I can," answered Neville, as he sat down and began to peruse it carefully.

The gang watched him eagerly as he went through it, and their impatience and curiosity were not a little heightened on observing Neville start several times with an exclamation of astonishment as he read on.

"What is it?" said the pirate, eagerly, as he saw that Neville had come to the end.

"It is a wonderful thing," answered the latter. "It is an account of the first booty taken by the crew of the Flying Hawk, at the sacking of Alpuxarra — a Spanish settlement on the coast of Brazil."

"Ay, ay!" said the commander; "I was there, and a bloody day it was. But let that stand by. Where is the booty? I thought it was long ago at the bottom of the sea — the iron box that held it, and all."

"It is here in this castle," said Neville; "at least if we are to believe what is written on the parchment by my unfortunate uncle."

The eyes of the wild crew sparkled at this bit of welcome news.

"Believe his written word!" almost roared the fierce commander. "Why, man, if all the world gathered together, and took their oaths to the contrary, I'd believe him in preference. Young man, whatever your uncle might have been, he was never known to break his word, no matter for what he pledged it. What else does he say?"

"He says," answered Neville, "that when you have found the booty, you must bring a few casks of powder from the ship, and blow up the castle. He says also that the booty must be fairly divided amongst the crew of the Flying Hawk, according to each man's degree."

"Good!" said the commander. "Now read the directions he gives for finding it."

Neville read the passage in English: —

"When you stand at the stair-foot, and look upon the unholy figure that the Spanish sculptor carved during his madness, mark the spot in the wall above at which the demon's spear points. In that spot you will find the booty of Alpuxarra."

"Throw some fresh brands upon the fire," said the commander. "We must make them serve as torches to light the spot our old captain speaks of."

It was done; and in a few moments the whole throng were standing under the massive porch beneath, facing the staircase. It was a wild scene. The burning brands held aloft, casting their red and fitful light upon the rude walls around, and upon the stern faces of the wild gang of desperadoes, who now peered upward with eager scrutiny to the point indicated by the huge spear, while at the same time the terrible colossal figure seemed to gaze down upon them in return, with a cold, stony smile of demoniac satisfaction at their greed.

"This will never do," said their commander. "There is the spot near the landing above; but we cannot pick the wall till we get some implements from the ship. Come, Jack Bolton, off with you with nine men to the Flying Hawk, and bring back the necessary things, together with a mining fuse and two barrels of powder. You should be here at least by sunrise."

Jack dashed his brand on the floor, and then, calling off nine of his comrades, led the way down to the boat, which was soon dancing over the still rough water. The remainder, with Neville, returned to the chamber above, and waited by the fire till morning, at which time Jack Bolton and his comrades returned with the several things ordered by his commander. They picked the wall at the spot which was so remarkably and strangely pointed out, and there found a huge iron coffer, in which, on breaking it open, they found what they sought — the booty taken at the cruel sack of Alpuxarra. It consisted of a huge heap of Spanish coin in gold and silver, with several valuable stones and ornaments, all of which, before the sun of that day set, was divided according to the dying instructions of their old commander on board the Flying Hawk. They placed the barrels of powder in one of the vaults of the old castle, and attached to them a mine fuse, which they carried down the slope to the shore. On gaining their boat, they applied a match to the fuse, and in a few moments the grim and ancient structure was blown in fragments into the air, with a roar that was heard for many a mile along the barren coast and desolate moorlands. The inhabitants of a far-off fishing village came over during the day to see the cause of the explosion, and their horror may be well conceived when they saw the black figure still standing uninjured amid the ruins. They dragged it from its foundation with a strong rope, and then cast it into the sea, where it was lost forever.

Bernard Neville's career was a short one. He crossed the seas, but about a twelvemonth afterwards fell on board the Flying Hawk, in an action fought somewhere on the Spanish Main.

MUN CARBERRY AND THE PHOOKA;

OR, THE RETURN ON NEW YEAR'S EVE.

THERE was not a man through all the wide fields of Munster, from the gray slopes of Sliav Bloom to Brandon Hill, that had such a light heart as Mun Carberry. Neither would you see, from Youghal Harbor to Garryowen, a fairer face than that of his young wife, Nancy, nor hear a merrier voice than hers, as she ordered out her two strapping servant-maids to the milking bawn on a fine May morning. It is often said by wise people, that "a bird in the hand is worth two in the bush," and that "a blackbird in the pot is better than a wild goose on the wing," and also that "a clean conscience, a clean shirt, and a guinea are no despicable possessions;" and all these saws were well illustrated by Mun Carberry and his wife; for they took what Providence sent them without murmuring, and jovially made use of the little they possessed without wishing and repining for things beyond their reach; and as they

each had an honest heart, and enough to live upon
through either hard or prosperous times, you would
not, on the whole, find a happier couple in a nine
days' ramble.

But all people have their failings. Mun had two.
The first — which certainly was no failing, except in
the eyes of the old and spiteful — was a love of music and dancing, which was shared in equally by his
wife, said music being particularly the lilt of the Irish
pipes, and the dancing the powdering away at an
eight-hand reel, a slip jig, or a moneen. There was
not a night of their lives, from Christmas Day to St.
John's, and over again to Christmas Eve, that some
wandering musician did not sit in their chimney corner; and it is there upon the dry earthen floor you
would hear the footing about, the shuffling, and the
jolly pattering of heel and toe, as Mun and Nancy,
the servants, and the neighbors rattled away to the
tune of "The Cricket's Rambles through the Hob,"
"Allisdrum's March," "The Hare in the Corn," or
"The Pretty Girls of Coolroe," or some other tune
that it would delight your heart to listen to. At
fair, patron, and meeting they were also to be seen
footing it away on the "light fantastic toe;" and it
was said all over the country, from Corrin Mor to
Corrin Thierna, that there was not a piper in the barony that would not rather play for them for nothing
than skirl a tune for any other pair of dancers for
the brightest fi'penny bit in Munster.

Mun's other failing was a firm belief in the supernatural, in the existence and appearance of ghosts, fetches, cluricaunes, sheevras, and phookas. To the latter — a phantom that generally appears to people in the shape of a mighty horse, a huge bearded he-goat, a kid, a great black bull, or a calf — he was particularly partial, and often, on going home at night from a fair, from the market in the neighboring town, or maybe from a wake, he would peer fearfully around him, expecting to catch a glimpse of the phooka in some dark hollow or glen; but for a long time his half-shuddering curiosity remained unsatisfied. Notwithstanding this, at the mowing time the greenest and tenderest grass upon the upland remained behind, by Mun's especial orders, for the regalement of the phooka; and for the same purpose, when the spalpeens dug out the potatoes, towards All Hallowtide, some of the best and brownest cups, and the soundest and whitest lumpers, were left behind upon the ridge. For a like intention also, you would see every evening, scattered over the farm-yard and the paddock, wisps of sweet-smelling hay, and handfuls of the cleanest and whitest straw; so that nothing was neglected on the part of Mun to render a meeting between himself and the phooka an amicable one, in case of such an event occurring at any time of his life.

It is a nice thing to be contented, and a good thing, as the song says, to be merry and wise; and, as I have said before, you would not find, within the five corners of old Ireland, a happier and more jovial heart than Mun Canberry's; but the old people will tell you, that have proved it and know it well, that, let a man's path be ever so smooth and flowery in the beginning, it may, before the end, become rough and thorny, that the longest lane has a turning, that there never was a summer that a winter did not follow, and that the stream which glides and winds through the green, flowery meadows, like a thread of glittering silver or a bead of pearls, may be dashed into smithereens over the rocks before it falls into the ocean. And what happened to Mun carried out the old people's sayings to a T.

One fine summer morning, while Mun and the neighbors, who had come to help him, were out saving hay in the meadow, his wife, with the milk set, the house swept clean, and all her work done, was sitting upon her *siesteen* at the door, crooning the "Cooleen Bawn" to herself with a happy heart, and looking out over the long, straight boreen, that, with its two rows of overshadowing beech, and green, feathery ash trees, led up to the farm-yard from the broad, sunny plain beneath. After coming to the end of her song, she turned to Noreen Gal, the servant-maid, and told her to prepare the potatoes for dinner. A moment before, not a living thing could be observed upon the boreen; but now, as Nancy turned, and was about to resume her song once more, she beheld a great funeral moving slowly along its whole extent upwards from the plain, with cars, and horsemen, and footmen, and a great gilded hearse in front, from the top of which waved four snowy plumes of feathers in the light wind that blew across the sloping uplands.

Unable to speak a word, and with a heart throbbing fearfully, Nancy continued to gaze upon the mournful and unwonted spectacle, till at last the hearse rumbled into the yard, and stopped in the midst opposite the door. Four tall, dark-looking horsemen then dismounted behind, took a coffin from the hearse, and were bearing it towards where Nancy sat, in fixed and unutterable terror, when a little red cock, that was perched upon the barn-top, flew down between her and them, clapped its wings, and began crowing loud enough to break its gallant little heart. At its voice the men turned round slowly, and without a word laid the coffin in the hearse; and as the brave little bird advanced, clapping its wings and crowing louder than ever, the four great black horses that drew the spectral funeral car were turned round by the drivers, and at length the mighty concourse that accompanied it turned also, moved back again down the boreen, and finally faded from poor Nancy's sight out upon the plain below.

That night, although the dancing went on as usual, the piper played in vain for Nancy Carberry in the chimney corner. In vain Mun and the neighbors asked her the cause of her melancholy. Terror kept her silent, and not a word would she say concerning the spectral funeral. Next morning the same thing occurred. The little cock flew down from the barn-top, clapped its wings and crowed, and the fearful spectacle faded away from Nancy's eyes as before. Still she did not tell her husband. On the third morning the funeral came up again, the four men dismounted, and brought forth the coffin; but now no saving bird of mercy flew down from the barn-top. As the men came forward, Nancy's terror at length found voice.

"Noreen, Noreen Gal!" she screamed, "where is the little red cock that ought to be on the top of the barn? Noreen, Noreen — where is he? Quick, quick, or your misthress is done forever, if he isn't to the fore!"

"Wisha, faith a vanithee!" answered Noreen, who stood unsuspectingly filling a pot with potatoes by the fire; "the little imp o' the divvle was makin' such noise about the yard these days past that I thought it onlucky, an' kilt him for the masther's supper."

"Lord bethune us an' harm!" exclaimed Nancy, in her terror. "You have killed your misthress too, Noreen. O, wirra, wirra! — what'll become o' me? Save me, save me, Noreen! Look, look!"

Noreen looked, and at the sight she beheld, darted into an inner room, screaming with fright, and hid herself beneath a bed.

"Is there no one to save me? O, Mun, Mun! — where are you?" shrieked Nancy, as she sat chained to the spot in the agony of terror.

No Mun appeared; but at the call a huge gray

goat, with its long, snowy beard sweeping the ground, danced, with many a caper, round the corner of the house, and in between her and the four men, where, raising himself upon his hind feet, he began to butt and present his sharp horns at the intruders, and with such effect that the latter turned, as before, and laid the coffin back in the hearse. And now, with wilder antics than ever, the goat danced round the yard, charging and butting at horse and man, till at length the great funeral turned, moved slowly and mournfully down the boreen, and faded, as before, out upon the sunny plain. The moment they had disappeared, the goat turned round, trotted up to the door, and fixed its great black eyes upon Nancy Carberry. Fascinated by the look, Nancy arose, and followed the weird-looking animal round the corner of the house, and into the garden. Dinner time came on, and Mun came in with his hay-makers; but no vanithee sat at the table head to make their hearts merry with her bright smile. That night there was loud lamentation in poor Mun Carberry's house, for the young vanitbee did not return; and for many days after they searched through wood and glen, village and town, and over the wide and dreary moorlands that stretched up the slopes of the hills, but never a sight of Nancy did they see, high or low. The wise ones — the old people, those who ought to know — shook their heads, and said that she was surely alive and well, — in Corrin Thierna, maybe, or in the old Fort of Lisdorney, — with the fairies.

Still Mun Carberry kept up his heart, and, although he mourned in secret, the neighbors, and those whom he met on the Fair Green, had always the light word and the pleasant smile, for he said to himself that a pound of sorrow never paid an ounce of debt, that a man in a pond must swim or else he will drown, and that, if he ever was to win back his young vanithee, it was not by moping at home in grief and melancholy.

Now o' nights, when returning home, he looked around more eagerly than ever, in order to catch a glimpse of the phooka, for he said, —

"One who I've thrated so well ought to be my friend, an' p'r'aps may give me news o' the vanithee. Howsomever, if he's not, there's an ind to it. Sorrow kilt a Dane, an' good-humor is the sowl o' long life. God help me this blessed night!"

His good humor and trust in the phooka's friendship were soon, however, to be put to the test. One night, as he was coming home from the wake of Saer-gorm, or the Blue-mason, — 'tis a *quare* name, but I can't stop to tell stories, — he crossed the river at Aha-na-slae, and took the short cut homeward through the fields. After ascending the side of the glen from the green *inches* beneath, he came to a formidable barrier, in the shape of a huge, double fence, with its two well-filled ditches. Mun Carberry's light legs, however, were not to be stopped by any such impediment. He leaped over the first ditch, climbed up the side, through the hazels and thick briers, stepped across to the other side, gave a flying leap to reach the green meadow beyond, and landed upon the back of the phooka, this time in the shape of a great black horse, with streaming mane, and long, sable tail, that switched the heads off the flowers which bloomed upon the meadow behind him.

"Be the sowl o' my body, but I'm in for it at last!" exclaimed Mun, as he stooped forward, clutched the phooka's long, black mane, and squeezed his knees, like the bold rider that he was, and thus holding on, prepared himself for the worst. "Howsomever, the darkest an' most *grumach* face may have the kindest heart ondher it, and 'tisn't the smilin' friend that'll always help one in his need; so here goes for the sake o' the vanithee, and the blue skies over Grena!"

With that the phooka darted off, with a hilarious neigh, now doubling and rearing, now floundering and splashing with headlong speed through the quagmires and morasses of the low grounds, now rushing quick as lightning across the craggy ridges on the uplands, and then plunging through the winding river below. At length, after sweltering through the river about the sixth time, he suddenly stopped upon the *inch*, reared upon his fore legs, and, with a neigh like the blast of a trumpet, pitched Mun Carberry into the air, and landed him, unhurt and safe, upon the smooth, flat top of Corrig-a-Phipera, or the Piper's Rock, a solitary crag that rises over the north-eastern bank of the stream.

Well might it be called the Piper's Rock; for, as Mun landed upon it from the back of the phooka, there sat upon a boulder, at one side of its flat summit, a diminutive little atomy of a man, clad in red body-coat, waistcoat, and breeches, with a pair of small top-boots that seemed once to have belonged to a horse-rider, a somewhat weather-beaten caubeen, set jauntily over his right eye, and a chanter resting upon his knee, said chanter belonging to an elegant set of bran new pipes, which he was that moment in the act of tuning. After an infinite variety of flourishes, stops, and wild skirls of music, he at length finished the tuning of his instrument, and then looked at Mun.

"Be the hole o' my coat, Mun!" said he, "but you're just come in the nick o' time, an' you're as welcome as the flowers o' May. What'll you have—a thribble, a slip, or a moneen? 'The Thrush's Nest,' 'The Bay an' the Gray,' 'Jackson's Bottle o' Punch,' or 'Norah Ciestha'? Allow me to insinivate that the latther is by far the most hilaarious an' lively in comparisment with the others, an' that your fut will keep time to it as merlifluously as the jinglin' of a sixpence on a tombstone."

"Whatever is most plaisin' to yourself, sir," answered Mun, politely. "Let it be 'Norah Ciestha' for the sake o' the ould times whin I an' the vanithee often danced it forenint aich other."

"Be this chanther in my hand but ye may often dance it again together, if it lies in the power o'

Drinaun Brac to do ye a good turn!" said the little piper. "But here goes for good luck, as the game-cock said to the sparrow whin he picked out his eye;" and with that he rattled up "Norah Ciestha" in a wild and joyous tone that would make the dead shake their toes under their green sods in Religa Ronan.

"Hurroo!" shouted Mun, as he powdered away at the moneen with a gusto and a nice and careful attention to time that made the eyes of Drinaun Brac twinkle with satisfaction. "Be all the stones in Corrin Thierna, but that's nate intirely!" and he footed it about, sprang up into the air, came down lightly upon his toes, drummed with his heels, and then executed step after step, too numerous and various to describe.

"That's it! straighten the chest, back with the elbows, and cover the buckle!" cried the little atomy encouragingly, and in high delight, as Mun now shuffled away like mad — "that's it! Honom an dhial! but in all the forths in Munsther there isn't the likes of him for a janius at the fut!"

At length Mun gave an athletic spring upward, came down with a resounding clash of his brogues upon the hard, smooth rock, executed another stampede round and round, and then, bringing the right foot behind the left, and taking off his caubeen, bowed to the little piper, thus ending the moneen with the height of politeness and urbanity.

"Well," said the Drinaun Brac, as he stood up

and bowed gratefully in return, "I've often wished to see you at a moneen, Mun Carberry. Allow me to express my onquinchable an' uproarious delight an' shupernathral plisure at your performance of it. Go home for this night in pace an' quietness, an' to-morrow set out upon your thravels to look for the vanithee. The time p'r'aps isn't yet come, but when next we meet, I may be able to do somethin' for you, for I'm your friend, an' have intherest with one who has power to do you good — manin' bethune ourselves, my masther, Farreen Shrad, who thrains the phookas for the King o' the Fairies. Good night; and may the most amberosial an' unspeakable good forthin attind on your peregrinations!"

With that he bowed once more, and, in the twinkling of an eye, vanished from the astonished gaze of Mun Carberry. Mun then descended the rock, crossed the stream, and went home with a lighter heart than he had known for many a long and weary day previously. Next morning he arose, told the servants that he was going from home for some time, warned them to take care of the cattle and the farm, and to be sure to have a piper in the chimney corner for a hearth-warming at his return, and then set off upon his wanderings in search of his lost wife.

One morning, about a month afterwards, as he was sitting on the top of the old castle of Kilcoleman, and gazing out sad and sorrowful upon the lake, he saw a small but intensely bright rainbow resting before him upon the water. Underneath this a figure, at first vague and shadowy, rose into view; but becoming at each successive moment more substantial and distinct, it at length assumed a form, the sight of which made his heart beat with a wild feeling of gladness. It was the very face and figure of his young and lovely wife Nancy, but now seeming far more fair and beautiful than ever. She seemed to be wrapped in a light robe of blue, all glistening over like the coat of one of those gay birds that flit like living sunbeams through the primeval woods of the torrid Eastern climes. She stood lightly on the glassy surface, gazing around at first upon the green shores; but at last turning to poor Mun, who stretched out his loving arms towards her, she advanced a few steps, stood, and then pointed three times up to the pass of Aha-na-Suilish, or the Ford of Light, a gorge in the mountains behind the castle. After resting near him for a short time, the apparition began to recede, and, when it reached the middle of the lake, the rainbow, rising slowly into the air, mingled with the light morning vapors, and the lovely figure of his wife disappeared again beneath the crystal, waveless water.

"Be the blessed stone of Ard-na-naov, but 'tis herself at last!" exclaimed Mun. "An' now I know by the way she pointed, that she is in the ould rath o' Lisdorney; for, sure enough, there it lies above in the middle of the pass of Aha-na-Suilish. If watchin' an' waitin' there will do, night, mornin', an' noon, it'll go hard with me if I don't bring her back some time or another, anyhow!"

He then came down from his perch upon the old castle, and morning, noon, and night, for a long time after, watched for the appearance of his wife beside the fairy rath of Lisdorney in the pass. One fine December evening, as the sun was setting in a blaze of red beyond the summit of Corrin-Mor, Mun sat in a thicket at the skirt of the wood, from which, although concealed himself, he could observe every object beside the rath. As he was ruminating gloomily upon the sad fate that separated himself and his wife, he was suddenly started from his reverie by a wild skirl of a chanter outside; and sure enough, on looking out, he beheld his acquaintance of the rock sitting upon a stone beside the pathway. This time, however, Drinaun Brac was not alone. A figure sat beside him, whom Mun at once recognized, from his habiliments, as the trainer of the Phookas to the Fairy King, namely, Farreen Shrad, the master of Drinaun, the piper. A blazing red hunting coat fell down upon his slender, bowed legs, which latter were encased in a pair of top boots, the *facsimile* of those worn by the little piper, differing only in the spurs that ornamented them. A scarlet riding cap decorated his head, and beneath its peak, his eyes, like two sparkling carbuncles, lit up a jovial round face, from the midst of which projected a splendid bacchanalian nose, with an extremity red as a ripe cherry in autumn. After a few attempts, Drinaun Brac seemed to give up the tuning of his instrument in despair; and then the two fairymen began conversing on various topics.

"Well," said Farreen Shrad,—which means the Little Man of the Bridle,—"purshuin' to me if I can stand the work at all at all, as I used to do in ould times. Five hundhert years ago, when the blood was hot in my veins, I could do a'most anything; but now I'm afeard I must give the thrainin' business up into younger hands!"

"Thrue for you, masther," returned the piper; "whin ould age comes on, everything looks quare an' gloomy. To my mind there is no plisure, whin a person comes to that, but in makin' acquaintance with the sowl-sootherin' potheen bottle! 'Tis the only cornucopy of plisure that warms my heart, anyhow."

"Sthrike us up a tune!" resumed Farreen Shred, abruptly. "Sure enough, the pipes an' potheen are my only comfort now, whin I'm gettin' ould an' stiff!"

"Wisha, where is the use in playin', after all," said Drinaun, "whin I haven't a dancer to keep time? If I only had Mun Carberry here now!"

"Never say it twice!" exclaimed Mun, starting up from his hiding-place. "Here I am; so ráttle up Norah Ceistha again, an' be the lafe o' my hat I'll do it justice, in compliment to the civil way you spake of me!"

Drinoun Brac tuned his pipes and struck up Norah Ceistha, and Mun rattled away as before, to the great delight of Farreen Shrad, who gave vent to his pleasure in a series of yells and hunting shouts that made the pass ring.

"An' now," said Farreen, as Mun bowed to him at the end of the jig, "as civility and perliteness is the ordher o' the day, an' as merriment an' the most obstbreperous joviality must reign shuprame bethune us, I'll sing you a song which I learned from ould Garodh Dorney, the poet, whom we had in the rath with us for nearly a month o' Sundays. Sate yourself fornint me there on the bank. Here goes. He made it in praise o' some place in the west which he called

THE GARDEN O' DAISIES.

I.

When first I saw my darlin' in the Garden o' Daisies,
   Fal urlium, ri durlium, muilearthach fa ral i!
I thought she was Diana or the beautiful Vainus,
   Fal urlium, ri durlium, muilearthach fa ral i!
I thravelled France an' Spain, an' likewise in Aashia,
An' spint many a long day at my aise in Araabia,
But never knew a place like the Lakes o' Killarney,
   Fal urlium, ri durlium, muilearthach fa ral i!

II.

'Tis there the mountains rise up with great imulation,
   Fal urlium, ri durlium, muilearthach fa ral i!
With the finest of ould timber an' foxes in the nation,
   Fal urlium, ri durlium, muilearthach fa ral i!
There the deers and bullocks browse, and the pikes in the
      wather
They mutilate the salmon an' throuts with great slaughther,
An' the cockatoo an' pheasant they crow in the mornin',
   Fal urlium, ri durlium, muilearthach fa ral i!

III.

Were I to numerate an' confess all the praises,
  Fal urlium, ri durlium, muilearthach fa ral i!
Of my darlin' that dwells in this Garden o' Daisies,
  Fal urlium, ri durlium, muilearthach fa ral i!
I'd want the pen o' Vargil, an' powers o' great Homer,
An' the tongue that kissed ould Blarney, an' riches o' Damer,
An' the eyes o' Rhadymantus, an' Bluebeard's pinethra-
    shion,
  Fal urlium, ri durlium, muilearthach fa ral i!

"Tallyho! there 'tis for you in the toss of a tinpenny bit! Lisdorney for ever and the blue skies above it — Tallyho-o-o!

"An' now Mun Carberry," said Farren Shrad, as he came to the end of his hunting shout, "bethune ourselves, you have some inimies where you know. 'Tis they that wanted to take your wife away the day they came up the boreen, and 'tis I out of an ould regard for you sent my favorite phooka, Goureen Glas, to the house to save her; an' he brought her here away from them, where she's safe and sound. But as our Queen has taken a fancy to her, it won't be so aisy to get her back. Never mind, howsomd-ever; I'll manage it. Next New Year's Eve, just at nightfall, be here at the Foord, where I'll lave the best-thrained phooka horse from here to the Rocks o' Skellig behind for you in the wood. Mount him without fear or consthernation, and whin you see your wife crossin' the Foord in the thrain o' the queen, rattle into the midst o' them, pull up your wife afore you, and then gallop away for your life. I'm now ould an' a particklar friend to the king, an' will stand the blame, and turn it all into ludiacrity!"

Mun stood up to make his bow and thank Farreen Shard; but when he looked again both the fairymen were gone.

At length came New Year's Eve with its white mantle of sparkling, feathery snow on hill and moorland, valley and lonely wildwood. Mun Carberry, with a stout heart, went up the pass of Aha-na-Suilish, and into the wood, where he found the identical phooka horse that had before pitched him to the top of the Piper's Rock, awaiting him. The moment he had mounted the great steed, he looked out, and there beheld the rath of Lisdorney in one blaze of splendor glittering before him, with a long glimmering and shining train of knights and ladies issuing from a blazing portal in its front, in the midst of which he saw his wife riding on a little palfrey behind the Fairy Queen. He waited till they were in the act of crossing the ford, then rattled forward, and amid the shrieks of the Queen and her maids of honor, seized his wife, drew her before him on his steed, and dashed away like lightning down the pass, out on the open moorland, and off towards his house, before the door of which they were safely deposited by the phooka, which now with a thunderous and joyful neigh darted back again to the moors to rejoin his companions.

That night the merriest dance that ever was seen was danced upon the kitchen floor in the light of their blazing turf fire by the light-hearted Mun Carberry and his wife, who were never afterwards troubled by either the Good People, the Phooka, or the Fairies.

THE OLD BACHELOR.

WE cannot define with certainty the nature of the feelings with which the antediluvians looked upon old bachelors. Probably they regarded them with contempt and scorn. This, however, is on the supposition that there were old bachelors in those days of war, revelry, and giving in marriage. "There were giants in those days," and, from all we have read and heard of those steeple-like specimens of humanity, we are led to think that they were far more given to matrimony than to single blessedness. Before the flood, then, an old bachelor must have been a regular *rara avis*, but we are not to imagine that on account of his scarcity (if we may so express ourselves), he was looked upon with any degree of leniency by his contemporaries. Let us suppose, for a moment, although it is very unlikely, that such an individual did exist, and, furthermore, that he was, for instance, a neighbor of Tubal Cain, the old artificer in steel and brass, to whom, in the common

course of events, he would have been likely to give
some employment. Well, let us say that, at the age
of five hundred years, which, according to the philosophers, corresponds to fifty in these degenerate days,
he bethought himself, one fine morning, of getting
his horse, or his behemoth, or whatever beast of
burden people then used, shod, and for that purpose
paid a visit to old Tubal's forge. Is it likely that the
gigantic blacksmith and his witty apprentices could
refrain from passing many a joke and jibe upon the
enormity of his remaining single up to such an age?
All we can say upon the matter is, that, notwithstanding their stature, they were men, and that, participating in the feelings common to all humanity,
their noses, which, if we are to believe some ancient
writers, were considerably over a fathom in length,
were often cocked up at their neighbor, and their
huge and begrimed physiognomies contorted into
many a sarcastic laugh at his expense, as he sat "like
patience on a monument" upon the hob, listening to
the bellows that roared beside him like a volcano,
and to the "ding-dong" of the mighty hammers
upon an anvil which, after a minute analogical course
of reasoning, we conclude must have been the size
of a respectable mountain.

The foregoing being all mere conjecture, we will
now glide up to a time after which the feelings of
society with respect to old bachelors assume a more
certain and definite aspect — we mean that "old
dusky time," when, as the prince of idlers, Thomson, says, in his poem of "the Seasons," —

"The deep cleft-disparting orb that arched
The central waters round, impetuous rushed
With univeʀsal burst into the gulf,
And o'er the high-piled hills of fractured earth
Wide dashed the waves in undulation vast,
Till from the centre to the streamy clouds
A shoreless ocean tumbled round the globe!"

Then, as the waters of the deluge subsided, and when Noah portioned out the green and smiling earth between his three sons, from that ancient period people seem to have looked upon old bachelors with no small amount of contempt, blended with a hot seasoning of animosity. Now, in all this we can see but little justice, and less of charity. Caligula is said to have wished the whole human race to have but one neck, that he might sever it with a single blow of his sword. Doubtless, although he never obtained his wish, the nefarious pagan often feasted himself by doing the deed in his imagination. For a far different purpose we have bundled up the whole mass of society, living and dead, before our mind's eye. We have held the scales of justice in our hands and weighed their opinions, and though we have found many of them fair and good, we triumphantly pronounce the aforesaid one regarding old bachelorism wanting — wanting in truth, kindness, and charity. Why should a man be blamed for what he cannot avoid; for what he has heroically striven against with might and main during many a long and weary year? People will answer, that a man becomes an old bachelor from mere choice, and will point the finger of scorn at many an unfortunate example of their assertions; but they who do so have studied the secret workings of the human heart but lightly.

A man who begins life with the avowed intention of never marrying, and apparently to the world "kicks against the goad" with his whole heart, is always sure in the end to become entangled in the flower-garlanded mesh of Hymen. Our friend Jack Browne, of Ballyskellig, is a good example of this. Jack is now a flourishing attorney, and a contented and benign paterfamilias. When he commenced to practise in his native town, he let "all and every" of his acquaintances know that he was determined to die a single man. This resolution of his did not proceed from lack of funds to support a family and keep up the credit of a matrimonial establishment, for Jack had a handsome property and a splendid house adjoining the town. His relatives, of course, although in secret they heartily despised him, entertained him with the utmost blandness and cordiality whenever he condescended to visit their domiciles, for, casting their piercing eyes into the future, they were in the daily habit of contemplating his last sickness, death, burial, and will, from the items of which delightful document they had no small expectations. But Jack Browne still went on "the even tenor of his way," adjusting the differences of his litigious neighbors with wonderful judgment and impartiality, and seemingly never dreaming that such a thing as a marriage-ring was ever beaten into shape by a goldsmith. The marriageable girls of Ballyskellig set their caps at him in vain, and even their plotting and match-making mammas, whose sagacious eyes might have been supposed capable of detecting a flaw in his resolution, at last gave him up in despair. And thus years rolled on, Jack all the while adding to his wealth, and ostensibly looking upon matrimony with the most rampant ill-will and hatred. At last Mrs. Tomkins, the banker's wife, gave a ball, and amongst the guests at this brilliant festival was Mary Somers, a black-haired, dark-eyed, rosy-cheeked, laughing beauty, without as much of a fortune as would "jingle upon a milestone." This quaint method of expressing the amount of Mary Somers's worldly gear was used by Miss Angelina Primrose, as that sweet-tempered old maid and I stood in a corner of the ball-room, looking at the dancers.

"But you may be sure, Mr. Hazlewood, she will not be long without a husband, for all that," added Angelina; "for if she hasn't the gold, she has an unlimited supply of brass. See how amiably she looks upon Mr. Browne, as he stands her *vis-a-vis* in the quadrille;" and Angelina nodded her head towards the far end of the room.

I looked, not at the beautiful Mary Somers, but, as it happened, at my friend Jack Browne, and, to my infinite amazement, saw him regarding the former with an unmistakable glance of admiration, as she moved through the mazes of the dance before him with an airy and inimitable grace that seemed peculiar to himself.

"However," rejoined the rather antiquated specimen of womanhood by my side, with a long-drawn sentimental sigh, which seemed to intimate that she herself had tried the powers of her beauty upon Jack, and failed: when she failed, how could others succeed?—"however, if she had ten times the tact and impudence that she has, she can have but small chance of catching Mr. Browne!"

The quadrille soon came to an end, and a universal polka began, during which my amazement was not a little increased to see Jack and Mary Somers, as partners, twirling round and round upon the well-waxed floor. Five mortal times that night they danced together, greatly to the consternation of the girls of Ballyskellig, to whom Mary Somers was a comparative stranger. Speculating mammas fanned their perspiring cheeks, pursed up their lips, looked sadly upon their bereaved daughters, and shook their heads at the expected result of those five Terpsichorean figures. The result was known soon enough, and far too soon for many. It fell, in fact, like a thunderbolt on Ballyskellig; for next day Jack Browne popped the question to Mary Somers, and was accepted. They were married within a month; and we may here state, as a remarkable proof of our theory, that since the memorable night of Mrs. Tomkins's ball, the ladies of Ballyskellig, blooming spinsters, old maids, and sagacious mammas, have all looked upon the protestations of the young men to become old bachelors as "airy nothings," and thereby have become far more cheerful and endearing towards us all, by which latter I mean those of us who are what is called eligible, in a matrimonial point of view.

Of your indifferent man, who sets out by saying that he does not care a straw whether he gets married or not, we have but little to say. An individual of that description is always sure, at some time or other, to be ogled into matrimony. Of him we have nothing further to remark. We pass him over in silent contempt, and come to a specimen of a far different class — we mean the hot-headed, warm-hearted, sanguine youth, who steps out on life's devious way, to him at first all bright and glorious, and looks around him upon evergreen woods and shining valleys, as he travels onward, with the delightful aspiration of becoming a Benedict ever burning in his joyous bosom. It is from such that the ranks of old bachelors are mostly recruited. They love, and live in paradise for a time; but by and by the world, the frosty and cruel code of pounds, shillings, and pence, comes between them and the objects of their young affections, withers up their hearts, and makes them miserable. A blight seems to fall upon them for a year or so. They live in darkness, despair, and sorrow, till once more the dawn appears, and they pluck up heart of grace, as the old romancists express it, and recommence their journey with renewed hopes. Another love, another walk through an enchanted and delightful land, lit by the golden sunlight of the heart. Then, mayhap, the ladies whom they worship play them false. The clouds again gather on life's horizon, and spread over the laughing summer sky. The lightnings flash, the thunder growls and bellows, and the storm pours down upon the poor wayfarers, who still journey on, their trust in woman's faith shaken to its foundation, their hearts seared and hardened, and their eyes opened to the guile and treachery that so often lie, like an artful ambuscade, before them. Once more they trust and are trusted, and now they are surely happy after their many sorrows. The bridal day comes on, a happy day for those who see it; but there are many who never see it, for death steps between, and smites down their idols with his unrelenting sword. Then, like a man who, when his last tie on earth is severed, throws himself into the tumult of war, careless of the future, those poor hearts, whom death has thus bereaved, step forward and join the little army of bachelors, whose fate it is to do battle ever against the ill-deserved contumely of the world.

As an illustration of the above, we take the liberty of giving here the history of our friend, Frank Esmonde. Frank is a gentleman of independent property, who, having grown weary of the country, now lives exclusively in town. The whole aim of his life, at present, seems to be to attend his club regularly and read the newspapers, to saunter on the sunny side of the street when the day is fine, to eat a good dinner, and afterwards, as he holds in his hand the single tumbler of punch he invariably indulges in, to drink happiness to the whole world — a happiness, alas, in which he is destined never wholly to participate. Frank, when I first knew him, was about eighteen years of age, and an only son. Never on the face of the earth existed a kinder, truer, or more honorable heart than his. Many a ramble he and I had together over his father's mountains, and many a pleasant story he told me of his youthful loves, as we sat by the verge of some green summer wood, or walked over the hill, side by side, to start the brown grouse from its purple covert of heather.

One bright October morning Frank and I went out shooting. The two previous months I had spent in town, and, as a matter of course, on that identical morning I made the most minute inquiries regarding the heart adventures he had undergone during my absence; for it seemed a settled principle with him to have a new sweetheart every month. To my surprise, he answered my inquiries in a very absent manner, and at length became quite uncommunicative. After several ineffectual attempts to get a story from him, I at last rattled away at my own adventures, at the end of which he appeared to relent somewhat, and seemed more inclined to take me into his confidence.

"As for me, Tom," said he, as we sat to rest ourselves on the grass on the verge of a glen, "I have nothing pleasant to tell you this time, at least what you would call pleasant."

"You don't seem much pulled down by sorrow, nevertheless," remarked I, looking into his fine eye and sun-browned face.

"Well," said he, "I suppose it is the case, for in my heart one feeling counteracts the other. I may say that I am happy and unhappy in the same breath."

"In other words," resumed I, "you are in love, Frank. With whom?"

"I am in love, Tom," answered he; "but this time it is a real feeling. I love her with my whole heart and soul, and shall never marry if I cannot marry her."

"Who is she?" said I, eagerly; for I saw by his face that he was in earnest.

"Kate Neville," answered he, with a sharp scrutiny of my face in return.

"Yes, Kate Neville," he resumed, somewhat bitterly, noticing my surprise. "Why should I not love her? Is she not good enough for me — for the best man in the land?"

Kate Neville was the daughter of one of his father's tenants. It will not be wondered at, therefore, that I started on hearing her name pronounced by poor Frank, knowing as I did that his father was one of the proudest and sternest men in the county.

James Neville, Kate's father, was a poor man, but his heart and head must have been in advance of his means, for he had contrived to give his daughter an education far beyond that usually given to young girls of her class. Kate was, in point of beauty, a most remarkable girl; and when we add to this her mental accomplishments, which were considerable, it will not appear strange that, however they happened to meet, she captivated the heart of Frank Esmonde, young, impetuous, warm, and romantic as he was at that most critical period of his life.

"Now, Frank," said I to him, "you had better pause before you go farther in this matter. I see no hope from your father; and thus you can easily understand what a mad course you are pursuing. It is only destroying your own happiness and hers, both together; for no matter how long you wait, your father will never consent."

"I suppose so," said he, sadly; "but as for drawing back, that I cannot do. We are pledged to one another, Tom. She loves me, if possible, far better than I love her; and think you that I could break her heart by basely forsaking her? It would break my own heart to do so. Therefore I will wait — and wait —"

"And wait for what?" I interrupted. "Depend upon it, Frank, that when you leave home, as you are about to do, and enter the army, your sentiments will soon change."

"We will see," said he, determinedly, as he stood

up. "There," continued he, as if wishing to change the conversation; "see! there goes a pack of grouse, whirring over the hill. Let us follow them;" and with that he strode off, at a surprising pace, up the side of the rugged glen by which we had been sitting.

"Poor fellow!" said I, commiseratingly, as I followed on the path at his heels; "he is mad; but the world will soon cure him."

"The world will never do so, Tom," said he, turning suddenly, and laying his hand on my shoulder; "for I have sworn, in my inmost heart, to love Kate Neville, and none other, forever more."

When we returned that evening, we were rather surprised to see James Neville, Kate's father, coming down the avenue. He seemed in a troubled state of mind as he passed us. I immediately suspected what had taken place. The sturdy old farmer, however he had come to the knowledge of it, had informed Frank's father of the whole affair. The latter, however, made no allusion to it; but I noticed that his look was sterner, and his manner more reserved than ever that evening. Next day he left home, and did not return for a fortnight. In about a week after his coming home, Frank was gazetted to an ensigncy in the ——th regiment of foot.

After a few days' preparation, Frank Esmonde bade farewell to his home, and proceeded to join his regiment. How he parted from poor Kate Neville no third person ever knew; but it must have been a sad leave-taking. Six years afterwards old Mr. Esmonde died, leaving Frank his sole heir. The latter, who had risen to the rank of captain, sold his commission, and returned to his native home. On his arrival at the neighboring town, he bade his servant drive off to Esmonde Hall to notify his coming, and said, as the evening was fine, that he would walk home. In doing so, he took the path that led through the ancient and beautiful church-yard of Temple-Darren. As he passed through this solitary abode of the dead, a new and handsome tombstone caught his eye, and, feeling a natural curiosity to ascertain who it was that had been stricken down during his absence, he turned aside to read the inscription. To his grief and horror, he found it was "to the memory of Catherine Neville, who departed this life at the early age of eighteen years," just one twelvemonth after he had left home. It is scarcely necessary to say what followed. Finally, poor Frank left Esmonde Hall, came to reside in town, and has since lived, as I have said, the lonely life of a confirmed bachelor.

THE GOLDEN BUTTERFLY.

AFTER visiting the stupendous cliffs of Moher, the tourist who proceeds inland and climbs to the summit of a certain steep mountain in the parish of Kilnaboy, county Clare, will see, shining beneath him in the summer sunlight, the beautiful Lake of Inchiquin, with its solitary island and its ruined castle. This lake is nearly three miles in circumference, and with the wild tier of mountains that rises abruptly over its western shore, and the varied succession of woody glens, fern-clad slopes, green meadows, and heather-empurpled moorlands that meets the eye from their summits, the traveller who gazes upon the scene will scarcely fail to pronounce it a picture of beauty equal to the best he has seen during his wanderings amid the fair hills of our romantic isle. Not alone from the circle of beautiful scenery of which it forms the centre, is this fair sheet of water interesting. Hoar tradition still lingers by its shores, and the solitary herdsman who sits with you on the brow of the mountain, or the sun-embrowned peasant in the cornfield beneath, who returns your salute with the warm response peculiar to his native land, will treat you to a number of legends associated with that delightful neighborhood, many of which the careful inquirer will find to be connected with some historical incident of olden time. The poet, too, has not left it unsung. One of our most gifted bards has limned it in a poem of more than ordinary excellence and beauty — "The Monks of Kilcrea."

The point of land on which the ruin stands seems to have been originally an island. The castle, though now greatly dilapidated, is still interesting, both from its situation and from the historical and legendary lore connected with it. It was built by a powerful chief of the O'Quins, the ancestors of the present Earl of Dunraven. Passing from the date of its erection, which is involved in obscurity, we come to about the middle of the fifteenth century, some time previous to which the castle seems to have been taken possession of by the O'Briens. The first of that name who made it his residence was Thiege, Prince of Thomond, whose death, according to the "Annals of the Four Masters," occurred in the year 1466. From that date it continued to be the residence of the successive chiefs of that powerful family, the O'Briens of Inchiquin, whose title of earl is now merged in the higher one of Marquis of Thomond.

Like many another Irish lake, the waters of Inchiquin are said to roll over the domes and palaces of a submerged city. The solitary fisherman who rows his light skiff, or curragh, over its smooth expanse on a calm summer evening, still believes that he can see

> "The round towers of other days
> In the waves beneath him shining,"

and will tell you a tale of a remote ancestor of the O'Quins, in which that hero is represented in the act of being overwhelmed by the raging waters, castle, town, and all, on account of some offence against one of the fairy potentates of the locality. Be this as it may, we will now come to the last O'Quin who ruled over the wild and romantic territory of Hy-Ifearnan, his ancient patrimony, and relate the cause of his expulsion from that region of mountain and moor, lake and tumbling river, together with his migration at the head of his broken clan across the Shannon, and his settlement in the county Limerick, where his descendants, as we have remarked above, remain to the present day, still holding a considerable portion of the rich lands of which they originally took possession.

In the castle of Inchiquin dwelt Donal, an aged chief, whose youth and manhood had been spent in battle and turmoil, but who now, in his old age, determined to throw aside targe and spear and iron glove, and spend the remainder of his days governing his broad lands in peace and equity. Of all Donal's children, none remained to cheer his heart, as he trod the final stages of life's troublous journey, save his youngest son, Rory the Black, a youth of whom the old chief was very proud, and who was already renowned for both his personal beauty and for his many knightly accomplishments. At the period to which we allude, young Rory the Black was just after leaving the ancient monastery of Kilfenora, in which he had been educated from his childhood, and from which he had never been allowed to come forth, save on such times as he was sent to the wars to learn the profession of arms, or during the great days of festival held by his clan in their merry principality of Hy-Ifearnan.

One day, after his departure from Kilfenora and final settlement in his father's castle of Inchiquin, young Rory went out to hunt. Unattended by either henchman or horse-varlet, he crossed the rugged chain of mountains that overhung the lake, and rode down into a deep glen, through the bosom of which a murmuring brown stream rolled down sparkling in the sunlight. After traversing several miles of this glen with his four gray stag-hounds behind him, the green forest beneath which he rode gradually became more stunted, and at length disappeared altogether, when before him opened a wide, stern, and solitary valley, without a single shrub or tree to hide its grim rocks and barren hollows. On making the circuit round the base of a huge crag that towered over the turbulent stream, he looked up the valley, and saw a huge, red stag rushing down its eastern slope, with a man who ran with extraordinary swiftness in close pursuit behind him. This strange hunter was clad in the skins of beasts, and held a short, bright spear in his hand, which he cast at the stag as the latter with a bound cleared the broad bed of the torrent. He missed his aim, however, and the spear stuck quivering deep in the green sward on the farther bank, while the stag bounded swiftly up the other slope of the valley. And now the hunter, also with a single bound, cleared the stream, snatched up his weapon, and with chest bent forward and head erect, darted up the hill at a speed that soon brought him within his original distance of the panting stag. But beyond that distance he seemed unable to advance as both swept up the hill, till at last they disappeared from the view of Rory the Black beyond its verge.

The young chief now rode farther up the valley, expecting to see no more of the hunter and the stag; but after a short time they appeared retracing their headlong course, and enacting over again what had occurred at the crossing of the torrent. Six times was all this repeated, during which Rory had great difficulty in preventing his hounds from darting forward and joining in the marvellous chase. At the seventh time, just as the hunter had thrown his spear, and was in the act of springing across the glen, his foot caught in a looped ivy stem that stretched along the edge, and he was thrown headlong into the deep pool of water beneath. Rory knew that such a hunter had but little to fear from the narrow pool of a mountain torrent, and seeing the stag rush up the hill, he found himself unable to resist the temptation any longer; so, throwing the bridle loose and touching his steed with the spur, he called merrily to his hounds, and dashed in pursuit. The stag had got a good start, and as Rory gained the ridge or spine of the hill, was half way down the slope at the other side. But now both steed and hounds went bravely downward, and began to gain upon the deer, till the latter, coming to the base of an immense wall of rock at the bottom, turned upward in a circular course, and went back again in full career for the first valley, where, instead of directly crossing the stream, as he did previously, he now rushed obliquely along the slopes and rocks towards the extreme end, and there turning, came down at a thundering pace on the opposite side, with Rory and his baying hounds still close upon his track. Another round of the immense valley, and again the stag came down, now on the very brink of the roaring stream. Just as he had gained the spot where his first pursurer fell, however, Bran, Rory's best hound, seized him by the haunch, and after a violent struggle, during which the other dogs had come up, all rolled over the abrupt edge into the stream. Rory, on coming to the spot, dismounted, and looked down. The huge stag was stretched dead beneath upon the sand, and the hounds were quietly lapping the cool water beside him. The strange hunter, however, was nowhere to be seen, till Rory, after descending the steep side of the glen and making a close search, at last found him lying upon a damp bank, apparently dead from the effects of his fall.

After a copious sprinkling of water from the stream, the stranger at length began to revive, and was soon able to stand and account for himself.

"Knight of Inchiquin," he said, "thou hast done me a service, for which I will repay thee well."

"Who art thou?" returned Rory; "for I never saw a man in thy strange guise amid these mountains before."

"I am Merulan the Wizard," replied the stranger.

"Take thy stag, then," said Rory. "Wert thou another hunter, I might claim him for myself, seeing that my hounds have killed him; but, by my knightly faith, it were pity to deprive hunter like thee of such spoil. Take him — or stay. Come to my father's house, and thou wilt have good cheer during many a merry moon."

"I cannot go," answered Merulan, "but I thank thee none the less. Thou and thine were ever bountiful to the poor and friendless from generation to generation, since the day that the mighty Olliol Oluim put his sword in the scabbard, and made the wise laws for the sons of Inisfail."

"Why canst thou not come?" said Rory, looking kindly on Merulan. "Thou hast nought to bind thee to one spot; so come with me, and we will have feasting and merry revel for many a day in the halls of Inchiquin."

"It cannot be," returned Merulan. "I must spend a year and a day in the cave that lies beneath yonder crag. The stag the hounds have killed will give me food for a long time; and," continued he, with a smile of strange sweetness and benevolence, "when I want another, thou hast seen enough of me to-day to show thee that I cannot die with hunger whilst a single deer bides within these mountains. However, for the service thou hast done me, take this;" and putting his hand into his leathern pouch, he drew therefrom the semblance of a butterfly, carved in flashing gold, and handed it to Rory. One of the legs of the glittering little image was pointed like the pin of a brooch. "Take this," continued he, "and place it as a clasp for thy plume. As yet, thy heart is kind and full of equity, but when thou growest older, the world may change thee, as it changeth every mortal man. Wear this, however, above thy forehead, and as long as thou dost right, it will continue to shine brightly as thou seest it now; but the moment the doing of a bad deed enters into thy heart, it will cease to shine, and become dull and dark as the damp sod beneath our feet!"

Rory, looking with delight on the strange gift, placed it as a clasp to the plume of his light-barred cap. Merulan, with another smile, bade him farewell, and then both left the glen, Rory riding across the ridge into another valley, and the wizard bearing the body of the stag towards his solitary cave.

When Rory had crossed the range of mountains, the mighty and rugged spurs of which shot out into a wide plain, a great forest extended itself before him, within the mazes of which he wound his horn merrily and hunted all day long, till the sun seemed resting beyond, upon the far glittering waves of the boundless ocean. He then bethought himself of returning, but before he did so, dismounted and sat down upon a green bank, in a flowery dell surrounded by many a silver birch and waving rowan tree. At last the sun set, and the dim shadows of twilight began to steal upon the resting-place of the young hunter. He now took off his barred cap, and looked again upon the golden butterfly. Its two minute eyes seemed of diamonds, and as the dark shadows gathered down faster and faster, and made a gloom upon all the forest around, the wonderful image emitted a light that seemed to fill the whole glade, and enabled him to distinguish the smallest leaf or blade of grass, even to a point far in between the trunks of the encircling trees. After gazing and wondering for some time, he again mounted his steed, and calling his hounds, proceeded through the forest homeward, the magic plume-clasp lighting his way through dark recesses and tangled paths with a brilliancy far transcending that of the brightest star or the yellow moon of autumn.

On the farthest verge of the forest ran a broad, swift river, to which the turbulent stream of the desert valley was a tributary. As Rory came towards the bank of this river, he heard a wild and piteous scream, which seemed to proceed from some one struggling for life in the water. Down he rode to the bank, the magic butterfly still lighting his way, and looking out upon the stream, beheld in the midst the figure of a young girl as she floated helplessly with the tide, still, however, faintly endeavoring to keep herself upon the surface. In an instant Rory dashed his horse into the river, at a point below that where the girl was still struggling, and as she floated downward, caught her in his strong grasp, and carried her safe to the other shore. For a time she lay insensible on the bank; but she soon recovered, and thanked her deliverer in a voice of exceeding sweetness. She said that she was the only daughter of a kerne, or foot-soldier, who lived hard by, and who served the lord of Inchiquin, and that as she was crossing the ford, a little distance above, she had lost her footing and fallen into the river.

Rory, by the light of the golden image, had time to examine the features and form of the young girl, as she stood up and prepared to depart for her father's cot. He had never before beheld a being so beautiful. She seemed at first frightened at the strange light emitted by the image, and began to think that she owed her deliverance to some forest sprite; but, when again she looked upon the smiling, noble face of the young chieftain, and heard his kind words, she knew he was mortal, and invited him to partake of the hospitality of her father's cot beside the river. This invitation Rory thankfully accepted, and when they arrived at the wood-kerne's cottage, the surprise of the young girl knew no bounds, when she saw her father welcoming Rory as the son of the brave lord of Inchiquin.

The more Rory saw of the beautiful young girl, the more he admired her; and when he took his departure in the morning, it is not to be wondered at that he resolved to return frequently to the cottage. And he did return; and who will marvel when they hear that he was at last in love with the beautiful Enna, the daughter of the wood-kerne, and that he swore, come what would, to make her his wife? All this, however, he kept secret from his father, for he knew that the latter, though just and wise, would sooner see him dead than the husband of a low-born maiden such as Enna.

And thus a year passed away, at the end of which the old lord of Inchiquin, finding his health failing, and wishing to see his affairs settled before his death, began to negotiate a match between his son and the daughter of O'Brien, lord of Thomond. It was now that Rory found himself sorely beset, between his duty to his father and his love for the young peasant girl. In those times the wishes of children were not consulted, particularly by their parents; and so, after a few meetings between the lord of Thomond and his vassal chief, old Donal of Inchiquin, the match was made, and the day was appointed for the marriage of Rory the Black and the haughty Maud O'Brien.

The important day came; and Rory, who had secretly married the lovely Enna in the interim, refused, of course, the hand of the princess of Thomond, for which rebellious act, at the instigation of O'Brien, he was lodged in one of the strongest dungeons of Inchiquin by his incensed father.

Day after day the old chief visited Rory in his prison, expecting the latter to be brought to reason; and thus matters went on for nearly half a year, at the end of which time Rory grew tired of his confinement, and began to think, in his misery, of repudiating his low-born wife, and marrying the young princess of Thomond. The father, noticing the change, now worked upon his mind untiringly, until at length Rory gave his consent, though he knew that, in the far-off cottage by the forest river, his rightful wife would die when she heard the woful news. It was now all rejoicing in Inchiquin. Rory was liberated, and another day was appointed for the bridal that had caused so much trouble. The lord of Thomond's castle was situated a considerable distance away from Inchiquin, beyond the mountains, and that they might reach it about noon, Rory and his father, and their gallant train, set out on their journey before the dawn of day. On they went, and now some glamour seemed to influence Rory, for never a thought came into his mind of the golden butterfly, and the kindly warning of Merulan, in connection with it. At the crossing of a glen his horse stumbled; but there was now no light to guide his way — nothing but darkness before and around him. During the passage of a quagmire, again his horse stumbled, and almost fell forward into a treacherous pool of water; still he thought not of the golden gift of Merulan.

And now upon the plain, smooth road, the horse for the third time stumbled and fell forward, bringing Rory down with him.

"I would to Heaven," exclaimed the young chief, as he extricated himself from his horse, and then helped the animal to rise, "that it was on the road to the far-off forest I was, where dwells my loved and lawful wife!"

At that moment the golden butterfly cast a faint glitter upon the dark road.

"She will die, poor thing," resumed Rory, "when she hears of the base act I am about to do. I have half a mind to refuse once more, be the consequence what it may."

The gleam from the golden image became brighter.

"Yes!" exclaimed Rory, as he now noticed the change suddenly, "come what will, I will not advance a step farther towards the consummation of this bad deed. I will return and proclaim my wife to my father's vassals, and die, if necessary, to defend her!"

And now the light became like the rising sun, brightening all a-near. Rory sprang to his saddle, wheeled his horse around, and in a moment dashed away on the backward track, pursued by his father and the train of gallants who attended him. It was still dark, and the rays from the magic butterfly lit Rory's path as he fled fast and far towards the cottage of his young wife. His father was soon left behind, and the pursuit at length entirely ceased.

Rory reached his wife before the hot noontide, and lived concealed in her little cot beside the river for a month. At the end of that time his father died, and he was proclaimed chief of Inchiquin. He then avowed his marriage, when a fierce war followed between himself and the prince of Thomond, who swore that he would never rest, night or day, till the clan O'Quin was swept, root and branch, from the principality of Clare. And he kept his vow; for he never ceased till he had driven Rory the Black to such extremities, that the latter, with his young wife and his broken clan, was at length forced to bid farewell to his ancient patrimony of Inchiquin, and cross the Shannon into the county Limerick, where his line, as we have said, is still represented by the earl of Dunraven.

THE ADVENTURES OF HUGH AND BRIAN.

ONCE upon a time, when the land was in its prime, when turkeys sat in state, smoking dudheens black and great, when the rocks could speak and sing like cuckoos in the spring, when the cats could all foretell, like prophets, what befell and appeared, when the fairy, and the ghost, and the giant ruled the roast, and swallows built their nests in ould men's beard, there dwelt a great and mighty prince by the side of Brandon Hill, in the kingdom of Kerry, whose name was Tiernan of the Long Sword.

Now, this Tiernan of the Long Sword had twelve daughters, who surpassed in beauty and accomplishments all the fair maids who dwelt beneath the shadows of the hills of holy Ireland. Twelve daughters had he; but, to his grief and desolation of heart, no son to whom he might bequeath his broad domains, and whom he might see leading forth to battle the bold and stalwart vassals that inhabited the green valleys and fruitful plains encircled by his native mountains. Prince, and lord, and chieftain flocked from far land and near as suitors for the hands of those sweet daughters of Tiernan; but he, although he lamented the want of a son, loved his fair maids, and to chieftain, lord, and prince, made answer: —

"No! Let them live and die in their ancestral home, like the flowers of the green valley, that start into bloom and beauty in the sunny spring, and fade, as the snows of winter whiten the mountains!"

Of all Tiernan's daughters, Meergal, the youngest, was the best and the fairest, and had the greatest number of suitors. Not a prince or warrior, far or near, that had not thrown down his gage of battle to some other redoubted champion — little they recked to whom — in honor of her bright eyes and for the love of her beautiful face; and many a head-piece was sheered through by heavy battle-axe, and many a shirt of mail pierced by sharp sword or dagger, as the first propitiatory act towards the gaining of her lily hand. The eleven sisters of Meergal were not angels altogether, and therefore had in their possession at least some of the passions belonging to human kind in general, and especially to women. And so envy of Meergal's charms and the number of her suitors became their ruling passion, and their sweet tongues, educated to the use of many a foreign language, were most eloquent and

musical in the revilement of their lovely sister on
every possible opportunity. But little she recked,
as she moved to and fro in the dawn of her woman-
ly splendor, what they said, and always answered
their sweet and shrill remarks by reminding them
that youth and beauty availed them not, since their
father would never consent to see them the brides
of any champions, no matter how renowned and
valorous.

One night Tiernan caused the beacon fires to be
kindled on the summits of the hills, collected his
vassals in the morning, and led them off on a foray
into a far land, where he remained many days. One
fine sunny day during his absence, Meergal walked
forth into the forest till she came to a spot where
the bright river that ran by the palace tumbled
down over the mossy cliffs into the sea. Meergal
sat herself down on a fragment of rock beside the
crystal pool, took off her golden sandals, and commenced laving her small, snowy feet in the cool,
bright water. Far down in the glassy depths she
could see the glittering fishes darting to and fro in
their merry play, while, if she raised her blue eyes
and looked around the margent of the pool, there
lay scattered in rich profusion before her shells of
every imaginable shape and hue — shapes resembling
the calyces of flowers, twisted trumpets, or half-
opened lily-leaves, and hues like those of the vivid
rainbow or the golden sunset. When Meergal had
finished the laving of her feet, and was raising the

left out of the water to put on her sandal, a bright light for a moment irradiated the depths of the pool, and a salmon with silver-sparkling scales, and eyes diamond-lit and glittering, darted swiftly upwards, and became before her eyes a young prince of great beauty. And while her father remained valorously fighting and slaying at the wars, she went with him to a beautiful bright island on the sea, where she became his wife, and bore him two sons.

There was a certain old captain of Tiernan's gallowglasses, named Trean na Leam, who dandled young Meergal on his knee when she was a child, and who now, though she had incurred her father's anger, and was condemned to die for fleeing from her home, loved her well; and he went and guarded her children in the island. After a time, Trean na Leam went to the three Talking Masons of Glendorn, that they might build a castle for the sorrowful mother and her two little sons. Now, these three brothers were called the Talking Masons in irony by the vassals of Tiernan and other princes, because they were the most silent men to be found in all Ireland. Trean na Leam led them to a wild and trackless glen by the sea-shore, where they commenced to lay the foundations and build the castle. Day by day they worked, never speaking a word, till the first year was past and gone. Then Diarmid, the youngest, shut his left eye, and casting a sharp and critical gaze with the right at a huge arch they had finished, said to the second brother, —

"By the diamond eye of Croum-Crue, the God of Thunder, but that schamin' thief of an arch will disgrace us, 'tis so crooked!"

When the second year was over, Murrogh, the second brother, laid down his lifted hammer, and, looking on Diarmid with a reproving frown, said, —

"By the beard of Amergin, you crooked-eyed robber, but you'll break my heart! 'Tis as nate an' fair arch as the rainbow over Brandon Hill."

When the third year had passed away, Mahon, the eldest, with a malignant scowl upon his bronzed face, threw his plummet at the eye of a whale that was gamboling in the water by the shore, and then turned to his brothers: —

"By the head of the Goban Saer!" he exclaimed, "ye noisy thieves, but if ye don't stop yeer chatterin' tongues, I'll peg off to Trean na Leam, and give up the job, and then lave ye, and go away on my rambles as a journeyman!"

This threat restored silence; and so the castle was soon finished, and the three Talking Masons returned to their home.

In this castle Meergal dwelt with her two sons for seven long years. In her home, they thought that Cleena, the Fairy Queen, had taken her away to her diamond palace for a bower maiden; and they thought of her gentle ways for a while, but she was soon forgotten. When the seven years were past and gone, Tiernan and Trean na Leam were sitting on the summit of Brandon Hill, looking over the green valleys and the blue sea, and ever and anon talking of the wars and tumults that then prevailed in Erin.

"I am growing old, Trean," said Tiernan, "and my back is becoming weak beneath the war harness. Woe is me that I have no son to whom I might leave my broad domains, and who would lead our warriors, when I am gone, into the red crashy battle. Dost thou remember the prophecy of the Wise Man of Doon? It said that descendants should arise from the blue sea of Tiernan of the Long Sword, who would spread his name and theirs far and wide over the green fields of Banba!"

Trean na Leam paused for a while. "By the faith of my body, O Prince!" exclaimed he, suddenly, "but the prophecy is true." And then he explained to Tiernan the marvel that befell Meergal beside the pool on the strand; how he stole her away when she was condemned to die, how the twin sons were born, and how they lived with their mother for the past seven long years in the castle built by the three Talking Masons of Glendorn. "And now, O Prince of my heart," continued the faithful Trean na Leam, "bring them back to thy palace, and we will train up the two sons of Meergal like good knights and brave, and they will lead thy vassals yet, with triumphant spears, in the red van of battle!"

And so Meergal and her two sons were brought back from their lonely castle to the palace of Tiernan, and ever afterwards the two boys were called by prince, knight, and peasant, Hugh and Brian, the Sons of the Salmon!

As the boys grew under the tutelage of Tiernan and Trean na Leam, they became great knights and warriors of renown. When twice seven years more had passed away, — when wars had been undertaken, and had ended in triumph to the Sons of the Salmon, when many a single combat had been fought and won, and when the renown of their great deeds had spread throughout all Ireland, — one day, as they were walking amid the garden of the palace, Brian turned to Hugh —

"The spirit of peace hath spread her wings over the land, Hugh," he said, "and our swords are rusting in their scabbards; what deeds shall we do to gain more renown?"

"I know not," answered Hugh. "Of the shields hanging in Tiernan's hall they make dishes for the table, and of the helmets on which swords clanged and war-maces battered in the red combat, drinking-cups for the revel; but for ourselves, we can do nothing — nothing, Brian, but to dance the dull years away with the fair maidens, and turn our thoughts to love!"

"For love I had no leisure heretofore," said Brian, "and I'll have none now, for this very day I am determined to set off on my adventures, like a bold knight, and not to return till I have won a kingdom for myself. Therefore are you to remain, and inherit Tiernan's domains. Look at this ever-blooming rosebush," continued he. "Dost thou remember the day I brought this from the Enchanted Garden in the Isle of Man? Now, every day during my absence, come and look at this tree with all its bright, shining flowers, and if at any time thou seest it withered, branch and blossom, then know that my life is in danger, and take thy boat and glide over the blue sea to my assistance."

Hugh promised faithfully to abide by the direction of his brother, and Brian, clothing himself in his armor, and taking his sword, and spear, and shield, set off on his adventures. A fair wind was blowing from the shore as he set the white sail of his boat, and sent it dancing gayly over the merry blue water. When he had sailed away many a league on the wide ocean, when no land was in sight, and when the sun was setting in a flood of purple and gold beyond the far horizon, Brian heard a confused but jubilant sound beneath and around him, and suddenly all the fishes that range the illimitable sea, came up from the azure depths, and began to gambol around his boat, — whale and porpoise, shark and swordfish, — and all cast a kindly look upon him as they arose, and all cried, "Welcome! welcome, brother!" as Brian sailed along.

"By the breath o' my body!" exclaimed a sagacious-looking old seal, at the same time shutting one eye, and looking through the other, with the air of a connoisseur in statuary, at Brian, "by the Rock o' Skellig! but whatever his nose or chin may be, he has the very eyes of his father."

"Tare alive!" said a truculent-looking old shark, as he licked his rapacious chops, "what nate tindher flesh he's made of!"

"You murtherin' ould robber!" exclaimed a good-natured and pious-looking whale, "is it afther makin' a supper av your cousin you'd be? Bad luck to you, an' all your sort, you mane ould bodagh!"

"Arrah, you cowardly ould bosthoon!" answered the shark indignantly, "'tis no such thing. I was only thinkin' o' the tundherin' male I had last spring, whin the two ships wor wrecked on thé Cliffs o' Moher."

"You wor, inyagh!" said the whale, at the same time sending a squirt of water into the eye of the shark, and then giving a playful dive beneath the boat.

"Blood an' turf!" exclaimed a sentimental old porpoise, that was swaggering along beside the boat; "begad, but your welkim, Brian! May that soord by your side gain you a princess that'll make you a better wife than the wife I got. Mavrone, the day that she gallivanted from me, an' wint surnadin' off wid another husband."

"Wisha, dheeling!" said an old grandmother of the mermaids to one of her neighbors, "isn't he a nate boy? I wish to my heart, that wan o' them gambadin' sthreels o' granddaughters o' mine wor here. Praps wan o' them might have the chance o' captivatin' him for a husband!"

"Yerrah, be aisy, you old jade!" answered the

other, who was a grim-looking old virago; "what is he to Prince Connor, that my daughter Mora tuck away wid her an' married? Och, aghragal, what ails you?" she continued, clapping her hands and addressing a huge fluke that floated suddenly up between her and her neighbor; "what happened to your face since I saw you last, an' turned your mouth the wrong way?"

"Wisha, then, I'll tell you, Maureen Glas," answered the fluke, with a sigh of misery. "'Twas all on account of an ould grandfather of mine — bad luck to him, the ould schamer! Wan day, as he was taichin' us to swim properly, an' perform vaarious ornamintal swivvilutions in the water at a ford near where the Laune runs into the say, who should come down the road, in the middle of all our fun, but a great ould magician. 'Twas a brilin' hot day, and the magician was sweatin', an' all covered with dust."

"'Begor!' said a little fluke, risin' to the top of the wather, an' lookin' up the road, 'that's the quarest ould man I ever saw!'

"'Tare-an-ages!' sis another, 'look at his beard! 'Tis like a bunch of say-weed!'

"At this we all laughed, for we couldn't help it; the ould man looked so quare, as he marched down with his thravvilin' staff in his hand.

"'Whist, ye oudacious thieves!' sis my grandfather, with a knowin' wink. 'He's goin' to take a dhrink at the foord, an' if ye stop, I'll make some fun for ye in airnest!'

"Well, the magician came to the foord, put his knees on a stone, and stooped down to take a dhrink. The very minnit his mouth touched the water, my ould villin of a grandfather swam up ondhernathe an' hit him a slap of his tail in the face, spatterin' him all over. At this I thought all our hearts would break laughin', but the ould man stood up, an' soon changed our tune.

"'Ye onnatural and inhospitable vagabones,' sis he, 'is that the way ye thrate me? Yeer laughin' at me. Stop so, with yeer mouths at the wrong side an' crooked, as an everlastin' mark o' my anger. An' you, you morthial ould sinner,' sis he to my grandfather; 'out o' that with you, an' march up to the side o' the hill.'

"With that, my grandfather marched out without a word, an' up to the side o' the hill, where the magician changed him into a stone. An' ever since our mouths, an' the mouths of all the flukes in the uniwarsil globe, are crooked an' at the wrong side o' their faces!"

"O, mille gloria! wasn't that great an' wonderful?" said the two mermaids.

"Keep out o' my way, ye ould viragos!" said the whale, as he passed the two old crones, after returning from his dive. "Keep in yeer places behind the boat, an' let us all conduct Prince Brian, our cousin, in pace an' quietness, to the kingdom where he's goin!"

And with that they all gathered round, and in joy

and jollity escorted Brian on his way over the blue, expanded sea. Three days did they accompany him, till, at the end of the third, Brian saw land before him, — a green and lovely land, — with the palace of its king shining like a great star amid the mountains. Brian landed, and proceeded to the house of an armorer, who dwelt hard by, and who also dealt in horses, and there bought a steed, properly caparisoned for a knight. He then went to the palace of the king, where he found it a day of revel and rejoicement, for all the princes, lords, and champions, from far and near, were gathered there, and contending in deeds of valor and strength for the hand of the princess, the king's daughter. Brian entered the tilt yard where those deeds were a doing, and there, by the might of his lance and the bravery of his spirit, conquered all before him, thus winning the king's daughter. And so they were married, and lived happily for many days.

One day Brian took his horse and hounds and sallied out alone, amid the green, silent mountains, to hunt. At length he came to a wide-extended moorland — a lonely desert that he had never looked upon before. On the verge of this melancholy plain, Brian sent his hounds forward to find the chase, and, after some time searching amid the green fairy ferns and purple heather bells, they started a large snowy-white hare, whose feet were as swift as the light wind that courses over the curling billows of the blue sea. Away she went across the moorland, and away went Brian and his hounds after her, swift as the shadow of the light cloud that glides in spring-time along the smooth, grassy sides of the sunny mountains. Away they went o'er beds of white canavaun and blooming heather, o'er bank, quagmire, and hollow, till at length, the hare leapt in through the solitary window of a little hut on the other verge of the moorland. Brian dismounted at the door, and entered the little hut, where he found but a huge, wrinkled, black-browed, and fiery-eyed old hag, sitting in the chimney corner. She was coughing and panting, as if she was after going on a hot summer day in a furious run, to the top of the highest mountain in Ireland, as the prince entered, and there was a torn wound fresh bleeding on her shoulder. The hounds surrounded her, and, with savage yells, attempted to tear her in pieces, but the prince beat them back, and drove them outside the hut.

"Who art thou?" said Brian.

"I am Grumach the Witch," answered the hag; "an' as I was runnin' on a message for the Fairy o' the Goolden Chair, your vagabones o' hounds chased me across the moorland, an', afore I could reach my home, bit me in the shoulder — a sore day for them, the murtherin' thieves!"

"The sun is setting," said Brian again, "and I cannot find my way back to the palace in the coming darkness — wilt thou give me lodging for the night?"

"Yes," answered Grumach, as she looked at him

with a malignant eye, " an' for many another night, too. Here, take these," continued she, giving him three long hairs from her matted elf-locks, " an' with them tie up in the shed outside, your horse, your hawk, and your unnathral villains o' hounds!"

Brian took the hairs and went outside the door, where they immediately became three strong cords, with which he tied up for the night his baying hounds, his horse, and hawk. As he returned and reëntered the hut, the witch struck him in the forehead with her wand, at which he suddenly fell down on the floor, transformed into a long thin slab of stone. The witch took the slab and placed it as a threshold for her door.

" An' now," she cried, as she performed some weird-like evolutions in the form of a dance around the floor, "you son o' the say, lie there forever; an' every mornin' as I go out, I can have my sweet revenge in walkin' over your neck! An' now, my son, Tarn the Giant, can go to the palace an' win the princess for his wife."

On that very day, as Hugh, according to his wont, went out into the garden of Tiernan of the Long Sword, he looked upon the rose-tree, and found it withered, branch and blossom. He armed himself and went down to the strand, and there set his sail and shaped his course over the merry blue sea in search of his brother. He had not gone far, when the fishes rose around and welcomed him. After three days, under their guidance, he arrived at the far land, where his brother lay in the witch's thrall, and saw the palace of the king shining brilliantly amid the green forest-clad mountains. He landed, and sat down on the bare sea strand to eat his dinner. He was faint with hunger, and as he was hastily putting the first morsel to his mouth, a gaunt and hungry wolf ran down the rocks anear, stood before him, and began looking wistfully at the tempting food.

"Here," said Hugh, "poor thin ribs, it shall never be said that I feasted while you hungered so pitifully;" and he gave him the first morsel, and another, and another, till the wolf seemed satisfied.

"And now, O Prince!" said the wolf, "if thou art ever in danger, call upon the Wolf of the Black Isles, and he will serve thee gratefully and well for thy goodness of heart!" and with that he departed.

After Hugh had swallowed a few morsels, he heard a great whirring in the air, and immediately a huge white eagle, lean and famished, alighted before him on the sand, and looked mournfully at him.

"Poor hungry-beak," said Hugh, as he gave the eagle food, "take this and be strong."

"I am strong, Son of the Salmon!" answered the eagle, when he had finished; "and if thou art ever in a difficulty, call upon the Eagle of the Wailing Pine Tree, and he will help thee." He then flew away.

When Hugh had eaten a little more, a large dog, poor and lame, limped up to where he sat, looked at him, and began licking his hungry lips.

"Poor Lame-leg," said Hugh, "here, take this, and gladden thy heart of misery with one good meal!"

"My heart is gladdened," answered the dog when he had eaten; "and now, if ever thou wantest aid, call upon the Dog of the Sparry Cave, and he will help thee;" and with that, cured of his lameness, he began bounding in delight up and down the strand, and at length darted up the cliffs, and disappeared into the woods.

Hugh finished his dinner without any further interruption, and then proceeded to the king's palace. There he found them in great woe and trouble, mourning for the absence of Brian. He heard also that a giant was devastating the kingdom far and near, and claiming the king's daughter, Brian's wife, as a bride for himself. Hugh staid in the palace that night, and next morning went down to the stables and chose a steed, and then, taking the remainder of Brian's hounds, he went out to hunt, hoping that he might find his brother. Away he went among the mountains, hunting, and wandering hither and thither for seven days and nights. On the eighth morning he rode down the mountains, and at length came upon the verge of that broad weird moorland, where his brother had been entrapped by Grumach the Witch. He then put forward his hounds to look for game, and immediately up started the White Hare from the fairy ferns, and led him and his baying hounds in a mad and troublous chase across the moorland. The hare leaped in, as before, through the window of the little hut, and Hugh found the witch panting and bleeding inside. As Hugh entered, Grumach started up in her rage, and attempted to strike him with her wand, but Hugh called loudly upon his hounds for aid, and they, darting in, began, in their mad fury, to tear her to pieces.

"Spare me! spare me!" yelled Grumach, as she felt the sharp fangs of the hounds. "Let me live, you vag—, you nate darlint, an' I'll give you back your purty gorsoon of a brother."

"Where is he!" exclaimed Hugh, at the same time beating back the hounds.

"He's here, the murtherin' rob—, the bould young prince!" answered Grumach. She then went to the threshold of the hut, struck the slab of stone with her wand, and immediately Brian stood before his brother. The moment that Brian was restored, the spell was broken outside; his hawk screamed with delight, his horse neighed, and his hounds, breaking loose, rushed in, and, with the other dogs, tore Grumach the Witch into a thousand pieces. Then Brian and his brother embraced, and proceeded back to the palace.

But since Hugh's departure for the hunt, great changes had taken place in the king's household. Tarn, the mighty giant of the weird moorland, had at length come to the palace, and compelled the king to give him the princess for a wife, saying that her former husband, Brian, was dead. Tarn also forced them to give a great marriage feast in his honor, and in the midst of that revel, as he was sitting by the unwilling bride, he told her that he would always have the form of a man by day, but that he was to be an eagle by night. Now, this giant could not be killed, because he had his life hid, no one knew where, and, except it could be found, no enemy could vanquish him. These things Hugh and Brian learned as they rode along.

When they arrived at the palace, they secretly discovered themselves to the princess, then disguised themselves, and hired with her as two serving-men. On the day of their arrival there was another great revel, in which the princess pretended to be very much enamoured of the mighty Tarn, and to fondle him with smiles, and glances, and sweet-toned words, by which means she thought to coax the secret of his life from him. At length he told her, with a grim and sagacious smile, that he had it hid beneath the threshold, at the door of the palace. When night came, and while Tarn, as an eagle, was soaring away on the wings of the wind over the melancholy moonlit mountains, Brian, and the princess, and Hugh dug and searched beneath the threshold of the palace door to find his life, but found nothing. In the morning, when Tarn returned, he asked the princess what she was searching for beneath the door, and she answered him, with many sweet words, that she wanted to find his life, to be caressing and fondling it. In the revel of that day, he told her that it was hid beneath the hearthstone in the great hall, that it might be eternally warm; but they searched there that night, and could not find it.

On the next evening, when the gay harps rang in the hall, and the dancers moved to and fro to the merry measure, when the mighty heart of Tarn was softened with the sparkling wine, he became so enamoured of the princess, by reason of her sunny smiles, love-lit glances, and dulcet words, that he at length confessed to her the truth, — that his life was hid in the ancient oak tree outside the palace gate; that when the oak tree was felled, an antlered stag would leap from its heart; that when the stag was killed, a wild duck would arise with outspread wings from his torn breast; that when the wild duck was in the act of being slain, it would lay an egg, and that if the egg could be broken against the skin of his forehead, he should then die.

That night they felled the oak tree, and the moment it fell, out bounded a noble stag, and rushed away towards the interminable labyrinths of the forest. Then Hugh remembered, and called loudly for the Wolf of the Black Isles, and immediately the wolf rushed out from a thicket hard by, and darted off in pursuit of the stag, which he killed beside the verge of the forest. When the stag was killed, out flew from its torn breast a brilliant and fleet-winged wild duck, which spread its pinions, and flew out over the calm star-lit sea. Hugh called out a second time upon the Eagle of the Wailing Pine Tree, which at that instant appeared, far out over the smooth sea.

But as the wild duck was dying, she laid an egg, which dropped beneath her into the deep green water. Hugh then called upon the Dog of the Sparry Cave, and the dog appeared upon the shore, swam out, far away into the sea, and brought up the egg, with which he returned to the palace, and there laid it at the feet of Brian, as the proper champion of the princess. All then waited for the coming of the giant in the morning.

In the morning, when the fierce Tarn returned, and saw the oak tree prostrate before the gale, he ran into the palace before they were aware, and clothed himself in his armor of proof, and put on his helmet, so that neither his face or forehead could be seen. He then came out, and demanded, in loud and angry tones, why they had felled the great tree. Brian, also, after arraying himself in his armor, came forth, and, with his sword in his hand, demanded battle on the part of the princess, his wife. Then the green sward was torn up with their armed heels as they moved to and fro, and round and round in the furious combat; but at length the giant struck Brian a heavy blow with his ponderous club, full upon the shoulder, and sent him reeling headlong, till he fell beside the trunk of the prostrate oak tree. The giant, then, with a loud shout of exultation, rushed over, with his dagger in his hand, to despatch Brian, but as he stooped, a withered branch of the tree struck violently against his helmet, and knocked it off, thereby laying bare his forehead. Then Brian drew forth the egg, and struck Tarn between the two fierce glaring eyes in the forehead, at which the giant fell backward on the earth with a loud clang, nerveless, and without strength. And Brian, as he fell, started to his feet, and with his keen sword, cut off the head of his foe. And thus the mighty Tarn, the son of Grumach the Witch, died. And the king on that day, being old, resigned his throne in favor of Brian, to reward him for his bravery, and thus Brian came to reign, and with his beautiful bride lived happily.

And now Hugh, seeing his brother sitting upon the throne, thought to himself that he would return to the palace of Tiernan. So he bade them all farewell, went down unattended to the shore, set the white sail of his boat, and sent it dancing merrily on the playful billows. And the fishes all thronged around once more to welcome him; but seeing him, as they thought, returning without renown, without pomp or lordly show, without spoils, and, above all, without a beautiful princess for his bride, like the inhabitants of dry land to a comrade and friend when the cloud of misfortune hangs gloomily over him, their sentiments changed, and they began to speak slightingly of the prince as he sailed along.

"Begor!" said a dapper little pinkeen to one of his comrades, "but we're disgraced forever wid our cousin! Tare-an-ounkers! if I wint to seek my forthin, an' cum back like him wid nothin' at all for my pains, but I'd die wid shame, and retire aftherwards to some disarted cave, an' there hide my head ondher the curtain av oblivion!"

"What a nate harmit you'd make," said a jolly porpoise who overheard him, at the same time giving all the company round a knowing wink of his left eye, "you obsthrapurous an' oudacious little sprissaun; how daar you compare yourself to a hairo like him? Arrah, you rampagious little atomy; if he only lifted his soord an' made a chop, he'd cut the worldt in two! But praps you're offinded wid his actions, an' would like a fight wid him to settle the differince!"

The pinkeen strutted about for a moment, and then answered modestly, that he "wouldn't mind a ruction, av id was conwaynient to all parties!"

At this a huge young whale, who was lying on the water sunning himself, emitted a roar of laughter, like a peal of thunder, lashed his enormous tail about him in the fury of his fun, and then gave a wicked bound on his watery pillow that tossed an ancient merman, who was sitting on his back all the time in the luxurious enjoyment of a short black dudheen, half a dozen perches into the air. Down came the enraged merman with a souse into the water, dropping his beloved pipe in the fall, and, after regaining it, and placing it, newly lit, in his left jaw, he raised himself, and looked indignantly around him.

"You unpronouncible, an' murtherin' an' sacriliginous young bligard of a robber!" said he to the

whale, "how daar you thrate a patriarch o' the say
in sich an onsarmonious an' outragious manner?
An' how daar ye, ye thurminjous an' ongrateful set
o' sparrow-headed savages, resave your own born
cousin wid such onpolite an' ongintlemanly woocifer-
ations? I repate and reitherate," continued he, after
giving a few oratorical whiffs of his dudheen, "that
ye should look farther into the Pligethontic and
Erebucious ragions o' nathure an' ferlosophy, afore
ye take upon yerselves the oudacity ov purnouncin'
on the latitudinous an' multifaarious powers o' mind
an' body av a human craythur, let alone a born
prince an' hairo av valior an' baligerant renown like
him in the boat! I supplicate attinshun to my thame,
an' obaygince to my ordhers, which I now preshume
to give regardin' this bowld an' magnanimous young-
sther. Ye must all know, if ye pay proper attinshun to my orathory, an' if yer brains are unadum-
brated wid the clouds o' dulness, that at the present
minnit Cuchullin, and Curigh mac Dhari, an' Conall
Cearnach, an' other immorthial hairoes of terraque-
óus renown an' fame, are besiegin' a great castle over
the say, where there is goold, an' pearls, an' darlin
princesses — conshumin' to the much will be left
there whin they rattle in over the ramparts, soord in
hand! An' now what's to be done? Why, to lade
our cousin — for ye all know that blood is thicker
than the wathery illiment — off to that siege o' valior and magnitudinity, an' av we do, I wociferate,
wid the hoith o' confidence and prognostical knowl-

idge, that he'll come back wid spoil, wid onquinch-able an' refulgent renown, an' above all, wid a beautiful, bloomin', an oncontrarious princess for a wife!"

"By all the sperrits in the say! an' by the powers o' Moll Kelly!" exclaimed they all, "but old Padhereen Gurm, the merman, an' his dudheen is right!"

And so they conducted Hugh far away over the azure fields of ocean, to that mighty castle which at that time Conall Cearnach and the other heroes were besieging. Long and bloody was the siege, but at last came the day of the final assault. As Hugh rushed up the breach over heaps of slain he became aware of a warlike and beautiful young princess, who stood in complete armor, sword in hand, ready to oppose his further progress.

"Yield thee, fair lady!" said Hugh, "for the sword befits not thy hand!"

"Never!" answered the amazon, "to an unknown knight like thee!" and with that she proceeded to demonstrate the truth of her assertion by immediate action, cutting off the plume from Hugh's helmet with the first slash of her sword. But Hugh soon showed her that he was no unrenowned knight, for he dashed the sword out of her hand by a parry of his own, and immediately took her prisoner. After the sacking of the castle he made her his wife, and, filling his boat with an abundance of spoil, he set its white sail and prepared to depart. This time, with his spoil, and his increased renown as a warrior, and with his beautiful and noble bride, the fishes came round his boat as it danced along merrily, and welcomed him upon the water with most uproarious good nature and jollity. At length he returned to his mother, Meergal, where Tiernan of the Long Sword resigned his rule in favor of him, where he frequently afterwards went out on many a bold foray with Trean na Leam and his gallow-glasses, and where he reigned with his beautiful and martial bride for many a year in joy and happiness. And thus fared Brian and Hugh, the Sons of the Salmon.

WINIFRED'S FORTUNE.

A STORY OF DUBLIN LIFE IN THE DAYS OF QUEEN ANNE.

THE oft-repeated aphorism, that truth is stranger than fiction, cannot be better illustrated than by the following story, which we happened to light on amongst the papers of an old staff officer, who died not far from Dublin, a few years ago, and who was descended from the hero and heroine of the tale. Changing a few names only, we shall proceed to relate the story just as it is told in those papers, without altering a single incident.

In a certain ancient street, not far from St. Patrick's Cathedral, there dwelt, in the commencement of Queen Anne's reign, an old man, named Sam Grimes. It was no figure of speech to call Sam old, for, at the time our story commences, he had just attained his ninety-eighth year. And yet, to an indifferent observer, he did not appear like one about to turn his century, for he was still hale and vigorous, and was endowed with that continual and jovial flow

of spirits that tends, more than rude health, to make
a man look youthful, even when he has progressed
far beyond the stage generally allotted to us as the
final one on life's journey. Keeping Sam's age in
memory, it will be seen what a number of wild and
stirring events he had witnessed since the day he first
opened his eyes upon the world's stage — events
which, from the happy temperament aforesaid, he
had ever looked upon as things to be laughed at,
and profited by, rather than as matters of fear and
sorrow. The Parliament was victorious, and the king's
head fell upon the bloody scaffold. What did Sam
care? Certainly he was a trooper in one of Cromwell's regiments; but beyond the actual fact of giving the malignants a thrashing, for the mere fun or
profit of the thing, he was not a whit concerned.
Cromwell died, and the "Merry Monarch" was
brought home to stultify high and low, rich and
poor, his own royal self among the number; but
still Sam Grimes, although no longer a trooper, was
as jovial as ever. James the Second, and William
and Mary, came and passed away; but it was still
the same with Sam Grimes. And why? Simply
because he was the host and owner of "The Jolly
Drummer," a tavern of renown in the city, and one
which was frequented and patronized by all kinds of
cavaliers, bucks, dandies, spongers, rufflers, gamblers,
and so on to the end of the catalogue.

Sam Grimes was rich; for, besides being the host
of "The Jolly Drummer," he was also owner of ex-

tensive wine cellars in the neighborhood. For many years he had been a widower. His only son, Abel, with whom, long before, he had some disagreement, was living in England, and there carrying on a thriving business as a wine merchant. Of this the neighbors were not aware at the period of our story; so they thought that old Sam's possessions, and the undoubted fortune he had made, would eventually fall to the lot of Winifred Walton, the old man's grandniece, who was living with him at the time. But old Sam, in his secret heart, thought more kindly of the absent Abel, and determined, at his death, to leave "The Jolly Drummer" and the wine cellars to him, intending, of course, at the same time, not to allow young Winifred to remain unportioned.

Winifred Walton was the pink of handsome girls. At the period to which we allude she was still in her teens; and in the populous city of Dublin there was no more handsome face than hers, no heart merrier or more guileless, no locks more golden bright and beautiful, no form more fair, no step more graceful, and no hand whiter and prettier than hers, as day by day she assisted old Sam in dealing out the wine goblets and ale tankards to his customers; for in those good old times girls of her degree and expectations were not above attending to their business industriously and contentedly. Winifred had received a good education, and this, in conjunction with a naturally refined mind, gave her a manner winning indeed, but at the same time one which effectually shielded her from the unpleasant attentions of the coarser sort of customers that attended "The Jolly Drummer." But if the revellers of low degree, in consequence of what they thought her haughty and distant demeanor, looked upon her, some with envious aversion and some with indifference, she was not without a plentiful array of admirers among the higher bucks and exquisites that frequented the house.

Foremost of Winifred's admirers was a gentleman dandy, whose name was Charles Parsons, or, as he was called by his rather numerous acquaintances, "Handsome Charlie," from the clear and almost effeminate complexion of his well-cut face, and from the exquisite taste displayed by him in dressing *a la mode* at the time. It was a marvel to those who did not know him intimately how Handsome Charlie contrived to indulge his taste for dress to such a degree, seeing that he had, long ago, got rid of his ample fortune in the dissipations of town life. But to the initiated few all this was easily accounted for; for the worthy Charlie had means at his disposal by which he seldom failed to recruit his fortunes, even at their lowest ebb; and many successive broods of poor pigeons, — in other words, young country gentlemen, — after undergoing a process of plucking at his hands, had reason to deplore the hour they first entered some secret gambling-houses in the Liberties, for, by means of certain nice implements, called cards and loaded dice, many a bright guinea was transferred from their pockets to those of Handsome Charlie and his associates. But the sun of fortune cannot always shine upon a gambler, no matter how experienced he may be. For a few months previous to the time of the following incidents, Handsome Charlie had met with a continued run of ill luck; and thus it was that, with his affairs involved still more desperately than ever, he and some of his companions entered the drinking-room of "The Jolly Drummer," on a certain Saturday night, in order to drown care in a stoup of wine, and look out for some stray pigeon whom they might entice to his plucking in the gaming-house.

"Come," said Charlie, holding up his pint of mulled claret, "we will, for once, drink confusion to Dame Fortune."

"Right!" exclaimed his companion. "Here goes! Confusion to the blind jade!" and each imbibed a copious draught.

"Ah," rejoined another, "she has treated us shabbily. Since the night that Charlie there emptied the pockets of the college buck, in Rainsford Street, we have scarcely got a chance since."

At the mention of the college buck, a tall young man, at the far corner of the room, turned round upon his seat, and cast his bold, roving eye, with a half-defiant, half-inquiring gaze upon the speaker and his party. Noticing this, Handsome Charlie touched the foot of one of his companions under the table, and, by a slight gesture, directed his gaze upon the stranger in the corner.

"Look!" said Charlie, in a voice half audible to the stranger; "look, Tom Fenton; upon my life there sits a second edition of the poor pigeon of Rainsford Street!"

After this, the whole party turned and looked upon the stranger, who now returned their gaze with a somewhat indignant brow, and a rather vicious sparkle in his eye.

"He seems game," whispered one of the party to Charlie. "I think I have seen him before; and, if it be as I imagine, I will venture my life upon a rough guess that we had better let him alone."

"Be it so," said Handsome Charlie. "I know, by the cut of his shabby beaver, that his purse is not worth the throw of a die. So let him alone. Here is to the health of handsome Winnie Walton, who goes yonder to give his sleeping draught of beggarly beer to the scurvy fellow!"

The latter, who had been listening all the while attentively, heard and understood the remark of the gambling exquisite. He took the silvered tankard, which, by the way, instead of beer, contained a full measure of hot sack, and smiling kindly upon Winifred, as he received it from her small white hand, stood up, and walked deliberately over to the table, around which his satirists were sitting.

"To whom am I indebted for the cognomen of 'scurvy fellow'?" said he, giving a general stare to the company. "To you, sir, I believe," continued he, at last, turning full and fiercely upon Handsome Charlie.

"To me, sir!" answered the latter, with a supercilious glance at the stranger. "Yes, I think I may acknowledge myself as father to the phrase."

"Perhaps," said the other, with a sneer, "you will also have the goodness to acknowledge the name of the worthy parent?"

"My name is Charles Parsons," answered the exquisite, with another insolent look.

"Very well, Mr. Charles Parsons," resumed the other, quietly. "I am a college man. My name is Rupert Russell, and you will find my chambers at No. 24 Old College Square, in Trinity. Take this to aid your memory;" and with that he dashed the measure full of hot sack right over the face and elaborate shirt-front of Handsome Charlie.

In an instant the latter was on his feet, the sack wiped, as well as his fury would allow, from his face and eyes, and his sword drawn, for we need not remind the reader that every gentleman in those days wore a rapier under his coat-tail. Charlie's companions had all imitated his example, one and all turning upon the stranger, who, with his face towards them, and his weapon extended, after the most scientific mode, in his right hand, now began to retreat to the corner of the room, in order to prevent himself from being surrounded. The moment he had gained that desirable spot, his assailants, headed by the now furious Charlie Parsons, were upon him, and the clashing of steel, as the brave young Trinity man parried the thrusts and lunges made at his chest and face, soon made itself heard in the outer room of "The Jolly Drummer," where, at that particular time, old Sam Grimes happened to be sitting in his huge arm-chair. Up started old Sam, with far more agility than might be expected from one of his age, and grasping a strong ashen staff, his constant companion, he strode into the inner room, where the unequal combat was, of course, promising to go soon against the bold Trinity man, although, however, he still held out stoutly, giving a few scratches to his assailants, and receiving a few slight ones in return. But old Sam had been preceded by young Winifred, who, seeing a general rush about being made upon the handsome stranger, darted between the combatants, in order to prevent further bloodshed, and was just in time to receive a sample of the reward of almost all pacificators in such quarrels, namely, an involuntary sword-cut in the arm from the weapon of Tom Fenton, the bosom friend of Handsome Charlie, and which cut was, of course, intended for the heart of the young Trinity man. At this juncture, old Sam Grimes came upon the scene, and, flourishing his ashen staff with a hand that had not lost its old dexterity at the broadsword, in an instant succeeded in striking up the rapiers of the assailants.

"Recover swords!" shouted old Sam, who, to the day of his death, never lost the military phraseology he had learned in his youth. "Right and left flanks, fall back in quarter troops; and centre retire in close order!"

This antique command was obeyed, sooner than it otherwise would, chiefly in consequence of the accident that had befallen old Sam's grand-niece. Handsome Charlie and his companions dropped their sword-points, and scowled sullenly upon the young Trinity man, who, supporting the drooping form of Winnie Walton with one arm, extended the other, with his naked sword, towards the group, and glared upon them in return, with a look of mingled scorn and defiance.

And now Charlie and his compeers had taken their departure, and Rupert sat upon a chair, still supporting the young girl, while Sam Grimes essayed, with a practised hand, to stop the blood and bandage the wounded arm.

"Keep your shoulder steady, Winnie," said old Sam, affectionately. "There, it's only a flesh wound. I trust a courageous girl like you for not being frightened at such a little scratch! Hold her elbow, good sir, for she shakes the limb so that I shall never be able to get this handkerchief properly round it."

"I was frightened," said Winnie, now recovering herself; "far more frightened than hurt, when I saw such a brave young gentleman about being run through the body."

A slight but sweet thrill shot through the heart of Rupert Russell, as he heard this acknowledgment from the beautiful young girl, who, suddenly conscious of his look, now blushed as red as the blood that was still trickling slowly from her arm, old Sam in the mean time applying some lint, which was brought by one of the attendants.

This was a nice situation for a warm-hearted and hot-headed young man like Rupert Russell to be placed in. After raking up our memory of all the novels, romances, and even philosophical treatises we have read on such subjects, after looking for innumerable historical incidents and parallels bearing upon the same, and throwing our own experience of the working of human hearts into the balance, we have come to the deliberate conclusion that there never was a young man placed in such a position that did not fall in love. At all events, all we can say at present on the subject is, that before leaving "The Jolly Drummer" that night, Rupert Russell delivered himself of a few affectionate, but rather confused phrases, to Winnie Walton, and then drank two rousing tankards of mulled sack to her health. He then proceeded, in an ecstatic state of heart and mind, along the street, and meeting and joining a set of his college companions, got into a thundering affray with a party of watchmen, which tumultuous scene had the effect of ridding him of some of his exuberant spirits, and after which he was enabled to retire to bed and sleep soundly. Early next morning he was awakened from a romantic vision, in which Winnie Walton figured as a fairy queen, by the voice of his college *chum*, Bob O'Mahoney, who was engaged in an animated conversation in the outer room with Tom Fenton, Handsome Charlie's friend. Bob was a tall, somewhat gaunt, but handsome student, with a head of curling, raven hair, and a pair of black eyes, which were ever sparkling with fun and devilment.

"I understand it all," he said, after Tom Fenton had laid the facts of the case before him. "It is useless to think of an apology from Rupert Russell, so the affair must be settled between himself and your handsome friend in the usual way. But what of the young girl's wounded arm, of which I have heard from my friend? Is that to be thrown into the shade altogether? As for my part, I say that it would be a sin and a shame to let it pass; for you know such a nice and delicate point of quarrel may not turn up again for a twelvemonth. In my opinion, then, the best, most friendly, and most delightful way of settling the whole affair is this, namely, to have Rupert Russell fight your friend for the cup of sack, and you to fight me at the same time and place on account of the wounded arm you gave to the fair maid at 'The Jolly Drummer.' Does this arrangement suit?"

"Admirably," answered Tom Fenton, who, whatever else he might be, was a man of courage. "For my part, I am quite content;" and after settling the remaining preliminaries, he took his departure.

We shall not go into the details of the double duel which was fought early next morning at Bully's

Acre. All we can say upon the matter is, that Handsome Charlie appeared at "The Jolly Drummer," about a week afterwards, with a lame step, and one of his arms in a sling, and that when Tom Fenton made his appearance, his sword-hand and his face showed many a deep mark of the amicable settlement he had entered into with the victorious Bob O'Mahony.

It is now full time to give some account of Rupert Russell, whose visits at "The Jolly Drummer," after the above occurrences, became day by day more frequent and regular; and for this purpose we must go back to those stormy days when old Sam's general, Oliver Cromwell, led his iron legions, with fire and sword, throughout the length and breadth of the land. At this period there lived in the ancient town of Tredagh, or Drogheda, an old gentleman, who, as a merchant, was one of the richest men in the town, besides being owner of a fine estate in a certain district near the shore of the Boyne. This old man had an only son, at that time a cavalry officer, fighting under the banners of the Kilkenny Confederation. After the investment of Drogheda by the army of Cromwell, and before the actual siege commenced, the old merchant contrived to escape; but so hurried was his flight that he was forced to leave his papers and most of his ready money behind him. In the general sack that followed, the house in which he had lived did not, of course, escape. It was plundered, in fact, from threshold to garret, and remained for many a year afterwards a frightful *souvenir* of the destruction committed during that terrible siege. Soon after his escape the old gentleman died, and when his son returned from the wars, he found the estate that should by right descend to him in the possession of a distant cousin, who had somehow or other gained favor with the government. After the Restoration, the poor cavalry officer entered into a suit at law to obtain possession of his patrimony; but, although he went so far as to prove his identity, and his right, in all justice, to the estate, the title-deeds had been lost in the sack of Drogheda, and the want of them turned the tables against him, after almost beggaring himself with the expenses of the suit. At length he died, leaving behind him, also, an only son. This son, following the example of his father, tried every means in his power to obtain possession of the estate, and in a lawsuit, which he had entered into during King William's reign, again succeeded in bringing affairs up to a point at which the production of the title-deeds would have made him successful. The loss of this suit broke his heart, and he died, leaving to mourn his loss a wife and daughter, both of whom soon followed him to the grave, and a son, by whom the losses of his progenitors were not a whit forgotten. This son was Rupert Russell, who was now living in Old Trinity on a somewhat scanty income.

We need scarcely say that, when the smallest member, even of a delicate machine, is put out of order, the whole construction is usually rendered unable to perform its stated evolutions. It was so with Handsome Charlie's hand, and we must remark, by the way, that a finer or more delicately constructed implement did not exist in the city of Dublin than that same member. One of the muscles that moved it had been almost cut in two in the encounter with Rupert Russell in Bully's Acre, and its master, being thereby rendered unable to handle either card or dice-box with his wonted dexterity, was reduced, during the month that followed, to the lowest state in his financial affairs. He still, however, frequently visited "The Jolly Drummer," but, of course, never either spoke, or gave cause of insult, to his late antagonist, except a stern look of hatred when occasionally their eyes met.

"Charlie," said Tom Fenton to him one evening, as they met together in the shabby garret that now served for their lodging, "I have been thinking seriously of your affairs lately, and have come to the conclusion that there is only one method by which to free yourself of your embarrassments. What do you think it is?"

"I am sure I don't know," answered Charlie, "except it is to cure my hand as speedily as possible, and take to box and dice once more."

"You must guess again," said Tom. "Your method is far too uncertain in your present need. Old Solomon's bill will be down on you before six weeks are passed, and when that time comes, you are sure to be disgraced and in prison. There is another plan."

"Out with it, then," returned Charlie, somewhat testily, "for I am in no humor for guessing at the present moment, I assure you."

"What would you think of marriage?" remarked Tom.

"Marriage!" exclaimed Charlie. "With whom, pray?"

"Let us see," said Tom, reflectively. "Of marrying in your own station there is now no chance. You must, therefore, descend a little, and try to make up in fortune what is wanting in birth and breeding. What do you say to Winnie Walton?"

"Between us both," said Charlie, "I have been thinking of her for some time past. But I cannot reconcile myself to bring disgrace upon an old family like mine by marrying one so far beneath me, be she ever so beautiful. Besides, I can see no way of bringing it about. Old Sam is too shrewd not to be aware that I have ruined myself long ago."

"Well, if it can be brought about, I advise you to proceed in the matter at once," returned the sage Tom Fenton. "If you were once married, and had the money in your hands, it would be easy to get rid of both wife and uncle-in-law. Away with us, then, say I, to 'The Jolly Drummer' at once, where you can pay your court, in the best matrimonial fashion, to the handsome Winnie, while I sound your praises in the ears of old Sam;" and off went both worthies without further delay.

As they were sitting over a preliminary cup of wine at the far end of the room, a number of students entered, and took their seats in the opposite corner. Among them was Rupert Russell, who, after gazing somewhat cavalierly on Tom and Handsome Charlie, sat down amidst his companions, and called for a supply of sack.

"You can now judge for yourselves," said Rupert, gayly, while they were waiting for the wine; "you, I say, that have not been here before, can see with your own eyes if she is not the handsomest girl in Dublin."

"'Pon my honor," said Bob O'Mahony, "I that have seen her will go farther, and say that she is the prettiest girl in Ireland."

"They are both in love," remarked another student. "Which, do you think, is most likely to win the affections of this lovely Hebe?"

"O," said Bob, looking under his swarthy brows a mock look of despair, "I resign my claims in favor of Rupert. You know she perilled her life for him; and in such a case no one has a chance when he is in the field. But here she comes."

"No staring," whispered Rupert, as his companions, one and all, bent their gaze upon Winnie Walton, who now entered with a large vessel of wine and some drinking tankards. "Come, come! She is a lady, every inch of her, and it is unfair to cause her a blush, especially as she looks so lovely to-night."

"Do you hear that!" whispered Tom Fenton to

his comrade in the corner. "Mark me, Charlie; you will have to look to it sharply, else you lose your best and last chance, for yonder crack-brained Trinity man is mad in love with the girl."

"I will look to it," answered Charlie, in a low but vehement whisper; "and if it were only to thwart him in his passion, — yes, him I hate as I hate the demon of darkness, — I will look to it, and win her, although he thinks himself so safe and pleasant in the matter. Come, my last crown is gone, and we cannot afford to have it known at 'The Jolly Drummer' that Charlie Parsons is at last penniless." With that the two friends stood up and left the house, Handsome Charlie revolving in his mind the best manner of gaining the good will of old Sam Grimes, in order that he might make known to the latter his intentions regarding Winnie Walton. Before he had reached home, however, he had come to the self-consoling conclusion that old Sam would be only too glad to have a gentleman of his birth and powerful family connections as a nephew-in-law; and it was finally resolved that night, between himself and his worthy adviser, Tom Fenton, that once the ceremony was over that bound him forever to Winnie Walton, the moment he got her fortune into his hands, he would get rid of her in some way or other, and set off for London, in which El Dorado the two villanous associates hoped to live a jolly life on the proceeds of their scheme.

A circumstance happened soon after that seemed

to aid gloriously their nefarious plan. At this time
the only theatre in Dublin was in Smock Alley; and
here the lively citizens thronged, night after night,
and made the roof resound with their applause of the
merry company that then occupied the stage. Among
the other play-going people was Sam Grimes's next-
door neighbor, Donat Connor, whose three blooming
daughters usually accompanied him on each merry
visit to Smock Alley. About a week subsequent to
the night whose incidents we have related above,
these three jovial girls not only persuaded their
father to take them to the theatre, but also coaxed
old Sam Grimes to allow Winnie to accompany
them; and away they all went, as happy a party — if
happiness can be measured by amount of laughter —
as could well be seen in the whole city. The play
was at length over, and the audience were in the act
of leaving the theatre, when they found the narrow
street outside half blocked up by a rude timber stage,
on which a merry-andrew, painted and bedizened in
the most grotesque and extraordinary fashion, was
playing off his capers, and bantering the dense crowd
around with an infinite amount of wit and volubility.
In this individual, as he now made the most ludicrous
grimaces at some over-dressed exquisite in the crowd,
and again gave forth the name, the life and actions,
and many of the secret affairs of some swaggering
buck beneath him, or made witty jokes on the rotun-
dity of some fat citizen, few would recognize Bob
O'Mahony, senior wrangler in Old Trinity, and bosom

friend of Rupert Russell. Bob O'Mahony it was, nevertheless; but of his identity not a single soul, either in Trinity College or in the whole city, was aware, not even excepting Rupert himself, who happened that evening to be away at a dinner party beyond the suburbs. Were he known, however, it would occasion but little wonder amongst the crowd, for the students of those days were in the habit of playing off some of the wildest tricks and antics imaginable.

The crowd around the stage had now become so dense that not a soul could make his or her way down the narrow street, and several dandies, who were accompanying ladies home from the play, were forced to stand with their fair charges opposite the porch of the theatre, without being able to advance a step. One of the exquisites, who had been bantered rather pointedly on his failings by the merry-andrew, by dint of elbowing and pushing, at length succeeded in advancing through the crowd opposite the rickety stage.

"Come," he exclaimed; "are we to remain here till morning, while that imp of sleight-o'-hand abuses us as if we were all begging impostors like himself? Down with him! Down with the ruffian mountebank, stage and all, and clear the street, if you are men!"

"Yes," exclaimed Bob O'Mahony, with a hideous grimace at the speaker, at which the crowd laughed uproariously; "yes, vade! begone! Clear the street, till Bully Jackson dances the hornpipe that his grandfather, the old posture-master of Marrowbone Lane, taught him. Clear the street, I say!" and he grinned again at the enraged Bully Jackson, turned a summersault, and grinned once more, till the whole crowd burst out into a roar of laughter that seemed to shake the ancient walls around them.

Bob now turned towards the throng of dandies before the porch of the theatre; but they, not relishing a similar display of wit at their expense, after whispering a few moments, all gathered together, and rushing forward in a body with their drawn swords, drove the crowd before them, the impetus of which in an instant overturned the rude stage, and Bob O'Mahony with it; he, however, with the agility of a cat, alighted on his feet amid the throng beyond, where he proceeded deliberately to disencumber himself of his spangled habiliments, at the same time exhibiting beneath a suit of most unexceptionable broadcloth. After whispering to a few students, who, in their turn, spread the intelligence he gave to their companions around, Bob, with a rapier which somehow or other he had possessed himself of, began forcing his way towards Bully Jackson; and at last a regular and uproarious scrimmage commenced in the street around the fallen stage. Men and women swayed to and fro, swords clashed, and clinched fists resounded upon sturdy chest and forehead, when, just as the uproar was at its highest, Donat Connor, who was a corpulent and aged man, found himself, with his three daughters and Winnie Walton, in the very centre of the fray. As he stood, perplexed and fearful, looking from side to side for some way by which to extricate himself and his charge, two gentlemen, who, we may as well say at once, were no other than Handsome Charlie and his friend Tom Fenton, pushed their way up to him, and bade him be of good cheer, promising at the same time to conduct himself and his charge safe through the roaring crowd.

"This way, this way, good sir," said Charlie, with great politeness, as he and Tom Fenton made their way before him towards the wall opposite the fallen stage. "Quick, or yonder break in the crowd will be filled up in an instant."

Donat Connor puffed and pushed onward, the four terrified girls following, and Charlie and his companion clearing the way in front, and at last had the satisfaction of seeing himself and all safe on the other side of the crowd. Charlie and Tom now offered their services to escort the party safely home. The latter they accomplished without further adventure, and that night Handsome Charlie had the satisfaction of receiving, over a tankard of wine, the marked and especial thanks of old Sam Grimes for the services he and his companion had rendered to Winnie Walton.

Next night Charlie attended duly at "The Jolly Drummer," and over another tankard of claret began making his overtures to old Sam with regard to

Winnie. The cautious old fellow listened for a long time without a word, merely nodding his head with a shrewd wink at the brilliant pictures and alluring episodes of domestic happiness, of which the eloquent Charlie was delivering himself.

"My estate is not entirely gone," said Charlie, "not so far sunk but that a little money would redeem it."

"I understand," said Sam, at last venturing to speak.

"And," resumed Charlie, "if I marry your niece, who, I must say, is fit for any man in the kingdom, you, of course, would get rid of this business, convert the whole concern into ready money, and come to live with us in the country, for I am heartily tired of the wickedness of the town."

"Probably," echoed old Sam, with another sagacious wink.

"Then," said Handsome Charlie, "we had better, I think, come to business at once. What fortune will you be able to give Winnie? I am thus particular, seeing that my estate stands in need of present redemption."

"Well, sir," answered Sam, shaking his head dolorously, "I am much grieved to disappoint your expectations on that score. I am a far poorer man than they say; and the fact of it is, I think, if my niece were to get married to-morrow, I could scarcely leave her even my old boots, which I haven't worn since the sack of Drogheda, where I had the honor of serving as one of Cromwell's troopers."

This answer Charlie at first pretended to take as a good jest; but when it was repeated by old Sam, with perfect earnestness and solemnity, he became convinced that the chance of redeeming his estate, or, in plain language, of enabling him to pursue his career of dissipation by means of Winnie's fortune, was but a poor one indeed; and after another cup of wine, hastily took his departure, and repaired to his garret, where his bosom friend, Tom Fenton, was awaiting him.

"Well," said the old fellow, with an additional wink at a huge arm-chair opposite, as Charlie went out, "if that is not as sweet-tempered and angelic a young man as I ever met in the whole course of my life, my name is not Sam Grimes! Good as he is, though, I do not think I can give him Winnie and the old boots."

Handsome Charlie, on getting the rather disheartening answer from old Sam which we have related above, for some time gave up all thoughts of Winnie Walton, and once more turned his attention to the alluring vicissitudes of the gaming-table.

Now it was that he hated Rupert Russell with that bitterness and intensity of which only a man mad in love is capable of feeling towards a successful rival. He sought, however, no occasion of public quarrel with Rupert; but from the depths of his own burning heart he swore to be avenged upon him at the first opportunity. And that opportunity speedily presented itself.

One night Charlie and three of his companions were returning from a masquerade, and, entering a narrow and deserted street that led beside "The Jolly Drummer," saw, by the indistinct light of a solitary lamp that burned in the distance, the figure of a man approaching.

"Now," whispered Charlie, "we cannot be recognized in our masks and strange dresses, and if this be a Trinity man coming down the street, we will give him a little pinking to accelerate his motions towards Alma Mater."

The figure had at length approached within a few perches of where they were.

"Hush!" whispered Charlie, peering sharply through the gloom. "By my soul, but it is the very man I want! It is Rupert Russell! Now, boys, stand to me for once, for I swear that man shall never leave the street alive."

Rupert — for it was he — was coming down the street, with his right hand to the wall. According to the custom of the time, it was his right to pass inside Charlie and his comrades; but it was not their intention to allow him that almost universally conceded privilege.

"Stop, sir!" hissed Charlie, in a feigned voice, as Rupert came up; "out with you, and let your betters take the wall."

"You'll have to fight, then, for the right of way," answered Rupert, stepping back, and instantly drawing his rapier. "The wall I must and will have; so I warn you, gentlemen, to pass on, else —"

"Else what, sir?" hissed Charlie again, now quivering with passion, as he found himself face to face with his hated rival.

"Else I will run you through the body," answered Rupert, making a sudden lunge at him, which Charlie succeeded in parrying without a scratch.

"Pink him! pink him!" shouted the companions of the latter, as Rupert placed his back to the wall, and prepared to defend himself.

"Yes, pink him!" echoed Charlie. "Toss the base hound's body into the gutter!"

"Some of you will go first," retorted Rupert, undauntedly, as he succeeded in plunging his rapier through the shoulder of the man nearest to him. "How do you relish that, my friend?"

The man literally gave a yell of agony as the cold steel was withdrawn from his flesh, and now attacked Rupert with implacable fury. The result of the contest was, that the four masqueraders, taking away with them some signal marks and tokens of Rupert's prowess, left the insensible body of the latter behind them, lying in a pool of blood upon the solitary street. About half an hour afterwards, as a belated bacchanal was making a number of sinuosities down the street, he stumbled over Rupert's body, and the fall sobering him somewhat, he scrambled to his feet, and called eagerly for assistance. Rupert's body was immediately borne back to "The Jolly Drummer," and there laid upon old Sam's capacious arm-chair to await the arrival of a surgeon. When the latter arrived, he found that Rupert exhibited still some symptoms of life. He bandaged up the several serious wounds that the young student had received upon face and limb; but there was one near the region of the heart which he paused over for a long time before making a decision regarding it. At last, after a most minute and careful examination, he pronounced it not mortal; and when it was dressed, poor Rupert, still almost insensible, was conveyed to bed.

It was broad daylight when he awoke to consciousness. When he did so, he was barely able to give an account of the transaction as it had occurred; but he could not give the slightest guess as to the names of his assailants. The news of the affair soon spread, and a vast amount of indignation was thereby aroused in Old Trinity amongst the students, by all of whom Rupert was greatly beloved.

Rupert was in good hands, without any mistake; for Winnie Walton nursed him through the long illness that followed, as only a loving heart could nurse the object of its adoration. At length he arose from his weary bed, and witnessed, with a throbbing heart, the joy displayed in every way by the guileless and lovely Winnie at his recovery. One morning, as she left the room in which he was sitting, with a sweet smile upon her bright face, he registered a vow within his burning and grateful heart, that, come what might, he would, when strength returned, ask her to become his wife. And he kept his vow, and was, as the reader will easily guess, accepted by the loving Winnie.

The next business was to communicate with old Sam Grimes. Rupert felt a little perturbation at the thought of encountering the shrewd old fellow regarding such a delicate affair; but Sam seemed to take it all after the best fashion, merely answering, however, in the precise words with which he had put off Handsome Charlie. But Rupert was not to be disposed of so easily.

"I care not," he said, "what you can give her. I will now turn my thoughts to a profession, and trust to be able to marry her independently after a short time."

"I advise you to marry her at once," returned old Sam, with a wink of mysterious meaning at Rupert. "My will is made, and believe me, neither you nor my grand-niece will regret its wording when I die, notwithstanding the old boots."

And Rupert did marry her at once; and we will venture to say that a lovelier bride than Winnie was not seen for many a year by the Liffey shore. Sam Grimes, on the wedding day, wrote a letter to his absent son. Whether it was that the old fellow drank too much of his own sack that night, our authority does not say; but however it was, Sam Grimes died the day after the wedding, and was buried with all due solemnity in St. Patrick's. About ten days after the old man's death, Abel Grimes came over from England to act as executor to his father's will. The latter was opened in the presence of Winnie and her husband and a few witnesses, and after the usual preamble, Abel read out, in a full-toned, satisfied voice, the words that gave and bequeathed to him his father's property, without a single reservation, save one. This went on to say that —

"Forasmuch as my grand-niece Winifred Walton has lived with me since her infancy, has been to me even as a daughter, and perchance better, and has always been obedient to orders, from reveille to shutting up of camp, I therefore give and bequeath to her my old boots and their contents, which are locked in the black cabinet in my bedroom, and which I have never worn since obeying my lord the protector's orders at the sack of Drogheda."

The black cabinet was opened, and the huge pair of old jack-boots brought to light and examined. They were both filled with coins of silver and gold, chiefly of the latter, one of them, namely, the left, having only a top layer of silver, the remainder being all gold. When this glittering heap was removed, Rupert found, in the foot of the right boot, a mass of papers and a parchment, which, on his examining them, to the infinite astonishment of all, proved to be the title-deeds of the lost property of his fathers.

Aided by the persuasive contents of one of the old jack-boots, Rupert soon entered into another lawsuit, worked it up to a certain turning-point, as his father did before him, then produced the title-deeds, and won the long-contested property. To his splendid mansion beside the Boyne he then removed in triumph with his beautiful wife, and there both lived happily during many a bright day and revolving year.

Handsome Charlie, some time after, failing to recruit his fortunes at the gaming-table, was lodged, by the old Jew Tom Fenton had threatened him with, in a debtor's prison, where, for two years, he continued daily and nightly chewing the cud of sad experience, at the end of which time, by the death of an old aunt who had not forgotten him in her will, he was enabled to release himself, and came forth a sadder, but a wiser man. The lesson he had brooded upon in prison effectually cured him of his gambling propensities; but he still relished the town, and lived there till his death, always the most fastidious and exquisitely dressed old bachelor in the merry city of Dublin.

LEGEND OF TIERNAN;

OR, THE BLUE KNIGHT.

LONG ago, when vale and mountain were clothed all the same in the great primeval forests with their hues of green and gold, there dwelt a chief in Mumha,* — young Tiernan was his name, — and his castle towered full grandly by a weird and dreamy wold, where the streams leaped glittering down, like linked lines of silver flame, to the feet of Cnoc-an-Affrin gray and old. And happy were his days in that castle on the height, hunting boar or wolf at morning, making love full fond at e'en — ah! all that e'er in human kind was beautiful and bright in the face of that youthful knight was seen! One early dawn, as blithely through the woods he led the chase, the span of two brown mountains he had left his train behind, when he came by deep Lough Mora, on a lonely fairy place, where the leaves wooed the

* Munster.

pleasant cooling wind; where around him dells mysterious spread from hill to crag-crowned hill,—a region wild and lonely, a land of airy dreams,—where you could hear that morning clear but the blackbird's bugle shrill and the sounds of the gushing golden streams!

And there, in that blithe sylvan place, amid the summer mountains, he reined up his golden-bitted steed, Bran Finneirg,* and halted at the foot of a great oak tree. The huge branches of this mighty tree towered up in a thousand gnarled and fantastic spirals towards the blue heavens, and, then spreading out, formed a thick canopy of glistening emerald leaves over the northern verge of a blooming meadow, that, gleaming all over with its gay mountain flowers, extended in one unbroken and verdurous belt around the stilly margent of the lake.

As Tiernan looked out through an opening in the branches, whom should he see but the Fairy Princess Mora, leading out her kine from her home beneath the lake to pasture upon the blooming meadow! Few mortal eyes have beheld those beautiful kine since that blessed morning; but those that have seen them — the favored ones, the seers, the double-sighted, the beloved of the Children of the Air, or Daoine Siodhe (the visitors to the merry raths and golden meads of Tir-n-an-Oge) — say that their bodies and limbs are smooth, glossy, and white-glittering as the wintry

* Bran, the Wine-red.

snow upon the top of Stackeen-na-Mona,* all without spot, stain, or blemish, save their delicate, sleek, wary ears, which are rose-red as the lips of my sweetheart when she smiles upon me at the jovial dance by the boundary stone of Aha-na-Rinky.†

Tiernan held his breath in delight and wonder as the lovely herd emerged upon the meadow. Behind them walked the Princess Mora in the light of eternal beauty, a garland of ever-blooming flowers encircling her radiant brow, and her long, yellow hair flowing down over her robes of eery and sunny splendor. As he looked upon her the heart of Tiernan filled to overflowing with a sudden, gladsome, and uncontrollable love, as a golden bowl brims over with the generous wine brought by the dusky foreigners from the sunny lands of the south to the green shores of holy Ireland. And there he gazed and gazed in a fit of rapt and silent happiness till the beams of the early sun began to smite upon the fresh meadow over the tops of the tall forest trees. The moment the first beams fell upon the snowy herd, Mora put a glittering little diamonded whistle to her rosy lips, and blew a tune sweet as the singing of the birds in the dewy April wildwoods. At the sound her obedient kine turned and moved to the shore, to regain their enchanted home beneath the lake, all save one, the monarch of the herd, which, taking

* The little Summit of the Bogs.
† The Ford of the Dances.

some refractory vagary into his head, after smiting the green grass with his hoofs, and lowing till the caverned hills around replied in a thousand echoes, darted in an opposite direction across the meadow, passed the great tree under which Tiernan sat concealed, and then disappeared, like a flash of light, amid the thick, leafy labyrinths of the forest.

As she saw the favorite of her herd thus escape her, Mora gave a wild cry of mingled surprise and anguish that smote sadly upon the love-laden heart of Tiernan, who now, without a moment's delay, gave the spur to Bran the Wine-red, and darted off in pursuit of the fugitive with a swiftness that soon brought him close upon the track of the latter.

"Ha!" exclaimed Tiernan, as he at length caught a glimpse of the white bull beneath him in a valley. "Now I see that I have not chased the wild cattle in vain over the rough slopes of Crotta Claith and the highlands of Sliav Gua. Now my wood-craft will stand me in good stead in the hour of need!"

With that he unwound a mighty thong of tough, dried bull-hide from around the bow of his saddle, to the end of which was attached a round iron ball. Holding this ball and the coiled thong in his hand, he put Bran the Wine-red to his topmost speed, and at length came up with the swift-footed bull, as the latter dashed down an open glade beside the stream that ran through the valley. Quick as the lightning flash that darts through Barna on a stormy night in autumn, he now cast the iron ball from his hand, and then, by a sudden jerk, whirled it backwards, bringing by its means the far end of the thong, coiling and coiling a dozen times around the foremost legs of the bull, which fell forward heavily on the grass. In an instant he was out of the saddle, and by the side of the prostrate bull; and there, after uncoiling the thong, and twisting it securely around the horns of the now subdued fugitive, he jumped once more upon Bran the Wine-red, and led his captive back in triumph to the green meadow by the lake.

There Mora stood to receive him, and, as a reward for his gallantry, took him and his brave steed to visit her enchanted home beneath the lake. And when they reached her bright palace, where it stood on the ever-blooming borders of Tir-n-an-Oge, she said,—for her heart began to fill with love for the graceful and brave young knight,—

"O Tiernan, choose thee between the region thou hast left, and this bright and lovely land—choose thee betwixt my love, which will last forever, and the fading love and the fading beauty of the maids of Mumha—of the earth!

And Tiernan chose to remain with her in her bright home.

"And now, O Tiernan, the beloved," she said, "thou canst visit green Mumha betimes, to give aid to the poor, the forlorn, and the down-trodden. Many are the widows that shall weep soon in that lovely land, for the strangers—the pirates of Normandy—are coming across the sea to glut themselves, by falsehood and treachery, in the blood of the free-born Irish clans."

"Then," said Tiernan, "it befits me not to remain inactive here, for by my vow as a good knight and true, I am bound to succor my native land, and fight for her, like a brave man, in her day of distress."

"Thou shalt go forth in her hour of distress, I tell thee," answered Mora; "but remain here till the evil day comes. When thou goest I will arm thee as befits a knight, and woe to him who shall meet thee breast to breast in the red van of battle!"

And Tiernan dwelt with her for a time in her fairy home. But the evil day came too soon. The Norman robbers landed in Wexford, and in many another coast town of Ireland, and commenced to pillage, and burn, and slay, after the manner of the ruthless Danes, whom Brian smote upon the bloody field of Clontarf.

Then it was that Mora clothed her young knight in a suit of blue glittering mail, put the sharp-shearing, double-edged sword of justice and valor in his hand, gave him her hawk Sulgarra,* which ever sat motionless with outspread wings upon his helmet for a crest, brought him his steed, Bran the Wine-red, and sent him forth from Tir-n-an-Oge to aid the oppressed, to comfort the forlorn, and to do battle, like a brave knight, for his native land. And when he again appeared in Munster, the husbandman who

* Sulgarra — *Sharp-eyed.*

tilled the land by the wayside, the shepherds who tended their flocks upon the green hills, and the soldiers — the kerne, the galloglasses, the hobbelers — who marched forth to battle, looked upon him with wonder wherever he appeared, and called him the Blue Knight, from the color of his mail.

And now, Strongbow and Raymond le Gros laid siege to Waterford. The brave citizens fought with stout hearts for the defence of their country and their homes, but their bravery availed them not, for the Normans made a wide-gaping breach in the wall, and dashed into the town, slaying all whom they met, — child and soldier, maid and wife, — till their career was stayed for a while at Reginald's Tower, which Gillemaire, a brave Dano-Irish chief, with the Lord of Desies, held against their fiercest onset. At length the stronghold was also taken, and Gillemaire, and the Lord of Desies, who fought side by side upon the gory stairway, were surrounded and about to be slain, when the Blue Knight suddenly appeared between them, cut a path for them through the thick press of the savage Normans, and led them out over the slippery breach, and into the open country, where he left them in freedom and safety, and there disappeared amid the lonesome glades of the thick forest.

Many a time afterwards he appeared in that war-wasted country, and was always the doer of some deed of mercy, of justice, or of valor. At the battle of Bierna, in Offaly, where O'Dempsey defeated the

Normans, it is said by the Seanachies and Minstrels that it was by the Blue Knight's sword that Robert de Quincey fell — he who was the son-in-law of the mighty Strongbow.

In those days there lived in the county Waterford, beside the Suir, a Dano-Irish chief, named Olaf Gluniarn, or Olaf of the Iron Knee, who had one daughter, Christine, the loveliest lady in the land. She secretly loved young Hugh of Raynagh, an Irish knight, who was away at the wars of Thomond. Now, her father, Gluniarn, had his own ideas of matrimony, and on a certain day sent heralds through the country with the intelligence that the bravest man should have his daughter in marriage, and that for the proof the chieftains, Norman, Danish, and Irish, were to assemble in the great bawn of his castle, and see the matter out with sword or spear amongst themselves.

A sad heart had young Christine for the absence of her lover, when, on the third and last day of the tilting, Hugo de Ridensford, an old Norman knight with one eye, was about to be declared the victor. But when Gluniarn was just putting his daughter's hand into that of old Hugo for the betrothal, a trumpet sounded at the gate, and the Blue Knight, with the hawk Sulgarra sitting proudly upon his helmet crown, rode into the bawn. The trial was short and deadly, for the Blue Knight ran his spear through the remaining eye of old Hugo de Ridensford, and slew him on the spot. Then the victor took the beautiful Christine by the hand, placed her suddenly before him upon Bran the Wine-red, and ere gillie, henchman, or chief could bar his way, dashed out through the gate, and into the forest, amidst which he was soon lost to their pursuit. The minstrels say that he took her to the lake, and gave her to the keeping of Mora for a time; and truth was in their saying, as you shall soon hear.

One day, as Roderic O'Connor and Donal O'Brien, Prince of Thomond, were marching towards Durlas O'Fogarty, where Strongbow had challenged them to battle, young Hugh of Raynagh, who was with the vanguard of the Irish forces, sat himself down, sad and sorrowful, beneath a tree at noon, when the army had halted to rest and refresh themselves. There he thought upon young Christine with many a melancholy sigh, for the news had reached him of what had befallen her. Suddenly he was aware of the Blue Knight sitting anear him upon Bran the Wine-red, beneath the cool shade of the tree.

"Sigh not, Hugh of Raynagh," said the Blue Knight. "Bear thyself like a true Irish soldier in the coming battle, and thou shalt have thy true-love back again at thy return."

Then Hugh of Raynagh took heart, and swore on the hilt of his sword to avenge his country like a man.

Next morning the two armies met face to face at Durlas O'Fogarty. Then came the war-cries, the fluttering of advancing banners, the clattering of

spears, the whizzing of arrows, and the clashing of
the good swords upon the rings of chain armor, and
the stout corselets, as foe met foe in the swaying and
raging battle. At first the Normans prevailed, for
the Irish line was broken in passing over some un-
even ground; but suddenly the Dalgais were aware
of the Blue Knight in their midst, rallying them and
leading them on, Bran the Wine-red overturning
horse and man in his way through the Norman
ranks, and Sulgarra clapping his wings and screaming with a shrilly and unearthly voice that rose high
over the deafening clangor of battle. But now
the Normans gave way, and the Irish, victorious
right and left, pursued them, and slew and slew, till
scarcely ten knights were left by the side of Strongbow as he fled from the bloody field of Durlas O'Fogarty.

Hugh of Raynagh bore himself that day like a
man, and received his true-love, young Christine,
some time afterwards, from the hands of the Blue
Knight.

In the songs of the bards and minstrels, and in the
stories of the Seanachies, it is said by some that the
Blue Knight often appeared afterwards amidst the
Irish troops in the hour of peril and misfortune, leading them on to victory, and showing them that they
were not to fight for clanship, or creed, or gain, but
all for the welfare of their native land; by others,
that when he found them battling amongst themselves, and sometimes even aiding the foreigner, he

disappeared from Mumha of the Green Valleys, to live with his chosen love, the Fairy Princess Mora, in Tir-n-an-Oge, and that he is to appear again when the people, with stout hearts and hands, and the dauntless souls of freemen, shall arise to fight the battle of right and liberty upon their native soil.

THE RESCUED BRIDE.

A LEGEND OF THE CUMMERAGHS.

THERE is not in all Ireland a range of mountains grander, more savage, and at the same time more abounding in the elements of the picturesque, than the Cummeraghs — that gigantic tier of summits, which, beginning in abrupt bluffs and swells beside the "lovely sweet banks of the Suir," stretch southward through the county Waterford, and slope down to the very seaboard beside Dungarvan. The wild territory embraced in this range is an unknown land to the tourist. Yet here nature can be contemplated in all its grandeur, and the traveller who ventures to explore those wild scenes, when he returns to his comfortable hotel in one of the adjacent towns, will scarcely fail to express his satisfaction at what he has witnessed. Commencing at the romantic valley of Glenpatrick, near Clonmel, should he make a circuit round the entire range, he will meet about a dozen lakes or tarns, some of considerable extent, and each with a name suggestive of its own peculiar characteristic. Over these solitary lakes the mighty crags rise in perpendicular ridges, in many cases to the height of several hundred yards, and throw their black shadows upon the still and lifeless water beneath. Nothing can be grander than to stand upon the desert shore, strewn with its naked boulders, and gaze up to the stony pinnacles overhead, where the hawk whistles shrilly as he prepares to dart upon his prey, and the gray eagle expands his strong pinions, and floats majestically upward through the blue, silent, summer sky.

The wanderer who wishes to obtain a true idea of solitude has only to ascend to the highest point of one of those giant summits and look around him. There nature seems entirely dead. No sound will break upon his ears upon a calm day, save the drowsy hum of the mountain bee, rising like the low tone of a fairy trumpet in the distance, and dying away again over the golden moss or purple heather, only to render the solitude more silent than before. But a calm day is of very rare occurrence in those elevated spots. When the wind is strong, wild and indefinable impressions of vastness, awe, and loneliness will crowd through the tourist's brain, as he sits upon some fragment of rock looking at the black volumes of cloud flying before the gathering storm, and listening to the blast booming amid the fissured crags, and whirling and bounding from the sharp edge of the ridge down upon the lowland moors and deserted valleys.

This region is rich in legendary lore and tradition. The enchanted prince of O'Donoghue is said to hold state beneath the blue waters of Killarney, the great earl, Garret of Desmond, abides with his spell-bound knights and barons in a cave beside the sunny waters of Lough Gur, amid the broad champaign of Limerick, and according to the same popular belief, O'Brien of the Silken Bridle has made his home in a vast pinnacled crag that rises like some ancient and barbaric castle at the entrance of Coum Airach, a savage, rugged, solitary, and basin-shaped valley, containing three small tarns or lakes, and appearing as if it had been scooped out by the hand of some Titan of old from the breast of Moneyvolla, or the Boggy Summit, one of the most elevated mountains of the great Cummeragh range. Many a strange tale is told of this enchanted prince. The peasantry still firmly believe that on certain nights he rides down the mountains at the head of his mailed warriors, as if to make a progress through his principality; and, not content with this, many of them will tell you that they have had actual ocular demonstration of the reality of these nocturnal pageantries.

"What's the name of that rock?" said I one day to a young peasant girl, whom I met by the shore of the Clydach, a stream that has its source amid the steep Cummeragh valleys. I pointed to the huge crag at the entrance of Coum Airach.

"Sure, sir," answered she, "I thought every one knew that. That's the palace of O'Brien, the fairy prince o' the Cummeraghs."

"Is he ever seen in these parts?" I asked again.

"Wisha, faith, he is, sir," she replied; "an' I have good raison to know, for I seen him myself, wid all his men, last November eve!"

"That's more than I thought any one in the whole county could say. Where did you see him?"

"I'll tell you how it was, sir," she resumed. "Myself an' Nancy Power, our servant girl, went down to the ford, beyant there, late that night, to bring home a can o' water. I was just goin' to raise the can upon Nancy's head, when we both heard a sound upon the lonesome road that lades down from the mountains to the ford. It was for all the world like the tinklin' o' bells. You may be sure we got afeard the minnit we heard it, an' both of us ran into the grove beside the ford to see what would happen. We waited there for some time, till the tinklin' an' jinglin' became louder an' louder; an' at last what did we see comin' down the road in the moonlight but a long string o' horsemen, like an army, with the most beautiful young man in the world ridin' in front o' them, his sword in his hand, an' a mighty lot intirely of darlin' blue feathers wavin' on the steel cap he wore on his head. The horsemen that followed had also their swords drawn, an' every man o' them — the young gentleman an' all — wore blue cloaks, ondher which, as they passed the ford, we could see their bright steel jackets glittering in the moonlight. Their bridles an' trappins were all jinglin' an' ringin' wid grandeur, as they came down an' began to cross the stream. Nancy an' I were shiverin' wid fear as we looked out upon them, but they spoke never a word, an' they looked neither to the right nor to the left, but passed on till they were all across the ford. They then wound up the bridle-path to the mountains, towards Coum Airach, an' when they reached the mouth o' that valley we lost sight o' them altogether. I suppose they shut themselves up in the palace till next November eve!"

There are, however, stranger tales even than the above connected with O'Brien's fairy palace.

Many and many a year ago, as the story-tellers have it, there lived at the foot of the Cummeragh mountains a rich farmer, named Dunlevie, who had one daughter. Mary Dunlevie was a very beautiful girl,—just as good as she was handsome,—and as she was known to have a good fortune, her hand was sought in marriage by many of the richest young farmers in the barony. But it was hard to please her in a husband. At last, however, a wooer came in the person of Tom Power of Glenora, who pleased both father and daughter. The match was soon made, the wedding day came on, and they were married. Tom Power was the happiest man in the county, and on the day of the "Hauling Home"—in other words, the day of the removal of the bride to her husband's dwelling—there never was such a "let out," as the peasantry call it, in the pleasant valley of Glenora.

Three days after the "Hauling Home" Mary disappeared mysteriously from her husband's house. None knew whither she had gone, or what had befallen her. Search was made throughout the whole county, and even her distracted husband went across the Suir to search for her through the fertile plains of Tipperary, but still no traces of her could be found. At last poor Tom, in his despair, paid a visit to a celebrated fairy man, or herb doctor, who lived in Glenpatrick, and asked him for tidings of his missing bride.

"If you came to me before," said the fairy man, "you'd have but little trouble in finding her; but now I fear it is too late."

"Why is it too late?" asked Tom. "Just tell me where she is — you'll be paid well for it — for if I once knew, no mortal man would keep me from bringing her back!"

"Alas!" answered the spaeman, "she is at present in no mortal hands. Tom Power," he added solemnly, "your wife is at this moment in O'Brien's palace, nursing the young fairy prince that was born the other day; it is now the first of March. You'll have to wait, I fear, till May eve before you'll get a chance of bringing her back. Meantime, take this little purse. It is full of the dust of a certain kind of blossom that has great power. If you can throw that dust upon your wife's head, she will be restored to you; so you had better watch near the palace as often as you can. You may see her even before May eve if you watch well. But," added the spaeman, "it will be impossible for you to see the fairy palace without my help. When you go up to the mountains, take the path that leads by Lough Mora, and never show a faint heart at what may happen you on your way."

May eve came, and in its dim twilight Tom took the path the wise man had told him of to the mountains. As he reached the shore of Lough Mora, a boundary ditch between two estates stretched before him. He climbed the fence, and gave a bound to reach the green turf at the other side, but instead of reaching the ground, alighted upon the back of a huge black horse, which seemed as if it had arisen from the solid earth beneath. And now, by the glaring eyes of the animal, and the thundering sound of its hoofs, Tom knew that he was on the back of the Phooka, or phantom horse of Lough Mora. Remembering the parting advice of the old spaeman, he kept up his heart, stooped forward, clutched the long flying mane of the phantom steed, and thus holding on, prepared himself for the terrible run that he knew was before him. Away darted the Phooka, now rushing quick as lightning up the hills and across the giant crags, or plunging through lake and torrent, till, after what appeared almost an age to his rider, he stopped suddenly, reared on his fore legs, and pitched poor Tom into a dark, damp hollow, in what seemed to him the midst of a wide and unknown forest. With a loud neigh of triumph he then disappeared.

Tom sprung to his feet, shook himself, and finding himself unhurt, looked around him. Above him still towered the savage crests of the mountains, with their yawning valleys between. Up to one of these latter, which Tom recognized but too well, he saw a bright and noble road, leading through the sloping forest, and down this was walking, at a stately and leisurely pace, a withered little atomy of a man, with a cocked hat and a beautiful set of bagpipes under his arm. Tom waited in wonder till the little man had reached where he was standing.

"A happy May eve to you, Tom Power," said the little fellow as he came, with a dignified and polite bow.

"The same to you, sir," returned Tom. "May I ask you where that road leads to?"

"Why, you omadhawn," answered the little atomy, much hurt, "oughn't you know by this that it lades to the palace of O'Brien of the Silken Bridle? Howsomdever, come on. I'll lade the way, and the devil may care who pays the piper!"

With that he put his instrument in order, and marched up the bright road, Tom following.

"What tune do you like?" asked he, turning suddenly round.

"'The wind that shakes the barley,'" answered Tom, scarcely knowing what he said.

"'Tis a lucky tune!" rejoined the atomy; and with that he struck it up with a joyousness that made Tom feel as if he could fight all the fairy princes in the world for the sake of his lost wife.

"Now," said the little piper, as he finished the tune, "I'd play you up the tidiest *moneen* you ever heard in your life, only I haven't time. Look up. There is the palace afore your eyes. One you know bid me to tell you to stand in the porch an' wait till the company comes out upon the lawn. You'll see your wife comin' out with them. A word is as good as a sermon. You have the purse o' Lusmore dust in your waistcoat pocket. All I can say is, use it when you see your wife." With that he struck up the "cricket's rambles through the hob" on his instrument, and marched straight back again down the road, on which he soon disappeared.

The fairy palace was now blazing in all its splendor before Tom's astonished eyes. He ran over to the grand porch, and concealing himself behind a tall pillar, stood waiting for the revellers within to make their appearance. He had not long to wait, for in a few moments a splendid train of lords and ladies began to make their exit from the palace, in order to have a moonlight dance upon the green lawn outside. Tom's heart bounded, as he at last saw his wife with the baby prince in her arms, walking out in the midst of the procession. He had emptied the contents of the purse into his hand, and now waited cautiously till his wife came opposite to where he stood. Then, in an instant, he cast the whole handful of Lusmore dust upon her head. The moment he did so, a wild and angry yell burst through the hollow chambers of the palace, the fairy babe was snatched away, the bright throng disappeared, and Tom Power and his wife found themselves standing alone, and clasped in each other's arms, at the foot of the mighty rock that guards the entrance to Coum Airach!

There was joy once more in Glenora, and it need not be said that Tom Power did not forget his promise to the successful spaeman.

THE BIBLE OATH.

OF all the passes leading from Cork into Limerick, Barna Dearg, or the Gap of Blood, was the most steep and perilous. It lay at the eastern extremity of Sliabhe Ballyhoura, — the Mountains of the Dangerous Ways, — not inaptly so called, for in the old wars many an escort and detachment were cut to pieces amidst their boggy and treacherous defiles. A beautiful mountain peak, with a continuous ridge of rocks stretching from base to summit, rises at the eastern side of the pass. This mountain was anciently called "Sliab Caoin," or the Hill of Lamentation, either from the numerous battles fought at its base, in the pass, or from the mourning of the Irish warriors over their prince, Mahon, who, according to tradition, was murdered here, in the tenth century. Towering over the pass at its western side, and crowned with huge detached masses of gray crag, rises Cnoc Aodh, or the Hill of Hugh, a celebrated outlaw.

A calm September moon was shining along the

silent ridges of this hill, as a solitary sleeper lay in a recess at the base of one of those piles of rock near the summit. The moonlight half illuminated the recess, and showed the dark, stern features of the sleeper, as he lay in a somewhat uneasy posture, his head resting against the naked crag. His large frieze coat formed a safe protection from the night dews; his hat had fallen off, and lay near his right hand, which clasped one of those rusty, long-barrelled hostler pistols, many of which since, perhaps, the wars of King James, have remained among the peasantry. His sleep was fitful and unsettled, for he knit his brows, and muttered from time to time incoherent sentences; and again, after a short interval of rest, clutched the pistol firmly in his hand, or stamped against the opposite wall of rock. Gradually his words became more distinct. " Peggy an Gleanna, why did you lade me—why did I lade you—asthray, is id? Do you remember your 'tarnal ould villin of a father, an' his doin's? Who laid my fusht cousin low, on Mologga Green? an' who kilt my brother? My black revinge on ye all! That's id, Shemus Mor! Ajm the timple—no place like the timple for a sore blow. Thrample him! Hurroo! *Thurrum a skian!** Ha, ha! Mihaul Dhuv, take that, an' that, an' that between the ribs!" The dreamer started to his feet with a sudden spring, thinking that the fight was actually raging around him; but nothing met his eye except the large rocks

* Give me a knife!

with their black shadows and the undulating expanse of heath, with its purple bells, stretching silent and drowsily beneath the moonbeams.

"My sweet curse on you for a drame, body an' sowl, to wake me out o' my nate sleep, an' I wantin' id so much! *Mo churp an dhioul!* there goes the dead-bells again. I heard id twice before this blessed night, an' for good or for bad 'tis plain enough now — but no!" Here he crouched forward, put his ear to the ground, and started again fiercely to his feet, as the tramp of horsemen and the jingle of their accoutrements rose distinctly from a deep ravine, running in a slanting direction towards the summit, from the foot of the hill.

"'Tis the bloody yeomen, the cowardly set o' mudhawns! They can't hunt a man in the middle o' the day, but for fear he'd turn on 'em with a bould face, they'll ever an' always thry an' cum on him in his sleep, the thraitors. I hear your voice too, Dhonal Brien! — the blood o' my brother an' cousin is on your head; but Diarmid Dhu Sheehy isn't the son of his father if he dosen't settle your accounts for you, an' that soon an' suddint!"

In a few moments he could hear the step of the horses more plainly, and see the swords and carbines of the yeomen glittering in the moonlight, as they moved up towards the rock, led by a tall, dark figure, a few paces in front. Diarmid crouched low in the shade, moving along the base towards a huge dark rent, which led to the highest point of the crag. He succeeded in clambering up unobserved, and placed himself among the heath and long sedge at the brow, where he felt himself secure of retreat; for a dark expanse of heath, intersected by deep drains and glens, extended behind him almost as far as the eye could reach. A body of about twenty yeomen soon made its appearance upon the hill, and formed a semicircle in front of the rock beneath him. Dhonal Brien now stepped forward from their centre, and stood, when within a few yards of the recess which Diarmid had so fortunately for himself abandoned.

"My nate fox, that was so 'tarnil cute, you're caught in your dhrames at last. Come on, gintlemen; you can't see him in the dark; but as sartin as my name is Dhonal, the murtherin' villin is inside."

Diarmid now moved still farther towards the edge. A savage and exulting light shot from his eyes as he aimed the long hostler pistol at the breast of Dhonal. Its loud report rang wildly among the crags, and Dhonal Brien, the father of Peggy an Gleanna, rolled and kicked in the throes of death, between the horses of the yeomen. These redoubtable champions, when they saw the fall of Dhonal, turned their horses, and fled in the wildest panic and disorder down the sides of the hill. But, in a short time, finding no enemy upon their track, they returned and bore away the body of the fallen man. Diarmid, too, had turned and fled, but, of course, in a different direction. Finding himself at length a safe distance from his late sleeping place, he sat down at the bottom of an abrupt glen, through which a clear brown stream danced merrily by him from the mountains, and, about a mile from where he sat, strayed out with many windings and glintings into the beautiful plain of the Blackwater. Less than a furlong beneath him, the glen widened into a low, rushy meadow, in the midst of which lay the ruin of an old farm-house, adding in its desolation to the wild loneliness of the scene.

While Diarmid is sitting in the glen, occupied in his sombre meditations, it is necessary that the reader be brought into somewhat closer acquaintance with him. His mother was a celebrated fortune-teller and herb woman, whom the peasantry called Breadh an Lus, or, Bridget of the Herbs, and who dwelt in a lonely hut at the bottom of the pass of Barna Dearg. In his boyhood he lived with his mother and brother — his father, a famous faction fighter, being dead at the time — in a still more lonely hovel, on the southern declivity of a hill which rose nearly a mile northward of the pass. Here, one evening, while his brother was away in the neighboring village, his mother, for some trival cause, beat him while in the field, and in a fit of rage he struck her in return, and rushed into the house. His mother looked after him, and soon saw him issuing from the door, with a cloud of smoke behind him. He had set the house on fire. From this time, as he grew up to manhood, he associated with, and became the prime favorite of, all the fighters and sovereign-gatherers of the surrounding villages. At one time he had to fly the country on a charge of murder, and his mother heard no more of him for a year or so, till one night he was brought home by his comrades to her hut in Barna Dearg, dangerously wounded in an attack upon a gentleman's dwelling, a few miles away. But to return to the legend.

Diarmid sat by the stream. "I have done for him at last," he said, "the bloody-minded ould informer. Him an' his murtherin' faction was the manes o' killin' my brother an' cousin; but he at laste will never inther a fair field again. Them misfortunate dead bells, they're never out o' my ears! Ha! *homon-an dhioul!* I have id at last, what was weighin' on my mind! I made my ould mother tell my own forthin once, an' I have reason to remember id now. She tould me, the ould thief, whin I heard three dead bells in wan night, an' the last rung upon a soord, to prepare for my reck'nin' in a month. I *have* heard um this night, an' no wander it makes me unaisy, for the ould woman was just beginnin' to cry, an' she tellin' me. Whist! what's that?" Here he bent forward to listen. A low, weak cry, accompanied by one louder and more plaintive, stole up the glen from the walls of the old ruin. It soon ceased, and a figure, bearing in its arms something like a child, issued into the moonlight from the broken doorway, and moved in the direction of where Diarmid sat, up the meadow. He could now distinguish it more plainly. "'Tis the Banshee! As sure as I hould

this pishtil in my hand, 'tis the Banshee! But no;
who ever heard of a Banshee carryin' a child in her
arms?" By this the figure had moved up the glen,
and stood within a perch of Diarmid. He started up.
"Peggy an Gleanna, is id you an' your child? and
what brought ye here!" Peggy an Gleanna — for it
was she — stood like one rooted to the spot. She
clasped her child convulsively to her breast, and for
some time could make no answer. "Is id you, I say?
an' what brought you before me this time o' night?
Answer me, or by the morthial 'twill be worse for you."

At length she spoke: "I little thought, Diarmid,
that whin I seen you, this was the welkim I was to get.
My own misforthin' an' your doin's that brought me
here, whin they dhriv me like a wild baste from my own
door. But no matter. This place is disolit an' wild
enough for one like me, an' myself an' my poor child
can die in pace in our scailp * below in the ould ruin!"

"There is wan, at laste," said Diarmid, suddenly
and strangely changing his mood; "there is wan, at
laste, who can never be to you like the black world;
an' that's myself. I thought to have my wild revinge
on ye, seed, breed, an' gineration; but you — at laste
regardin' yourself — have changed my black hate
into fondness. I led you asthray, Peggy, but you
know well how my heart warmed to you before an'
afther id."

"Yes, Diarmid, that's your way ever since the

* *Scailp*, a little hut made of sods and branches.

evenin' we met first at the dance on the Green of Daragh; fair an' fond whin you're near me, but carin' little when you're away. Sorrow an' disolation came wid your fondness, an' have stuck close to me ever since. Home an' me are strangers now; but there'll be an ind to id all soon, for the heart widin me is broke at last."

"As for the matther o' home, Peggy, what can I do? I am chased an' hunted day afther day, an' from place to place, like a wolf o' the glins, an' have to burrow in the mountains at night like a fox. Ha! that reminds me. Dhonal Brien, your job is dun. Black-hearted thraitor, you'll never more bring the cowardly yeomen on the track o' Diarmid."

A shrill and piercing shriek here interrupted him, and Peggy an Gleanna fell senseless to the earth, her little child tumbling from her arms, upon the grass, at its father's feet. Diarmid ran and brought some water in his hat from the stream, some of which he sprinkled over her temples, and she soon revived. She took the child in her arms again, and stood up faintly.

"You have dun for him — is id? The ould father that nursed me on his knee whin I was a child, an' depinded on me, and prided in me, whin I grew up an' my mother died! May the heavy curse of an orphint an' deluded an' broken-hearted girl light — but no, Diarmid, there are curses enough on your head idout adding mine!"

She turned and fled from him with her child, down

the glen, and Diarmid, with her wailing and the death-bells ringing in his ears, turned also, and strode away in an opposite direction.

About three weeks after his meeting with Peggy an Gleanna, Diarmid sat in his mother's hut, in the gap of Barna Dearg. It was a dark and stormy night, and he could hear distinctly, as he sat, the blast tearing through the brushwood that clothed the sides and bottom of the pass, or moaning and howling savagely through the chinks and caverns of the ridge of rocks that extended to the summit of the hill. His mother had placed a dun-colored, rickety table near the hearth, on which stood a large black bottle, looking proudly down in the red fire light, like a lord amid his vassels, upon a few glasses and two cracked teacups. There was a cloud upon Diarmid's brow as he turned to his mother.

"Mother, that was a black fate you foretould for me the night I made you find out an' tell my forthin."

"You onnathral vagabone, you," answered Breadh, "'twas too good for you. For what should I be marciful to you that niver was like a son to me, bud iver an' always bullyin' an' yowlin' at me, whin you cum back from your dipradashins!"

"To tell God's thruth, mother, I was a rale bad son, an' run bad coorses, an' must run them again, I suppose; but whin my black fits hadn't hoult o' me you know I always thrated you well."

Breadh now began to relent at her harshness, and

turned to console him, but was interrupted by three low yelps, like those of a young fox, which seemed to proceed from some spot close outside the door of the cabin. "That's Shemus Mor's call," she said, as she hastened to unbolt the door. In a few moments a tall, rough-visaged, red-haired man strode in, and after the usual salutation, commenced conversing in a low voice with Diarmid. A variety of other calls and whistles followed, to each of which the door was opened, until at length about a dozen men sat round the table.

"Here is tattheration to the bluddy magisthrates, an' may the wheels of our own carriages blind their cunnin' eyes with spatthers o' splindhur!" said a smart, fair-haired young fellow, at the lower end of the table, after the glass had circulated a few times. This produced a low laugh of approval among the auditory.

"An'," rejoined another, "may the coals from our pipes burn the noses off o' their sarvints, the tarnil fools o' yeomen!"

"Yis, the magisthrates," exclaimed Shemus, "only for thim an' their hangin', an' burnin', an' purshuin', the bluddy traitors, we'd have pace an' quietness; — we could settle our differences among ourselves, an' could go to fair, patthern, and meetin' wid light hearts, an' dance an fight to our hearts contints wheniver we wished."

"*Magister* — *magisthratus* — which, expounded scholastically, manes greatest — 'the greatest rogues,

I suppose,' said a little, imperious looking man with a hooked nose, at the upper end of the table. This was one of the hedge schoolmasters of the district, a classical scholar, and having at one time a flourishing school; but who, from his unlimited fondness for ardent spirits, had, perhaps, increased his popularity, but lost his scholars. In the company of Diarmid and his associates he could gratify his appetite for drinking to the fullest extent. "*Magisthratus*, indeed. 'Pon my bright soul, *Magisthratii imperium regunt, nunc dierum*, which, illuminated to non-scholiasts, manes that the magisthrates have come to the chief sway at present — a nate and speedy descent to them from their iambics!"

"By gor!" whispered a black-visaged young fellow — a blacksmith — to the person next him, "thim sledge-hammers o' words o' Misther O'Regan's would be nearly heavy enough to weld a piece of red iron. Yerrah," continued he, addressing the man of learning, "can't you descind a little, sir, an' spake in a way we'll understand you?"

The master cast a look of speechless contempt at the blacksmith, and was at length about to reply, when Shemus Mor interrupted him.

"Don't mind that aggravatin' thief, Misther O'Regan, bud give us that purty song you sung at Bill Noonan's weddin' long ago. 'The Hurlin' Match,' was the name of id, I blieve."

"'The Brigade's Hurlin' Match' — yes. 'Pon my soul and imagination — an imagination, too, which my fraternal scholiasts were obligated to asseverate, was remarkable for the richness an' spontaneity of its effusions — 'pon my soul bud id gives me shupreme pleasure, *ad infinitum*, to enlarge upon the bravery an' magnanimity of those indomitable warriors — *homines bellicoses*, as the Latins say. They went to foreign and remote territhories from their native region; — *armis et castris rem tentare*, that is to try the forthin o' their arms, an' the terraqueous an' revolvin' globe is acquainted already with their Spartanic exploits."

He would, perhaps, have held forth much longer on his favorite theme, the bravery of the Brigade, had not several voices called out for the song. After swallowing another glass of whiskey, he commenced in a somewhat mellow voice —

THE BRIGADE'S HURLING MATCH.

In the South's blooming valleys they sing and they play
By their vine-shaded cots at the close of the day;
But a game like our own the Brigade never saw —
The wild sweeping hurlings of Erin go Bragh!

Our tents they were pitched upon Lombardy's plain;
Ten days nigh the foeman our army had lain;
But ne'er through his towers make we passage or flaw,
'Till we showed them the game played in Erin go Bragh.

Our sabres were sharp and the forest was nigh,
There our hurleys we fashioned ere morning rose high:
With the goal-ball young Mahon had brought from Dunlawe,
We showed them the game played in Erin go Bragh.

Our captain stood out with a ball in his hand,
Our colonel he gave us the word of command;
Then we dashed it, and chased it, o'er esker and scragh,
While we showed them the game played in Erin go Bragh.

The enemy stood on their walls high and strong,
While we raced it, and chased it, and dashed it along,
And they opened their gates as we nearer did draw,
To see the wild game played in Erin go Bragh.

We left the round ball in its roaring career,
And turned on the foe with a wild, ringing cheer.
Ah! they ne'er through our bright, dauntless stratagem saw,
While we showed them the game played in Erin go Bragh.

Their swords clashed around us, their shot raked us sore,
But with hurleys we paid them in hard knocks galore;
For their bullets and sabres we cared not a straw,
While we showed them the game played in Erin go Bragh.

The fortress is taken, our wild shouts arise;
For our land and King Louis they ring through the skies;
Ah! he laughed as he told us a game he ne'er saw,
Like the wild sweeping hurlings of Erin go Bragh!

"Here, Misther O'Regan," said Shemus Mor, when the yells of approval had subsided, after the finishing of the song, — "here is to your nate windpipe; an' may it become as sweet as the fairy's chanther that plays every night in the moat o' Glanisheen!"

"Cum!" exclaimed the young blacksmith, maliciously interrupting the reply of the schoolmaster, and trying to change the subject of conversation — "cum! here's that the divil may cut the toes off all our foes, that we may know them by their limpin'!" and in a loud, waggish voice, he began singing a stave of an old song —

" Their bodies an' sowls they'd sell,
Their bodies an' sowls they'd sell,
Bud the divil may care; at pattern an' fair
We'll meet them wid valior, an' bate them well! "

when the schoolmaster broke in — " Benighted ignoramus, whisht, I say!" But the blacksmith could not be stopped so easily —

" Bud the divil may care; at patthern an' fair
We'll meet them with valior, an' bate them well,
An' sind them both bodies an' souls to hell! "

"Whisht, hathen! Why should you, who can hardly repate a Pather — why should you, I reitherate, presume to spake about the burnin' ragions of Phlegethon an' Styx?"

"By gor, sir, if you say I know nothin' about sticks, your head must be gettin' light in airnest! Blud an' turf! man, who saisons all the fine tough old sticks for the fencin'-masther bud myself?"

The schoolmaster did not deign a reply, but struck the table. "Taciturnity — silence, I say. Have any o' ye ever heard an exposition regardin' the infernal ragions? — hell I mane."

Here Diarmid, who could not get rid of his warning of the death-bells, began to manifest some interest in the conversation.

"Have any o' ye," continued the schoolmaster,— "have any o' ye ever heard a dilation exthraordinary upon hell an' its torments? Seldom, I suppose. Listen. A flamin' an' roastin' prison extends foreniut my terrified and reluctant optics. Its flure is a burnin' lake, smokin' an' glarin' wid fire, in which the sowls of poor misforthunate sinners swim — navigate I mane — in torthure an' disolation. Have ye ever seen a man in armor — *homo perarmatus*, as the bright stars o' hathen times, the poets, say? — a man clad in mail — in a shuit of iron. I supplicate ye for an infinitismal period to imagine that shuit of armor, hated red hot, an' a man placed inside in it. His pain, an' anguish, an' torture in it would be unmarciful, an' widout ind or limitation; but if myriads o' ragin' madmen congregated round him, wid red, flamin' steel spears in their hands, an' thrust them through his softened and half melted shuit o' mail, tearin' an' conshumin' his flesh, what would be his tormints then? 'Twould be the most magnitudinous pleasure an' pleasing delectability to the tormints an' pains o' hell!"

Diarmid, during this sudden burst of the schoolmaster, began to exhibit signs of displeasure and somewhat of terror. "What!" he murmured to himself, "what if the warnin' be thrue, an' my time nearly out. Is there no way, or plan, to settle the matther? Yis, an' only wan, which I have been thinkin' of this long while." Here he started up, striking the table violently with his clinched hand.

"*Honom-an-dhioul!* man, bud we have enough to thrubble us idout your praichin'. I have run the worst, an' most sinful, an' misforthunate course of any one round this table, an' yer chruel account ought to be unwelkim to me. Bud, at any rate, this blessid night I'll set my own sowl on the safe thrack, if I can. Did you remimber what you towld us last year, when we wor all cum to prove Dan Moran free — that God wouldn't stand our false oaths, an' what's more, that He hates all lyin' an' perjury?" He strode down to an old cupboard in the corner of the cabin, returned with a worn, soot-stained old prayer-book in his hand, and knelt down beside the table. "God," he exclaimed, "hates perjury, an' that's rale gospel thruth. Now, upon this blessed an' holy book I make my Bible oath that I'll never go to hell, an' God is marciful, an' hates lies, an' will never make a perjurer o' me."

He started to his feet, dashed the prayer-book on the table, and looked triumphantly at his companions. But in their countenances, bad as they undoubtedly were, he could see no manifest approval of his impious oath. No one spoke; each looked at the others with a strange feeling of awe; but silence was at length broken by Mister O'Regan, whose brain the whiskey was beginning to lighten more and more.

"You're wrong, Diarmid, wrong *in toto*. The fallaciousness of your conclusion depinds upon an eternal and indestructible principle, which I'll repate presintly, after laying down the premises of my argument. *Primo*, if we lade a wicket life, widout sorrow for our transgressions, or emendation in our aetions, we deserve hell, an' shall get id. *Secundo*."

Here his syllogism was cut short by Breadh, who had by this time totally lost her patience.

"Yerrah, boys!" she exclaimed, "will ye spind the whole night listenin' to the sarmints o' that cracked ould villin? Ye came here to do somethin', an' the whole night is gone, talkin' an' drinkin'."

"Thrue for you, Missis Sheehy," said the blacksmith; "'twould be fitther for us before this to be inthratin' a few soverns below at Pad Murphy's o' the Moat."

"'Tis too late now, boys," broke in Diarmid, anxious to be left at ease for the night; "we settled to be there at eleven, an' 'tis now past wan at laste. Shemus Mor an' myself will meet ye undher this roof this night week." So the party broke up.

That night week came, and with it a storm as before. The moon was at its full, but a heavy sea of watery cloud overspread the sky, beneath which the valleys lay dim and plashy, filled with a dubious kind of light, worse than utter darkness. In the hut of Bridget of the Herbs the same party were met; but they did not sit so devotedly round the table as on their last meeting, though it stood invitingly with the bottle and its companions beside the fire. It seemed, by their elaborate preparations, that they were for setting out on some dangerous adventure.

Two ancient-looking, long-barrelled guns, which their exulting owners denominated "Queen Anne's," lay below the bottle upon the table; a group of three men stood in the red glare of the bog-deal fire, examining the locks or brightening their crazy old pistols; others stood round the hut, in various attitudes, some fastening the tops of scythes upon handles, in imitation of swords, some filling their old hats with hay, to ward off blows upon their craniums; but the most extraordinary figure of all stood right in the middle of the floor. This was Shemus Mor, who was that night to lead the party, Diarmid, by a previous arrangement, — perhaps remembering the warning of the death-bells, — having consented to act the part of a subaltern in the attack. Upon his head Shemus had fastened, in an inverted position, a small chair for a helmet, with the rungs of the back protecting his face, and two straw ropes, loosened from the bottom, sticking up and leaning jauntingly to one side between the legs, like a plume. For a corselet he had fitted a horse's saddle across his breast, with the stirrups carefully knotted behind; and as he stood, with his ancient "Queen Anne" in his left hand, and a huge rusty pistol in his right, he looked a most ludicrous representation of a knight of old — a *homo perarmatus*, as Mister O'Regan would say — a man armed cap-a-pie. The helmet was to protect his head from the murderous blow he was sure to receive when entering the door at Pad Murphy's of the Moat, and the corselet he intended to shield his breast from the still more fatal stab of scythe-blade or hay-fork, certain to be aimed at him the same time.

"By gor!" he exclaimed to his comrades, in immense delight at his appearance; "by the gor o' war, an' there's not morthial bein' more like him than I am myself this blessed minnit; bud I bein' ye're gineral, and Diarmid here my liftenant, we'd bate out the brigade that Mister O'Regan was gallivanthin' about the last night we wor here."

Mister O'Regan, who had swallowed a little too much whiskey in the beginning of the night, sat dozing by the fire. At the mention of his name, however, he roused himself somewhat; but, instead of Shemus Mor and his warriors, he fancied himself among his pupils.

"*Sol ruit, et montes ambranther*," he murmured, and then continued more audibly, " parse that, Charley Casey — yes. Decline *sol*, Billy Murphy. Nominative *sol, the sun* — yes. Genitive *solus, alone* — is id? 'Pon my immaculate honor, bud you're both alone an' unique in that declinsion, at any rate."

Here he sank again gradually into slumber, and the party, well knowing his want of valor, left him to his repose, and headed by Shemus Mor in his panoply, and Diarmid, proceeded on their expedition. They wound silently along the base of the mountain, and descended at the opposite side into a low, marshy glen, down which a stream, having its origin between two high hills, and now much swollen by the rains, dashed and roared through the darkness.

They followed the course of the torrent for some time, till at length, turning up a stony path to the right, they came in front of a large farm-house, the devoted garrison of Pad Murphy of the Moat. On they went, as stealthily as possible, over the scattered and broken pavement of the yard, till they arrived before the door; and here, as if disdaining further concealment, they spoke, and even joked, without the slightest restraint, and those that had them as a martial prelude to the attack, clattered the butt-ends of their guns upon the flags. They seemed to have come not unexpectedly upon Pad Murphy and his sons; for a few moments after the clatter, a light streamed suddenly on the darkness through a small cracked window, and as suddenly disappeared. Shemus Mor now advanced, and after banging the door twice with his "Queen Anne," demanded admittance. He was answered from the inside,—

"To cum in, is id? A poor disthressed thraveler, I suppose. Ye tarnil set, walk in iv ye're able, and maybe ye'd get the supper some o' ye got last Molagga fair."

Some now put their shoulders to the door, and more banged it again with their guns, but could produce no effect.

"Liftenant," said Shemus Mor, turning to Diarmid, "make your men bring hether that nate bame o' timber, that darlin' batherin'-ram that lies behind ye in the yard there, an' perhaps 'twould make the door relint a little."

Diarmid turned with half a dozen of the gang. They lifted the beam from the yard, and, after poising it for a space in the proper direction, with one push dashed in door and door-jambs upon the floor. Silence for a moment followed the crash, bnt it was broken by a volley through the now open doorway from the inside, which slightly wounded some of the party, but brought down Diarmid. True to his trade to the last, he half raised himself from the yard, and exclaimed, " Don't mind me, Shemus; don't give um time to load again, or maybe more o' ye'll be dun for like myself."

Shemus Mor took the advice, and dashed in the door, followed by his now infuriated men. As he strode inward, he received a powerful thrust of a scythe-blade upon his leather corselet, and a blow upon the helmet, neither of which took effect. A smouldering turf fire burned upon the hearth, and in its faint light showed him and his party Pad Murphy, his two sons, and four yeomen standing ready to receive them at the lower end of the kitchen. The fight now commenced in good earnest, but was soon terminated, for the "tarnil fools o' yeomen" were instantly overpowered, and Pad Murphy and his sons, seeing this, tried to escape by the door, in order to procure more effective help, but were captured. A light was brought by one of the gang, the captives pinioned, the "big chest" broken and rifled of its contents, — a few sovereigns, — and the robbers stood in silence, ready to depart. They now heard Diarmid's voice from where he lay in the yard.

"I knew id, I knew id! Thim misforthinate deadbells, an' the last ring upon the yeomen's swords tould me, sure enough, my thread was nearly run."

After securing their prisoners to the legs of bedposts, or whatever else they found convenient, the robbers left the house, and surrounded Diarmid. They found him bleeding almost to death from a bullet wound in the side. "No," said he, as Shemus Mor opened his coat, and attempted to stanch the wound with an old handkerchief, — "no, Shemus, 'tis too late now; 'tis useless, for I'm a gone man. Take me away wid ye," he suddenly exclaimed, as a spasm of sharp pain shot along his body. "Take me home, I say. The torthures o' hell, that Mister O'Regan was spakin' of, have seized on me, I bleeve, at last."

They lifted him between them, and bore him through the darkness and storm towards his mother's hut; but ere they reached it, Diarmid Dhuv Sheehy, the sovereign gatherer, the seducer, and the murderer, was a stiff corpse.

The cold, bright November moon was shining down upon the hills, as a thinly-attired female sat singing her child to sleep, beside a pathway, about two miles north from the pass of Barna Dearg. Between her and Barna Dearg stood a beautiful pointed mountain, in the form of a pyramid, rising over a solitary pass, called, in the poetic language of the country, Barna Geeha, or the Gap of the Winds. The song, with which she endeavored to lull her child to sleep, was in her native tongue, one of those sweet but plaintive nurse tunes, to the cadences of which many a Munster baby is yet rocked to slumber. The first verse, literally translated, runs thus:

> "I will put my own child to sleep—
> It is a fine sunny summer day—
> To sleep in his golden cradle on the smooth floor,
> With the green branches on it waved by the wind."

It was not, unfortunately for the poor child, the summer breeze that waved the long dark hair over its pale temples. A sharp wind blew up the valleys from the north, and made even its mother shiver as she continued the song in a tone tremulous and truly mournful. At length the child fell asleep, and the mother began weeping, and speaking to herself:—

"Where," she murmured, "is the bright home that I myself made disolit? 'Tis as dark an' disolit as myself, an' that's enough for it, this blessed night. The fire is quinched upon its hearth, an' the ould father that nursed me, an' the brothers that loved me are in their cowld graves. O, wirra! wirra! Peggy o' the Glin, did you ever think you'd come to this? They tould me, too, that he was dead and berrid — Diarmid, the father o' you, my poor child; bud I don't bleeve id. He was the murtherer o' my own father, bud he loved me still, an' I don't bleeve he's dead."

Here the child suddenly awoke, looked up into the face of its mother, and gave three low, wild shrieks. The mother looked around her in alarm, and beheld a tall, dark man moving slowly towards her, up the pathway. As he came up and stood before her, she recognized him, and exclaimed, —

"Diarmid! Is it you agin? I thought, after the night you kilt my father, that we wern't to meet ever more. But id can't be helped now. Where did you go since, for they tould me that you were dead an' berrid, though I didn't bleeve them?"

"Peggy an Gleanna," said Diarmid in a broken voice, "this at laste is to be our last meetin'. I have wandered in many a place since, in tormint an' burnin' faver, an' have come back to see the ould place — the misforthinate place for me. Cum," continued he, as he beckoned her to follow him up the path, — cum, an I'll show you where I was put, an' what put me on the bad thrack first."

Peggy felt a strange, shuddering fear creep over her; yet she took her child in her arms and followed. He led her through the Gap of the Winds, and in by a by-path to the ruins of a lonely cabin on the southern declivity of the mountain. Here he stopped in a little field before the ruin, and motioning Peggy a space away from him, exclaimed, in a voice that thrilled the very heart with terror, —

"Peggy an Gleanna, the mother o' my innocent child, here on this spot I struck my ould, grayheaded mother, an' on this spot I am to be seen on the earth by morthial eyes for the last time to-night! The heavy curse of a lost, an' torthured, an' damned sperrit be upon his head who raises his hand to his parent, for 'twill put him straight on the road to hell, as id put me. My oath! My oath!" he cried, as he tossed his arms wildly to heaven, and with glaring eyes began to sink slowly into the earth. "My black and cruel oath that put the flamin' chain o' damnation round my neck, to burn red an' hot round id forever!" As his arms and head only remained above the surface, he stopped moving for a moment, looked upward at the pale sky, and with a voice that rang shrilly along the valleys, shrieked out three times the words, "During eternal glory!" and then disappeared downward forever!

Peggy an Gleanna, with her child clasped in her arms, was found senseless near the spot by two herdsmen in the morning. They carried her to her uncle's house near, where she recovered her senses, but died in a short time, leaving her infant to the care of her aunt.

www.ingramcontent.com/pod-product-compliance
Lightning Source LLC
Chambersburg PA
CBHW032042220426
43664CB00008B/815